Reading Stories for COMPREHENSION SUCCESS

JUNIOR HIGH LEVEL

Reading Level 7-9

KATHERINE L. HALL

**THE CENTER FOR APPLIED
RESEARCH IN EDUCATION**
West Nyack, New York 10994

Library of Congress Cataloging-in-Publication Data

Hall, Katherine L. (Katherine Louise)
    Reading stories for comprehension success : junior high level, grades 7–9 : 45
high-interest lessons with reproducible selections & questions that make kids think /
Katherine L. Hall.
        p. cm.
    Includes bibliographical references.
    ISBN 0–13–022331–X
      1. Reading (Middle school)—Problems, exercises, etc.   2. Reading
comprehension—Problems, exercises, etc.   I. Title.

LB1632.H34 2000
428.4'071'2 21—dc21   99–045657

Acquisitions Editor: *Susan Kolwicz*
Production Editor: *Tom Curtin*
Interior Design/Composition: *Dee Coroneos*

ISBN 0-13-022331-X

**THE CENTER FOR APPLIED RESEARCH
IN EDUCATION**
West Nyack, NY 10994

On the World Wide Web at http://www.PHedu.com

DEDICATION

To my Mother, Doris L. Hall
Thank you always for your love, support, patience, and confidence,
not only during the writing of this book, but through all the
ups, downs, pains, and joys of our lives.

The author would like to extend special thanks to:

Her sister, *Elizabeth Chavez,* and her brother, *James Hall,* for the love and technical support they so graciously supplied.
Beverly McKinney for her advice, support, and friendship.

ACKNOWLEDGMENTS

LEVEL 7

The Luck of the Chimney Sweep: Story 1
Pam Francis/Liaison Agency
The Dust Bowl: Story 2
Photograph by Arthur Rothstein. Library of Congress-LC-USF34-4051.
Mystery of the Deep: Story 3
Al Grotell Underwater Photography
Buying Your First Car: Story 4
Photo Edit
Life is Sweet: The Story of Milton Hershey: Story 5
Milton S. Hershey with Robert Schaeffer, a Milton Hershey School student, 1923.
    Photograph courtesy of Hershey Community Archives.
Mina del Padre—The Lost Padre Mine: Story 6
Photograph by Katherine L. Hall. Franklin Mountains, El Paso, Texas.
Po Chieng Ma's Coded Pencils: Story 7
Kevin Horan/Stock Boston
Lowe's Intrepid: Story 8
Library of Congress-LC-B8184-2350
The Never-Fading Popularity of Levi's Jeans: Story 9
Courtesy Levi Strauss & Co. Archives
A Letter Home: Story 10
Hulton Getty/Liaison Agency
Quanah Parker: Story 11
Panhandle-Plains Historical Museum Research Center, Canyon, Texas. Ph1 1879-59/4
    Quanah Parker on Horseback.
Martin Luther King, Jr. Receives the Nobel Peace Prize: Story 12
Hulton Getty/Liaison Agency
Walking Stones in Death Valley: Story 13
George Gerster/National Geographic Image Collection
Can Sand Sing?: Story 14
John Beatty/Tony Stone Images
Thomas Flyer Arrives in Paris: Story 15
1907 Thomas Flyer, winner of the 1908 New York to Paris Race, on display at the National
    Automobile Museum (The Harrah Collection), Reno, Nevada.

LEVEL 8

Is Anyone Awake Out There?: Story 1
Ferris and His Wheel: Story 2
Carnegie Library of Pittsburgh-A-107.
Where Does the Money Go?: Story 3
Bob Daemmrich/Stock Boston
Hale House of Harlem: Story 4
Scott McKiernan/Liaison Agency
Sir Walter Raleigh's Lost Colony: Story 5
Hulton Getty/Liaison Agency
Lewis Wickes Hine: Story 6
Photograph by Lewis Wickes Hine. Library of Congress-LC-USZ6-1222

Mysterious Crash of Airship Akron: 73 Feared Dead: Story 7
The True Pooh: Story 8
From the Collection of the Central Childrens' Room, Donnell Library Center, The New
    York Public Library
Scott Joplin: Ragtime King: Story 9
New York Public Library for the Performing Arts-ICON-Joplin, Scott #4 Neg. D811
Betty Ford: A True First Lady: Story 10
Liaison Agency
Rachel Carlson: The Coming of Silent Spring: Story 11
Adam Jones/Photo Researchers
The Return of Supersonic Flight: Story 12
National Aeronautics and Space Administration
The Guest Star: Story 13
Chuck Place/Stock Boston
There Lives a Monster in the Loch: Story 14
Artist: Eileen Ciavarella
"D.B. Cooper—Where Are You?": Story 15
Hulton Getty/Agency Unknown

LEVEL 9

Omen in the Sky: Story 1
National Aeronautics and Space Administration
"Cosmic Rocket:" Soviets Winning the Space Race: Story 2
Corbis Images
Witches and Lies: The Salem Witch Hunt: Story 3
Courtesy, Peabody Essex Museum, Salem, MA.
Negative Number 16,068 (EI) *"The Trail of George Jacobs, August 5, 1692"* Oil painting by
    T.H. Matteson, 1855.
The Glorious Tombs of China: Story 4
Wolfgang Kaehler/Liaison Agency
Automaton: Story 5
Corbis Images
America Mourns: Story 6
Hulton Getty/Liaison Agency
Dreaming to Remember: Story 7
Photograph by Katherine L. Hall. Andrew James Hall.
Summer Camp Isn't What It Used to Be: Story 8
UPI/Corbis-Bettman
"Ma" Barker Gunned Down by F.B.I.: Story 9
Corbis-Bettman
Joseph Cardinal Bernardin: Story 10
UPI/Corbis-Bettman
What Does "QUERTY" Mean?: Story 11
Hulton Getty/Liaison Agency
Adopt-a-Senior: Story 12
Bill Aron/Tony Stone Images
1,200 Dead in Cameroon: Story 13
Corbis Images
Predicting the Next Earthquake: Story 14
Liaison Agency
Journalist of the People: Story 15
AP/Wide World Images

ABOUT THE AUTHOR

Katherine Hall attended the University of Texas at El Paso and earned her bachelor's degree in elementary education and special education in 1982. She has worked with students at the elementary school level for many years as a teacher for the first grade, English as a Second Language program, and resource room as well as a private tutor.

An interest in reading comprehension was first sparked by her experience in elementary school resource rooms. Disillusioned by her students' lack of progress, she found that the multiple-choice question format often became monotonous and did not excite students or offer opportunities for self-expression. The challenge of opening up the world of literature to her students, including the learning disabled, prompted the creation of a new format for teaching comprehension skills. Katherine developed *Reading Stories for Comprehension Success* to increase students' confidence, interest, and involvement in learning. She found that when she used high-interest, nonfiction stories, her students' curiosity about learning began to grow. From her own experience, she has found that *Reading Stories for Comprehension Success* also creates a rewarding teaching experience that can be implemented in schools, homes, and tutoring centers.

During the past ten years, Ms. Hall was an active member of the Texas State Council of the International Reading Association and of a Parent Teacher Association. Katherine taught and developed summer programs for the Learning Disabilities Association. She has presented inservices for teachers and was published in several magazines. In addition to reading and teaching, she also enjoys music and is an avid performer of the harp, flute, and piccolo. She resides in Hurst, Texas, where she continues to tutor students at the elementary to college level.

INTRODUCTION

USING *READING STORIES FOR COMPREHENSION SUCCESS*

Reading Stories for Comprehension Success includes an entire week or more of activities for each story lesson. Turn to the beginning of any of the three reading levels, and you'll see that they all follow this format:

CONTENTS

The *Contents* page lists all the story titles, along with the reading grade level of each story and the story's page number. The reading grade level tells the teacher the story's reading difficulty within the reading grade level.

ABOUT THE STORY

A brief description of the story introduces the teacher to the topic.

> **Moments in Time:** The *Moments in Time* series appears within the *Junior High* and *Senior High* volumes. Periodically, a story will begin with the *Moments in Time* title and a date in the upper left corner. The author wrote these stories in the format of a news article as it might have appeared during the event described in the story. Its purpose is to help students gain a fresh insight into historical events.

QUOTES OF THE WEEK

Every lesson includes one or more quotes from literary works or important people in history which highlight the subject of the story lesson.

INTERVIEW TOPIC

Every week the students receive an interview topic. They are to locate interview subjects, and conduct an interview using prepared literal and interpretive questions. The interviews give the students opportunities to experience viewpoints from a variety of people.

PREVIEW WORDS

The *Preview Words* are *not* words that the teacher drills before the lesson. These words allow the teacher to expose the students to words they may not know or are unable to pronounce. Teens should prepare for unknown words before reading in front of their peers.

Choose all or only a few of the words, based on your students' needs. Write the Preview Words on chart paper or on overhead projector transparencies before the day of the story lesson.

WORD-ORIGIN STUDY

As an exercise in vocabulary building, the *Word-Origin Study* teaches students the meaning of words through the terms' historical development, and prefix/suffix meaning. Students can apply this information to unknown words which appear in exams, such as the SAT.

Included in the *Word-Origin Study* is the student's vocabulary notebook. Each student keeps a notebook of words related to those presented in the list for a particular story along with their definitions.

THROUGHOUT THE WEEK OR PRIOR TO THE LESSON

Nearly all of the stories include these topics. *Throughout the Week* presents activities which continue throughout the story lesson; *Prior to the Lesson* tells you about any important preparations you must make before the week begins.

BOOKS TO READ

A list of books that relate to the subject of each story lesson is provided. These books are at many levels, from juvenile chapter books, to young adult books, to adult books, both fiction and nonfiction. Your librarian can provide you with additional sources.

*Important—Always review any books, videos, and other materials before introducing them to your students, whether they are on the *Books to Read* list or suggested by a librarian. What is considered appropriate for the students varies from state to state, or from school district to school district.

ARTICLES OR ORGANIZATIONS

Occasionally, magazine/newspaper articles with further information about the story topic are listed after the *Books to Read* section. Organizations offering further information are also listed.

VIDEOS

This section lists videos on the story lesson subject. Many public libraries lend videos without charge.

*Use caution, however, when showing videos to your class. Make sure your situation does not require special fees to show the film. Avoid violating copyright laws.

CDS, RECORDS, AND CASSETTES

Here you'll find other materials that coordinate with the story lesson.

BOOK CLUB

The *Book Club* section highlights books reflecting the story lesson topic. Reading books and discussing the stories with a group adds a new dimension to reading comprehension. You might find extra copies of a given title at your local public libraries, or through inter-library loan. In large classes, you might assign books from different story lessons to different book club groups, then rotate the titles. This method might help you provide enough copies of every title.

Another possible exercise to coordinate with the *Book Club* is the writing of critiques. Each student will rate the book, and discuss whether they would recommend the book to others.

INTRODUCTORY ACTIVITIES

Introductory Activities introduce the student to the story lesson. In Reading Level 7, *Po Chieng Ma's Coded Pencils*, the introductory activity includes a discussion of the reasons for, and repercussions of, cheating. The students also conduct a survey of fellow students on the practice of cheating. These experiences encourage more logical, well-thought-out answers to interpretive questions.

STORY LESSON

The stories—each with an accompanying photograph—are the foundation of *Reading Stories for Comprehension Success*. Prior to the lesson, make a copy of the black-line master for each student. If you choose question 11, "Write a title for the story" (Identification of the Main Idea), make one copy of the story. Erase the title of the story with correction fluid, then make the number of copies needed for your class.

The design of the story meets the needs of the learning disabled and students with poor comprehension skills. The margins are wide to reduce the clutter on the story page, and there are no pictures, questions, or illustrations on the reading selection. This helps students with perceptual problems, attention deficits, short attention spans, or other disabilities to see the text more clearly.

If a student has an extremely short attention span, cut the stories apart between paragraphs. Present only one paragraph at a time. When the student masters reading one paragraph without losing attention, increase the page length to two paragraphs. Continue in this way until the student reads an entire story at one sitting.

Following the lesson plan, choose the questions the students will answer. Mark out, or delete with correction fluid, any questions you do not wish the students to answer. Like *Reading Stories for Comprehension Success—Primary* and *Intermediate* volumes, where students wrote their answers on the question sheets, the *Junior High* and *Senior High* volumes require upper-level students to do the same or to write their answers on a separate piece of paper. If you select the latter, you might direct the students to keep a special notebook for this activity.

Follow the *Presenting the Story Lesson* instructions (p. xxi) for each story. Every story follows the same presentation procedure. The consistent format is important for learning disabled students and the many upper-grade students with only minimal comprehension skills.

The nonfiction, multicultural stories of *Reading Stories for Comprehension Success* are high-interest, and encourage the students to learn more. The biographies tell about such people as Charles Kuralt and Benjamin Banneker, who reached beyond themselves and their circumstances to achieve their dreams. The *Moments in Time* stories sprinkled throughout the volumes give students the insight into historical events as they happened.

EXTENSION ACTIVITIES

Each story includes a list of *Extension Activities* which allow the students to experience the subject beyond the story. Art projects and special activities which reach outside the classroom are offered.

QUESTIONS

The question format of *Reading Stories for Comprehension Success* requires students to answer in complete, well-thought-out sentences. There is no answer key because students create their own answers. Count any answer within reason as correct.

Note: According to the National Assessment of Educational Progress (NAEP), several factors contribute to reading comprehension improvement. The report pointed to the importance of "writing long answers in response to reading." The report went on to state:

> At all three grades (4, 8, 12), a positive relationship between writing long answers to questions on tests and assignments that involved reading and student reading performance is generally supported by findings from the 1998 NAEP assessment. Students who reported engaging in this activity on a weekly or a monthly basis had higher average scores than students who reported doing so only once or twice a year, or hardly ever. At the twelfth grade, students who reported doing such writing at least once a week demonstrated the highest reading performance.[1]

When presenting the Questions Sheet, encourage the students to debate possible answers to the interpretive questions. For example, the Identification of Cause question in the story about Martin Luther King, Jr. reads, "Why did Martin Luther King choose nonviolent protests over violence?" The students might present many answers to this question. Discuss everyone's answers. Each student's opinion is valuable, and they must know this every time they choose an answer to an interpretive question.

One exercise the students enjoy is a discussion group. The teacher acts as moderator, and the students discuss ideas presented in the story. Ask individual students interpretive questions about the story; encourage them to state their own opinions, and to back up their opinions with evidence. This exercise helps students to realize that not all questions have the same answer. After using *Reading Stories for Comprehension Success*, students can better evaluate the choices presented in multiple-choice tests.

Unlike many other reading comprehension programs, *Reading Stories for Comprehension Success* bases all of the comprehension questions on the text of the story. You choose the number and difficulty of the questions based on the needs of your students.

---

[1] Donahue, Patricia L., Kristin E. Voelkl, Jay R. Campbell, and John Mazzeo, "NAEP 1998 Reading Report Card for the Nation and the States," *The Nation's Report Card: National Assessment of Education Progress.* National Center for Education Statistics, March 1999, pp. 3–4, http://nces.ed.gov/nationsreportcard/pubs/main1998/1999500.shtml

Comprehension exercises include literal and interpretive questions using the following format. (Teachers in grades 7-12 need to make a chart-size copy of this information. As students prepare questions prior to their interviews and as they complete the Question Sheet, they should refer to the chart. Students become more proficient in answering higher-level questions if they understand the basis of the various question styles.)

Literal and Interpretive Questions

Literal Questions: The students find and retrieve answers directly from the text.

- ■ THE FACTS (or description): Questions 1-4 on the Questions Sheet present literal questions in which the student takes exact answers from the text.

- ■ SEQUENCE OF EVENTS: Questions 5-6 ask the students to demonstrate an understanding of the sequence of events in the story.

Interpretive Questions: The students are asked to draw logical conclusions based on the information presented in the text. Answers to these questions might vary from student to student.

- ■ DRAWING CONCLUSIONS (Question 7): These questions ask students to look at the facts of the text, then draw a conclusion based on these facts.

- ■ MAKING INFERENCES (Question 8): Here, students must look beyond the stated text to what is inferred by the author.

- ■ MAKING PREDICTIONS (Question 9): To answer questions dealing with prediction, the students must imagine a future influenced by the events described in the text.

- ■ IDENTIFICATION OF CAUSE (Question 10): The students speculate on the cause of an event or someone's actions.

- ■ IDENTIFICATION OF THE MAIN IDEA (Question 11): This seems to be a difficult concept for many students with or without learning disabilities. One of the best ways to teach this concept is to ask students to write a title for the story. The title must state the topic or main idea of the story in only a few words.

  1. Throughout *Reading Stories for Comprehension Success*, the question for the main idea is basically the same, "Write a title for the story. Use as few words as possible."

  2. First, remove the title from the story page with correction fluid, then make the number of copies needed for your class.

- ■ COMPARISON (Question 12): Students must compare subjects, concepts, and events found within the story.

- ■ SUMMARIZE (Question 13): These questions ask the students to summarize an event in their own words.

- ■ EFFECT (Question 14): The questions ask students to consider the effects of the events presented in the story.

■ FACT AND OPINION (Question 15): Students determine if a statement from the story is a fact or an opinion. The question also asks the students if they can prove their answers. For example, can they find sources in reference books to back up their answers?

■ ON YOUR OWN (Question 16): Students write questions of their own for a teacher or another student to answer.

STUDENT DATA SHEET

• Students track their progress on the student Data Sheet.

• All students record their time on task. Those with attention deficits see concrete evidence of their improvement.

READING ABILITY GUIDELINES

■ *Reading Stories for Comprehension Success* provides a chart enabling teachers to follow a lesson procedure that matches a student's reading comprehension ability.

■ Routines for Poor Readers, Average Readers, and Upper Level Readers further allow you to tailor the lesson to the student's abilities. As the student improves, move to the next level of the Guidelines.

*See important research information concerning reading comprehension skills of upper-grade students in the *Reading Ability Guidelines* (page xx).

COURSE SYNOPSIS

The reproducible *Course Synopsis* form helps students organize their materials, and record due dates for reports and other projects. The form also assists teachers in the presenting of objectives for the week.

WHO CAN USE <u>READING STORIES</u> <u>FOR COMPREHENSION SUCCESS</u>?

TO TEACHERS

While working in the public schools as a Resource teacher, I saw more of the educational responsibility for students with learning disabilities fall on the shoulders of the regular education teacher. Some of these teachers had important and valid concerns:

■ "Tommy's attention span is so short. What can I do when I have twenty other students in the classroom?"

■ "Julia reads two years below grade level. How can I modify my lessons to include her in a subject dependent on reading?"

I could give the teachers the same list of modifications: Reduce distractions. Seat Tommy close to your desk. Underline important information in Julia's books. These modifications, however, only emphasize the special students' disabilities in front of their peers.

Reading Stories for Comprehension Success has all the modifications built into the program. The entire class works on the same lesson without singling out the learning disabled student. These modifications proved effective for nondisabled students striving to improve reading comprehension skills. Therefore, this book works well for students in a variety of settings, including the following:

1. Public school systems

2. Private schools (both regular and special education)

3. Classes for the learning disabled

4. Behavior disorders classes

5. Bilingual education classes

6. Tutoring centers

7. Home schools

8. Adult education classes

According to the National Assessment of Educational Progress (NAEP), the majority of students in the upper-grade levels are not achieving at proficient levels in the area of reading comprehension. Student performance was scored on a scale from 0–500 ranking the students on three achievement levels: Basic, Proficient, and Advanced. The following chart illustrates the percentile performance of fourth, eighth, and twelfth graders on the NAEP reading comprehension assessment in 1998. Each percentage indicates students at or above the given level.[1]

GRADE LEVEL	4TH	8TH	12TH
BASIC	62%	74%	77%
PROFICIENT	31%	33%	40%
ADVANCED	7%	3%	6%

These results showing the majority of students scoring below proficiency in reading comprehension indicates a need to address reading comprehension in the upper grades.

---

[1] Donahue, Patricia L., Kristin E. Voelkl, Jay R. Campbell, and John Mazzeo, "NAEP 1998 Reading Report Card for the Nation and the States," *The Nation's Report Card: National Assessment of Education Progress.* National Center for Education Statistics, March 1999, pp. 1–2, http://nces.ed.gov/nationsreportcard/pubs/main1998/1999500.shtml

TO TUTORS

Students in tutoring centers can benefit from the use of *Reading Stories for Comprehension Success*. As a tutor, you can tailor the lessons to the individual student's needs.

The week before the story lesson, give the student a list of books, videos, and activities to which the parent should expose the student. At the end of the list, add activity suggestions from the *Introductory Activities* and the *Extension Activities*, which the parents can do with the child.

TO PARENTS

Parents can use *Reading Stories for Comprehension Success* to supplement a child's education. When using this program with your child, follow the instructions for the teacher. Ask your child's teacher to administer an Individual Reading Inventory and inform you of your child's independent reading level. Many teachers already have this information in your child's file.

Remember to be consistent. Use complete sentences whenever you talk to your child. For example, your child might ask, "Where are we going?" Answer in the complete sentence, "We are going to the mall." Do not answer with the sentence fragment, "to the mall." Reduce visual distractions and clutter around the home and use natural light whenever possible.

Read one story a week with your child. Before reading the story, complete the *Introductory Activities*, and take your child to the library to check out books on the story subject.

Follow the *Presenting the Story Lesson* instructions on the day you read the story. If your child has a very short attention span, begin with only one paragraph of the story, and only one question from the Question Sheet. Note the length of time the child stays on task on the Lesson Plan (Objective 3 on p. xxiii), and monitor progress on the *Student Data Sheet*. Over time, slowly increase the length of the story read, and the number of questions on the Question Sheet.

After reading the story, complete the *Extension Activities*. All the activities are great family projects, and a parent has more freedom than a classroom teacher to expose students to a variety of learning experiences.

CLASSROOM ENVIRONMENT

When creating a classroom environment, keep the distractions to a minimum. The classroom decorations don't have to be plain and dull—just not too busy. Some suggestions are:

1. Hang the same color of bulletin board paper throughout the room. White paper does not fade, so the same paper will last all year.

2. Use bulletin board borders that are not busy. Even plain borders can be attractive.

3. Play soft instrumental music as the students enter the room or while they are doing seat work. The music masks the random noises such as dropped pencils and squeaky chairs.

4. Use natural light whenever possible; students seem more at ease without fluorescent lights.

5. If you store your materials in open bookcases, put the materials into boxes. Cover the boxes with shelf paper without a busy design. Use the same design on every box.

6. Keep a few plants in the room. They add beauty and act as living air filters.

"IF YOU DO IT FOR ONE, DO IT FOR ALL"

The most important rule a teacher can follow is: "If you do it for one, you do it for all." Too often, teachers make modifications for special education students that are visible to the entire class. These modifications, which are put in place to help the student educationally, can destroy a student's morale. You *must* use modifications for learning disabled students; however, modifications should be subtly implemented. Publicly announcing a student's special needs in front of her or his peers embarrasses and demoralizes a student already struggling for acceptance. These students will withdraw in shame or act out to find approval from their peers.

Watch your special education student throughout the day; note how many times you make special allowances or modifications of which the entire class is aware. For example:

- Seating the student in an isolated area, even when there is no disruptive behavior involved.

- Stating the modifications when giving an assignment. Avoid statements like these:

  "Read Chapter One and answer questions one through ten. Frank, you only need to do questions one through five," or "Everyone read Chapter Six. Susan, I'll underline the parts you need to read after everyone begins working."

Later, look over your notes. Are there modifications that the entire class can participate in? If you do it for one, can you do it for all? For example, students with learning disabilities have difficulty keeping their work organized. If one modification is to set up a notebook with individual folders for each subject area and homework, all the students should have such a notebook.

Sometimes modifications can not be used with the entire class. It is best to meet with the student privately to discuss these modifications. When you meet with the student, write down all the modifications he or she can expect and how you will implement them. Remember to make the implementation as private and subtle as possible. After the student understands and agrees to these modifications, sign a contract. File it in the student's file; it will be invaluable as proof of modifications if school district or other officials ask for it.

ATTENTION DEFICIT DISORDER

Aside from the recent surge in drug therapy, few programs offer innovative teaching aids for learning disabled students, including those with ADD. Focus on strategies that go beyond medication, and remember to use these strategies with the entire class whenever possible. For example, the rate at which the teacher reads a story affects the student's comprehension level during auditory presentation. According to one study, hyperactive students were less active and stayed on task when the teacher read the story fast "without added nonrelevant detail." Comprehension improved, however, when the teacher read the story slowly without added detail.[2]

According to Fiore, Becker, and Nero, the following techniques are most likely to be effective in academic areas:

POSITIVE REINFORCEMENT

1. Social praise

2. Group reward contingencies

3. Parent rewards

4. Token economies

PUNISHMENT ("a contingency that reduces the frequency of behavior")

1. Hyperactive students remained on task longer using negative feedback. However, errors increased significantly.

2. Short, strong, and consistent reprimands reduced disruptive behaviors.

In her book *When Children Don't Learn*, Diane McGuinness states that educators must meet the following three needs before hyperactive students can change their behaviors and begin to improve their academic performance.[3] We should apply these needs to all students, with or without learning disabilities.

1. *Achievable Goals: Reading Stories for Comprehension Success* allows the teacher to determine "achievable goals" for each student on an individual basis. The teacher chooses the type and number of questions used. As the students achieve success, the teacher gradually increases the number of questions.

2. *Goals Based on Academic Subject Areas: Reading Stories for Comprehension Success* incorporates the needs of learning disabled students in an academic subject (reading comprehension) in a format that benefits every student in the class. Students can develop reading comprehension skills at any reading level.

The teacher chooses a reading level based on the learning disabled reading skills, and uses this level for the entire class. The high-interest, factual stories mask the true reading level. Everyone in the class, learning disabled or not, learns comprehension skills with modifications built into the program, without being aware of special provisions for learning disabled students.

---

[2] Fiore, Thomas A., Elizabeth A. Becker, and Rebecca C. Nero, "Educational Interventions for Students with Attention Deficit Disorder," *Exceptional Children*, v 60 (Oct.-Nov. 1993), 163 (II).

[3] McGuinness, Diane, *When Children Don't Learn: Understanding the Biology and Psychology of Learning Disabilities*. New York, NY: Basic Books, 1985.

3. *Frequent Praise:* As students progress through *Reading Stories for Comprehension Success*, they complete their assignments without undue stress. They participate in making the Data Sheets, proving to themselves that they can succeed. The factual, fascinating content of the stories inspires students to learn more, and possibly to set goals based on newly found interests.

TEACHING STRATEGIES

Teachers can use several teaching strategies with the entire class to improve the reading comprehension skills of students with or without learning disabilities. *Reading Stories for Comprehension Success* begins with one to two days of introductory activities before the story lesson. From these experiences, the students develop a better understanding of the story. The Extension Activities build on the students' comprehension; with them, you create a "total sensory experience."

LANGUAGE DEVELOPMENT

The Preview Words of *Reading Stories for Comprehension Success* introduce the students to new vocabulary words without drill. The students not only hear the words in the story, but continue to use them in speech and writing during the Introductory and Extension Activities. Encourage the students to find new words based on concepts presented in the story. They keep a record of the new words and their definitions in the vocabulary notebook. Remember to model the use of these words in your own speech.

VOCABULARY GAME

A stumbling block to proficiency in reading comprehension for secondary students is poor vocabulary skills. Most upper-grade exercises designed to build vocabulary rely on drill, memorization, and multiple-choice tests. One unique and effective way to build vocabulary is through games. The following vocabulary game echoes the familiar format of a common board game.

Setting Up the Game:

1. Collect a list of vocabulary words, and their definitions. The words might come from the students' vocabulary notebooks, a school district's required vocabulary list, or books, such as *The Reading Teacher's Book of Lists, 3rd ed.* by Edward Bernard Fry, Ph.D., Jacqueline E. Kress, Ed.D., and Dona Lee Fountoukidis, Ed.D. (West Nyack, NY: The Center for Applied Research in Education, 1993), or Murray Boomberg and Julius Liebb's *Hot Words for the SAT: The 350 Words You Need to Know* (New York, NY: Barron's, 1989).

2. Write each word on the front of an index card, and the definition on the back. Some computers print on index cards with professional results. Let the students help make the cards to reinforce the new vocabulary words.

3. Enlarge the Vocabulary Game Board on page xix.

   Note: Give the students a list of the vocabulary words to study before the game.

Play the Game:

1. Place the deck of vocabulary cards word-side up next to the game board.

2. Use one die or a spinner to determine the spaces moved.

3. The students line up their game pieces on **GO!**. You can use game pieces from old games, or use any small objects such as refrigerator magnets.

4. The first player reads the word facing up on the top of the deck. Another player picks up the card without revealing the definition. The first player must say the definition, and/or use the word in a sentence correctly. If the student is correct, he or she throws the die, and moves along the board.

5. There are several slides (☺↘ , ↖☹) scattered along the route. Landing on a slide causes the player to gain or lose ground.

6. The winner is the player to reach **STOP!** first.

Vocabulary Game Board

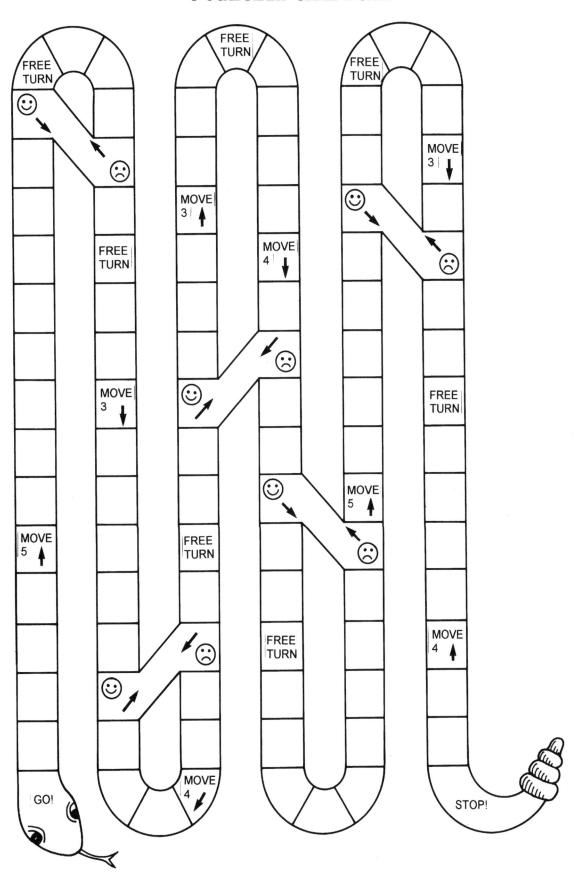

FREE TURN

FREE TURN

FREE TURN

MOVE 3

MOVE 3

FREE TURN

MOVE 4

FREE TURN

MOVE 3

MOVE 5

FREE TURN

MOVE 5

FREE TURN

FREE TURN

MOVE 4

GO!

MOVE 4

STOP!

TEAM LEARNING

Throughout *Reading Stories for Comprehension Success*, students work in groups or teams. This allows the learning disabled students to participate in an activity without depending solely on their own abilities. Break the class into groups. Subtly assign a higher level reader to each group. This student can help the others in the group with difficult words or passages, and learning disabled students don't feel singled out when other students in the group also ask for help.

Carole McGraw in her article "Teaching Teenagers?: 'Think, Do, Learn!'" discusses the impact of team learning in the secondary classroom.[4] McGraw suggests using labs or teamwork sessions in the upper grades at least 50% of the class time.

Set up a permanent book center in the classroom. Encourage the students to read books that interest them.

READ TO THE CLASS

Each story lesson in *Reading Stories for Comprehension Success* lists several books, fiction and nonfiction, in the Books to Read section. Choose a book from this selection or an alternate award-winning book to read orally to the class. Often overlooked in the secondary level, reading to the class models proper reading patterns as it fosters interest in literature.

READING ABILITY GUIDELINES

These guidelines suggest teaching procedures based on the students' reading comprehension skills.[5] These guidelines are particularly relevant in the upper grades due to the high percentage of students displaying mastery of only the most basic comprehension skills. (See the summary of the National Assessment of Educational Progress (NAEP) report on page xiii of this Introduction.) As poor readers improve, move to the next level.

A student's answers to interpretive questions may not be logically sound. Conduct a short, open discussion about other possibilities. Consider the answer correct, however, if the student arrived at the conclusion based on his or her best effort. Remember that the purpose of *Reading Stories for Comprehension Success* is to create joy in learning and expressing oneself.

*Note: Do not include interpretive questions in your question list until the student demonstrates mastery of literal questions. Then introduce only one interpretive question until the student shows confidence.

---

[4] McGraw, Carole, "Teaching Teenagers?: 'Think, Do, Learn!'," *The Education Digest*, February 1998, pp. 44–47.

[5] Based on information from: Durkin, Dolores, *Teaching Them to Read*, 3rd ed., Boston, MA: Allyn and Bacon, 1979, p. 442.

Poor Readers (at Basic reading comprehension level)

1. Read the literal questions orally.
2. Read the story silently.
3. Discuss the answers to the literal questions. (Encourage students to speak in complete, understandable sentences.)
4. Read the interpretive questions orally.
5. Read the story silently (second reading).
6. Discuss the answers to the interpretive questions.
7. The students complete the Question Sheet independently, writing all the answers in complete sentences.

Average Readers (at Proficient reading comprehension level)

1. Read literal and interpretive questions orally.
2. Read the story silently.
3. Discuss the answers to the interpretive questions.
4. The students complete the Question Sheet independently, writing all the answers in complete sentences.

Upper Level Readers (at Advanced reading comprehension level)

1. Read the interpretive questions orally.
2. Read the story silently.
3. Conduct a discussion based on the questions. (Guide the students in the use of complete, well-thought-out sentences.)
4. The students complete the Question Sheet independently, writing all the answers in complete sentences.

PRESENTING THE STORY LESSON

*Important: Remove all extra stimulation from the students' view or reach. The work area must be clear of distractions.

1. Review the Introductory Activities. Discuss what the student did and learned.
2. Display and discuss the Preview Words, then remove the words from the students' sight.
3. Display the story picture. Engage the students in a discussion about the illustration. Focus on the topic of the story and guide the students in such a way as to focus their attention on the subject.
4. Read the quote found in the Story Lesson section of each story. This question prepares them for the content of the story. For Example, "The title of the story we're reading today is *Predicting Earthquakes*. What do you think the story is about? What do you already know about earthquakes?"

5. Hand out the story pages.

6. Choose the lesson format in the guidelines that suits your students' reading ability. Remember to remove the story from the students' view when they work on their question sheets to avoid distractions. They can refer to the story if needed; however, remove the story from the students' view as soon as possible.

7. Grade the questions in front of the students when they complete their work. Because you monitor the work closely, there should be few errors.

8. Students record their scores on the Student Data Sheet, and the Course Synopsis.

PRETEST

Determine the reading grade level of each student in the class. Survey each student's reading grade level using your favorite Individual Reading Inventory (IRI). You are looking for the student's independent reading level, *not* the instructional level. *Reading Stories for Comprehension Success* aims to improve comprehension skills only. If you begin the program at the student's instructional level, the reading of individual words becomes the focus of his or her efforts. If you present the stories at the student's independent reading level, he or she comfortably reads the text and concentration is on the content.

Look over the IRI scores. Which score is the lowest? Begin *Reading Stories for Comprehension Success* on the level below this score, unless the lowest score is grade 1. In this case, begin on Reading Level 1. For example, if your students are eighth-graders, look at the lowest IRI score. If the lowest independent reading level is grade level 8, begin *Reading Stories for Comprehension Success* at Reading Level 7.

This procedure ensures that the student with the lowest reading level will feel comfortable reading with the rest of the class. Never tell the students the reading level they are working on. Because of the factual, high-interest nature of the stories, they will not realize that they are reading at a lower reading level. *You can teach any reading comprehension skill at any reading grade level.*

TEACHER LESSON PLAN

The Lesson Plan form in *Reading Stories for Comprehension Success* saves valuable teacher time. First, choose the type and number of questions you will ask the students. Begin with only literal questions on the first lesson, presenting one to no more than five questions in one lesson. The number of questions asked depends on the students' ability and attention span.

LESSON PLAN FORM

1. Basic Information

Fill in the class information at the top of the page.

2. Objectives

The lesson format of *Reading Stories for Comprehension Success* is consistent and predictable throughout the series. Therefore, each lesson teaches and reinforces the same basic objectives.

- *Objective 1*—Circle if the student is to read orally or silently.

- *Objective 2*—Circle if the student is to answer the questions orally or in writing.

- *Objective 3*—Fill in the number of minutes the student will stay on task. Use this objective to monitor students with short attention spans. By beginning with a short question list and increasing the number of questions over time, you can actually help the student to increase his or her time on task.

3. Comprehension Skills Taught in This Lesson

Check off the comprehension skills you will present in the lesson.

4. Materials

Every lesson uses all the materials listed.

LESSON PLAN

Date: _____   **Teacher Edition page** _____

Class: _____   **Student page** _____

Student: _____

Story: _____

OBJECTIVES:

(circle one)

1. The student(s) will read orally/silently the story.

(circle one)

2. The student(s) will orally state/write the answers to the following comprehension skills in complete, understandable sentences.

3. The student(s) will complete the given assignment in _____ minutes.

COMPREHENSION SKILLS TAUGHT IN THIS LESSON:

(check the skill to be taught)

   I.   Literal questions

   A. The Facts   _____

   B. Sequence   _____

   II. Interpretive questions

   A. Conclusion   _____

   B. Inference   _____

   C. Prediction   _____

   D. Identification of Cause   _____

   E.   Identification of Main Idea   _____

   F. Comparison   _____

   G. Summarize   _____

   H. Effect   _____

   I.   Fact and Opinion   _____

III.   Teacher-created question   _____

MATERIALS:

___ Story page   ___ Question Sheet   ___ Student Data Sheet

COURSE SYNOPSIS

A course synopsis gives students a sense of organization, and prepares them for required assignments. A synopsis also organizes a teacher's lesson, and insures the statement of the class objectives before the lesson begins.

1. Make multiple copies of the following synopsis page. Punch notebook holes along the left edge of the copies.

2. Give each student one copy for each week of the class to keep in a loose-leaf notebook.

3. Make an enlarged teacher copy, or make an overhead projector sheet for the teacher presentation.

4. Fill in the week's synopsis on the teacher copy.

5. On the first day of the week, present the synopsis allowing time for the students to fill in their copies.

6. As the papers and projects are graded, the students will enter the grades in the given space. At the end of the week, the students will average their grades, and enter their average onto the last line of the synopsis.

A sample form is provided for you.

Student: _____

Class: _____

Teacher: _____

Period: _____

Course synopsis

Week: _____

Story Topic: _____

Interview Topic: _____

_____

Interview Due On: _____ Grade: _____

Vocabulary Notebook Requirements: _____

_____

Vocabulary Notebook Due On: _____ Grade: _____

Book Club Title: _____

_____

Book Critique Due On: _____ Grade: _____

Field Trip (if applicable): _____

Special Project: _____

Special Project Due On: _____ Grade: _____

Materials List: _____

_____

Other: _____

_____

_____

GRADE AVERAGE: _____

Student: __Joseph Rey__

Class: __Reading II__

Teacher: __Mrs. Burns__

Period: __3rd__

COURSE SYNOPSIS

Week: __One__

Story Topic: __Superstitions__

Interview Topic: __Interview a person over the age of 60 who practices superstitious__ __rituals to bring good luck.__

Interview Due On: __9/27__   Grade: _____

Vocabulary Notebook Requirements: __List words which begin with the prefix super–.__ __Write the words and their definitions.__

Vocabulary Notebook Due On: __7/29__   Grade: _____

Book Club Title: __The Half Child by Kathleen Herson__
_____

Book Critique Due On: __9/30__   Grade: _____

Field Trip (if applicable): __N/A__

Special Project: __Complete "Good Luck Chart"__

Special Project Due On: __9/27__   Grade: _____

Materials List: __"Good Luck Chart"__
_____

Other: __None__
_____
_____

GRADE AVERAGE: _____

STUDENT DATA SHEET

Student: _____

Story	1	2	3	4	5	6	7	8	9	10	11	12	13	14	15	AVERAGE
Date																
The Facts																
Sequence																
Conclusion																
Inference																
Prediction																
Cause																
Main Idea																
Comparison																
Summarize																
Effect																
Fact/Opinion																
On Your Own																
Score																
Percentage																
Time on Task																

L I T E R A L (The Facts, Sequence, Conclusion)

I N T E R P R E T I V E (Inference, Prediction, Cause, Main Idea, Comparison, Summarize, Effect, Fact/Opinion, On Your Own)

STUDENT DATA SHEET

Student: ___Frank_____

Story	1
Date	4/6/00
The Facts	2
Sequence	1
Conclusion	1
Inference	0
Prediction	
Cause	
Main Idea	
Comparison	
Summarize	
Effect	
Fact/Opinion	
Score	4/5
Percentage	80%
Time on Task	6 min.

Consider a comprehension skill mastered when the student has five correct answers in a row. Move on to the next skill; however, intermittently include the mastered skills in the Question Sheet as review.

PURPOSE OF STUDENT DATA SHEET

The easy-to-use Student Data Sheet helps both teacher and students track their progress through *Reading Stories for Comprehension Success.* The Data Sheet serves several purposes:

1. The students track their own performance, which serves also as a motivational reward system.

2. The students track their time on task, and thus see tangible evidence of their efforts. This is also a powerful, yet often overlooked, reward system.

3. You can use the Data Sheet to monitor the student's mastery of comprehension skills.

4. School districts require teachers to keep written record of any provisions made for students who qualify as learning disabled. The Data Sheet is a good record to keep in your files.

USING THE STUDENT DATA SHEET

1. After the students complete their Question Sheets, grade the answers in front of each student. At the top of the page write:

$$\frac{\textit{The Number of Correct Answers}}{\text{The Total Number of Questions}}$$

For example, if a student answered four out of five questions correctly, write the following at the top of the page:

$$\frac{4}{5}$$

2. Give the student her or his Student Data Sheet.

3. Write the date under the number of the story read.

4. Look at the list of reading comprehension question styles listed down the sheet. In front of the student, enter the number of correct responses to each question style. Because of the presentation of the material, there should be few errors.

5. The student enters the score from the Question Sheet into the space marked Score.

6. Using the score numbers, enter the percentage into the percentage box. If the student has the skills to calculate the percentage, he or she will enter the number into the Data Sheet; otherwise, you must calculate and enter the percentage. (You can also use this number as the grade for the lesson.)

7. The student enters the time in minutes that he or she stayed on task in the Time on Task space.

8. At the end of the reading level, average the percentage scores and enter the total score under the Average box. For example, Frank's Question Sheet contained two facts questions, one sequence question, one conclusion question, and one inference question on Story 1. He answered every question except the inference question correctly. The score on his paper would read: 4/5. His time on task was 6 minutes.

IN CONCLUSION

The aim of *Reading Stories for Comprehension Success* is to incorporate modifications for learning disabled students into one program. It is of particular importance to address the reading comprehension skills of all upper-grade students because these exercises are generally overlooked, and the comprehension proficiency levels of these students remain unacceptably low. This program gives teachers maximum flexibility in lesson presentation. Unlike other reading comprehension programs, this book gives you the freedom to base a lesson on your students' needs. Always keep in mind the following:

1. Keep the room and work area as distraction free as possible.

2. If you do it for one, do it for all.

3. Always model complete sentences in your own speech.

4. Encourage the students to speak in complete, well-thought-out sentences.

5. Create an environment in which students feel free to develop and communicate their unique ideas. Allow them to debate the interpretive questions, and to learn from the variety of backgrounds each student brings to the class.

Katherine L. Hall

CONTENTS

INTRODUCTION / VII

Using *Reading Stories for Comprehension Success* (vii)   Introductory Activities (ix) Extension Activities (x)   Literal and Interpretive Questions (xi)   Who Can Use *Reading Stories for Comprehension Success*? (xii)   Classroom Environment (xiv) Attention Deficit Disorder (xv)   Teaching Strategies (xvii)   Reading Ability Guidelines (xx)   Presenting the Story Lesson (xxi)   Pretest (xxii)   Teacher Lesson Plan (xxii)   Lesson Plan Form (xxiv)   Course Synopsis Form (xxvi)   Student Data Sheet (xxviii)   In Conclusion (xxxi)

READING LEVEL 7

CONTENTS / 1

THE LUCK OF THE CHIMNEY SWEEP / 2

About the Story (2)   Quotes of the Week (2)   Interview Topic (2)   Preview Words (2)   Word-Origin Study (2)   Books to Read (3)   Book Club (3)   Introductory Activities (3)   Extension Activities (4)   Story Selection (7)   Questions Sheet (8)

THE DUST BOWL / 11

About the Story (11)   Quotes of the Week (11)   Interview Topic (11)   Preview Words (11)   Word-Origin Study (11)   Books to Read (12)   Book Club (12) Introductory Activities (12)   Extension Activities (14)   Story Selection (16) Questions Sheet (17)

MYSTERY OF THE DEEP / 20

About the Story (20)   Quotes of the Week (20)   Interview Topic (20)   Preview Words (20)   Word-Origin Study (20)   Books to Read (21)   Book Club (22) Introductory Activities (22)   Extension Activities (23)   Story Selection (25) Questions Sheet (26)

BUYING YOUR FIRST CAR / 29

About the Story (29)   Quotes of the Week (29)   Interview Topic (29)   Preview Words (29)   Word-Origin Study (29)   Books to Read (30)   Book Club (30) Introductory Activities (30)   Extension Activities (31)   Story Selection (33) Questions Sheet (34)

LIFE IS SWEET: THE STORY OF MILTON HERSHEY / 37

About the Story (37)   Quotes of the Week (37)   Interview Topic (37)   Preview
Words (37)   Word-Origin Study (37)   Books to Read (38)   Book Club (38)
Introductory Activities (38)   Extension Activities (39)   Story Selection (41)
Questions Sheet (42)

MINA DEL PADRE, THE LOST PADRE MINE / 45

About the Story (45)   Quotes of the Week (45)   Interview Topic (45)   Preview
Words (45)   Word-Origin Study (45)   Books to Read (46)   Book Club (47)
Introductory Activities (47)   Extension Activities (48)   Story Selection (50)
Questions Sheet (51)

PO CHIENG MA'S CODED PENCILS / 54

About the Story (54)   Quotes of the Week (54)   Interview Topic (54)   Preview
Words (54)   Word-Origin Study (54)   Books to Read (55)   Book Club (55)
Introductory Activities (55)   Extension Activities (57)   Story Selection (59)
Questions Sheet (60)

LOWE'S INTREPID / 63

About the Story (63)   Quotes of the Week (63)   Interview Topic (63)   Preview
Words (63)   Word-Origin Study (63)   Books to Read (64)   Book Club (64)
Introductory Activities (64)   Extension Activities (65)   Story Selection (67)
Questions Sheet (68)

THE NEVER-FADING POPULARITY OF LEVI'S® JEANS / 71

About the Story (71)   Quotes of the Week (71)   Interview Topic (71)   Preview
Words (71)   Word-Origin Study (71)   Books to Read (72)   Book Club (72)
Introductory Activities (72)   Extension Activities (73)   Story Selection (75)
Questions Sheet (76)

A LETTER HOME / 79

About the Story (79)   Quotes of the Week (79)   Interview Topic (79)   Preview
Words (79)   Word-Origin Study (80)   Books to Read (80)   Book Club (81)
Introductory Activities (81)   Extension Activities (81)   Story Selection (84)
Questions Sheet (85)

QUANAH PARKER: COMANCHE CHIEF / 88

About the Story (88)   Quotes of the Week (88)   Interview Topic (88)   Preview
Words (88)   Word-Origin Study (88)   Books to Read (89)   Book Club (90)
Introductory Activities (90)   Extension Activities (91)   Story Selection (93)
Questions Sheet (94)

MARTIN LUTHER KING, JR. RECEIVES THE NOBEL PEACE PRIZE / 97

About the Story (97)   Quotes of the Week (97)   Interview Topic (97)   Preview Words (97)   Word-Origin Study (97)   Books to Read (98)   Introductory Activities (99)   Extension Activities (100)   Story Selection (102)   Questions Sheet (103)

WALKING STONES OF DEATH VALLEY / 106

About the Story (106)   Quotes of the Week (106)   Interview Topic (106)   Preview Words (106)   Word-Origin Study (106)   Books to Read (107)   Book Club (107)   Introductory Activities (107)   Extension Activities (108)   Story Selection (110)   Questions Sheet (111)

CAN SAND SING? / 114

About the Story (114)   Quotes of the Week (114)   Interview Topic (114)   Preview Words (114)   Word-Origin Study (114)   Books to Read (115)   Book Club (115)   Introductory Activities (115)   Extension Activities (116)   Story Selection (118)   Questions Sheet (119)

THOMAS FLYER ARRIVES IN PARIS / 122

About the Story (122)   Quotes of the Week (122)   Interview Topic (122)   Preview Words (122)   Word-Origin Study (122)   Books to Read (123)   Book Club (123)   Introductory Activities (123)   Extension Activities (124)   Story Selection (126)   Questions Sheet (127)

References for Level 7 (130)   Quotation Footnotes for Level 7 (132)   Word-Origin Study Reference for Level 7 (132)

READING LEVEL 8

CONTENTS / 133

IS ANYONE AWAKE OUT THERE? / 134

About the Story (134)   Quotes of the Week (134)   Interview Topic (134)   Preview Words (134)   Word-Origin Study (134)   Books to Read (135)   Book Club (135)   Introductory Activities (135)   Extension Activities (136)   Story Selection (139)   Questions Sheet (140)

FERRIS AND HIS WHEEL / 143

About the Story (143)   Quotes of the Week (143)   Interview Topic (143)   Preview Words (143)   Word-Origin Study (143)   Books to Read (144)   Book Club (144)   Introductory Activities (145)   Extension Activities (147)   Story Selection (149)   Questions Sheet (150)

WHERE DOES ALL THE MONEY GO? / 153

About the Story (153)   Quotes of the Week (153)   Interview Topic (153)   Preview Words (153)   Word-Origin Study (153)   Books to Read (154)   Book Club (154) Introductory Activities (155)   Extension Activities (155)   Story Selection (159) Questions Sheet (160)

THE HALE HOUSE OF HARLEM / 163

About the Story (163)   Quotes of the Week (163)   Interview Topic (163)   Preview Words (163)   Word-Origin Study (163)   Books to Read (164)   Book Club (164) Introductory Activities (164)   Extension Activities (165)   Story Selection (167) Questions Sheet (168)

SIR WALTER RALEIGH'S LOST COLONY / 171

About the Story (171)   Quotes of the Week (171)   Interview Topic (171)   Preview Words (171)   Word-Origin Study (171)   Books to Read (172)   Book Club (172) Introductory Activities (172)   Extension Activities (173)   Story Selection (175) Questions Sheet (176)

LEWIS WICKES HINE / 179

About the Story (179)   Quotes of the Week (179)   Interview Topic (179)   Preview Words (180)   Word-Origin Study (180)   Books to Read (180)   Book Club (181) Introductory Activities (181)   Extension Activities (182)   Story Selection (184) Questions Sheet (185)

MYSTERIOUS CRASH OF AIRSHIP AKRON: 73 FEARED DEAD / 188

About the Story (188)   Quote of the Week (188)   Interview Topic (188)   Preview Words (188)   Word-Origin Study (188)   Books to Read (189)   Book Club (189) Introductory Activities (189)   Extension Activities (190)   Story Selection (193) Questions Sheet (194)

THE TRUE POOH / 197

About the Story (197)   Quotes of the Week (197)   Interview Topic (197)   Preview Words (197)   Word-Origin Study (197)   Books to Read (198)   Book Club (198) Introductory Activities (198)   Extension Activities (199)   Story Selection (201) Questions Sheet (202)

SCOTT JOPLIN: RAGTIME KING / 205

About the Story (205)   Quotes of the Week (205)   Interview Topic (205)   Preview Words (205)   Word-Origin Study (205)   Books to Read (206)   Book Club (206) Introductory Activities (206)   Extension Activities (207)   Story Selection (209) Questions Sheet (210)

BETTY FORD: A TRUE FIRST LADY / 213

About the Story (213)   Quotes of the Week (213)   Interview Topic (213)
Preview Words (213)   Word-Origin Study (213)   Books to Read (214)   Book
Club (215)   Introductory Activities (215)   Extension Activities (215)   Story
Selection (219)   Questions Sheet (220)

RACHEL CARSON: THE COMING OF A SILENT SPRING / 223

About the Story (223)   Quotes of the Week (223)   Interview Topic (223)   Preview
Words (223)   Word-Origin Study (223)   Books to Read (224)   Book Club (225)
Introductory Activities (225)   Extension Activities (226)   Story Selection (228)
Questions Sheet (229)

THE RETURN OF SUPERSONIC FLIGHT / 232

About the Story (232)   Quotes of the Week (232)   Interview Topic (232)   Preview
Words (232)   Word-Origin Study (232)   Books to Read (233)   Book Club (233)
Introductory Activities (233)   Extension Activities (234)   Story Selection (237)
Questions Sheet (238)

THE GUEST STAR / 241

About the Story (241)   Quotes of the Week (241)   Interview Topic (241)   Preview
Words (241)   Word-Origin Study (241)   Books to Read (242)   Book Club (242)
Introductory Activities (242)   Extension Activities (243)   Story Selection (246)
Questions Sheet (247)

THERE LIVES A MONSTER IN THE LOCH / 250

About the Story (250)   Quotes of the Week (250)   Interview Topic (250)   Preview
Words (250)   Word-Origin Study (251)   Books to Read (251)   Book Club (252)
Introductory Activities (252)   Extension Activities (253)   Story Selection (255)
Questions Sheet (256)

"D.B. COOPER—WHERE ARE YOU?" / 259

About the Story (259)   Quotes of the Week (259)   Interview Topic (259)   Preview
Words (259)   Word-Origin Study (259)   Books to Read (260)   Book Club (261)
Introductory Activities (261)   Extension Activities (263)   Story Selection (265)
Questions Sheet (266)

References for Level 8 (269)   Quotation Footnotes for Level 8 (272)   Word-Origin
Study Reference for Level 8 (272)

READING LEVEL 9

CONTENTS   /   273

OMEN IN THE SKY   /   274

About the Story (274)   Quotes of the Week (274)   Interview Topic (274)   Preview Words (274)   Word-Origin Study (274)   Books to Read (275)   Book Club (275) Introductory Activities (276)   Extension Activities (276)   Story Selection (278) Questions Sheet (279)

"COSMIC ROCKET": SOVIETS WINNING THE SPACE RACE   /   282

About the Story (282)   Quotes of the Week (282)   Interview Topic (282)   Preview Words (282)   Word-Origin Study (282)   Books to Read (283)   Book Club (283) Introductory Activities (283)   Extension Activities (284)   Story Selection (286) Questions Sheet (287)

WITCHES AND LIES: THE SALEM WITCH HUNT   /   290

About the Story (290)   Quotes of the Week (290)   Interview Topic (290)   Preview Words (290)   Word-Origin Study (291)   Books to Read (291)   Book Club (292) Introductory Activities (292)   Extension Activities (293)   Story Selection (295) Questions Sheet (296)

THE GLORIOUS TOMBS OF CHINA   /   299

About the Story (299)   Quotes of the Week (299)   Interview Topic (299)   Preview Words (299)   Word-Origin Study (299)   Books to Read (300)   Book Club (301) Introductory Activities (301)   Extension Activities (302)   Story Selection (304) Questions Sheet (305)

AUTOMATON   /   308

About the Story (308)   Quotes of the Week (308)   Interview Topic (308) Preview Words (308)   Word-Origin Study (309)   Books to Read (309)   Book Club (310)   Introductory Activities (310)   Extension Activities (311)   Story Selection (313)   Questions Sheet (314)

AMERICA MOURNS   /   317

About the Story (317)   Quotes of the Week (317)   Interview Topic (318)   Preview Words (318)   Word-Origin Study (318)   Books to Read (318)   Book Club (319) Introductory Activities (319)   Extension Activities (320)   Story Selection (322) Questions Sheet (323)

DREAMING TO REMEMBER / 326

About the Story (326)   Quotes of the Week (326)   Interview Topic (326)   Preview Words (326)   Word-Origin Study (326)   Books to Read (327)   Introductory Activities (328)   Extension Activities (329)   Story Selection (332)   Questions Sheet (333)

SUMMER CAMP ISN'T WHAT IT USED TO BE / 336

About the Story (336)   Quotes of the Week (336)   Interview Topic (336)   Preview Words (336)   Word-Origin Study (336)   Books to Read (337)   Book Club (337) Introductory Activities (337)   Extension Activities (338)   Story Selection (340) Questions Sheet (341)

"MA" BARKER GUNNED DOWN BY F.B.I. / 344

About the Story (344)   Quotes of the Week (344)   Interview Topic (344)   Preview Words (344)   Word-Origin Study (344)   Books to Read (345)   Book Club (346) Introductory Activities (346)   Extension Activities (346)   Story Selection (349) Questions Sheet (350)

JOSEPH CARDINAL BERNARDIN / 353

About the Story (353)   Quotes of the Week (353)   Interview Topic (353) Preview Words (353)   Word-Origin Study (353)   Books to Read (354)   Book Club (354)   Introductory Activities (354)   Extension Activities (355)   Story Selection (357)   Questions Sheet (358)

WHAT DOES "QWERTY" MEAN? / 361

About the Story (361)   Quotes of the Week (361)   Interview Topic (361)   Preview Words (361)   Word-Origin Study (361)   Books to Read (362)   Book Club (362) Introductory Activities (362)   Extension Activities (363)   Story Selection (366) Questions Sheet (367)

ADOPT-A-SENIOR / 370

About the Story (370)   Quotes of the Week (370)   Interview Topic (370)   Preview Words (370)   Word-Origin Study (371)   Books to Read (371)   Book Club (371) Introductory Activities (372)   Extension Activities (372)   Story Selection (374) Questions Sheet (375)

1,200 DEAD IN CAMEROON / 378

About the Story (378)   Quotes of the Week (378)   Interview Topic (378)   Preview Words (378)   Word-Origin Study (378)   Books to Read (379)   Book Club (379) Introductory Activities (380)   Extension Activities (380)   Story Selection (382) Questions Sheet (383)

PREDICTING THE NEXT EARTHQUAKE   /   386

About the Story (386)   Quotes of the Week (386)   Interview Topic (386)   Preview Words (386)   Word-Origin Study (386)   Books to Read (387)   Book Club (388) Introductory Activities (388)   Extension Activities (388)   Story Selection (391) Questions Sheet (392)

CHARLES KURALT, JOURNALIST OF THE PEOPLE   /   395

About the Story (395)   Quotes of the Week (395)   Interview Topic (395)   Preview Words (395)   Word-Origin Study (395)   Books to Read (396)   Book Club (397) Introductory Activities (397)   Extension Activities (398)   Story Selection (400) Questions Sheet (401)

References for Level 9 (404)   Quotation Footnotes for Level 9 (406)   Word-Origin Study Reference for Level 9 (406)

READING LEVEL 7

Story Title	Reading Level	Page
1. The Luck of the Chimney Sweep	7.00	2
2. The Dust Bowl	7.00	11
3. Mystery of the Deep	7.40	20
4. Buying Your First Car	7.42	29
5. Life Is Sweet: The Story of Milton Hershey	7.52	37
6. Mina del Padre, The Lost Padre Mine	7.59	45
7. Po Chieng Ma's Coded Pencils	7.65	54
8. Lowe's *Intrepid*	7.69	63
9. The Never-Fading Popularity of Levi's® Jeans	7.81	71
10. A Letter Home	7.83	79
11. Quanah Parker: Comanche Chief	7.84	88
12. Martin Luther King, Jr. Receives the Nobel Peace Prize	7.86	97
13. Walking Stones of Death Valley	7.86	106
14. Can Sand Sing?	7.90	114
15. *Thomas Flyer* Arrives in Paris	7.98	122
References for Level 7		130
Quotation Footnotes for Level 7		132
Word-Origin Study References for Level 7		132

1. THE LUCK OF THE CHIMNEY SWEEP
Reading Level = 7.00

ABOUT THE STORY

This story tells about the history and legends behind the superstitions surrounding the chimney sweep. It includes anecdotes from Germany, England, and France.

QUOTES OF THE WEEK

Quote 1:

"Superstition is a religion of feeble minds."[1] *(page 458)*—EDMUND BURKE

Quote 2:

"You know, Tolstoy, like myself, wasn't taken in by superstitions like science and medicine."[1] *(page 458)*—GEORGE BERNARD SHAW

Quote 3:

"There is a superstition in avoiding superstition."[1] *(page 458)*—FRANCIS BACON

INTERVIEW TOPIC

Interview a person over the age of 60 who practices superstitious rituals to bring good luck (knocking on wood, collecting lucky pennies, etc.). Prepare a list of questions including literal and interpretive questions: "Do you truly believe these rituals bring good luck or ward off bad luck? Why do you feel this way?" Compile a list of superstitious rituals your subject remembers from his or her childhood. Does he or she know when or where the rituals began?

Make a list of unique terms used by your subject and discuss them in class. Use the words often throughout the week of the lesson.

Research one of these superstitions and find its origin and original meaning. Use as many of the words from your word list as possible.

PREVIEW WORDS

superstition   *apprenticeship*   *undertaker*

WORD-ORIGIN STUDY

apprenticeship: *Apprentice* is derived from the same word as apprehend, or to take hold. An apprentice "takes hold" of knowledge passed on to him or her by a master. An *apprenticeship* is an agreement entered into where an apprentice works for a master craftsman in exchange for instruction in the craft.

---

[1] Refer to *Quotation Footnotes for Level 7* on page 132.

| superstition: | The prefix *super-* means "over, above, or on top." *Superstition* comes from the Latin *superstitio*: a standing still over or near an object or event as one would stand in awe at a time of amazement, wonder, or dread. |

List other words beginning with the prefix *super-*. Write the words and their definitions in your vocabulary notebooks.

BOOKS TO READ

Baring-Gould, Sabine. *The Book of Were-Wolves: Being an Account of a Terrible Superstition*. Detroit: Omnigraphics, 1989.

Cowan, Lore. *Are You Superstitious?* Princeton, NJ: Apex Books, 1969.

Davis, Kenneth W. and Everett Gillis (eds.). *Black Cats, Hoot Owls, and Water Witches: Beliefs, Superstitions, and Sayings from Texas*. Denton, TX: University of North Texas Press, 1989.

Delton, Judy. *It Happened on Thursday*. Chicago: Albert Whitman & Company, 1978.

Frazer, Sir. James George. *The Illustrated Golden Bough*. Garden City, NY: Doubleday, 1978.

Herson, Kathleen. *The Half Child*. New York: Simon & Schuster Books for Young Readers, 1991.

Jenkins, Steve. *Duck's Breath and Mouse Pie: A Collection of Animal Superstitions*. New York: Ticknor & Fields, 1994.

Maple, Eric. *Superstition and the Superstitious*. South Brunswick, NJ: A.S. Barnes, 1971.

Nevins, Ann. *Super Stitches: A Book of Superstitions*. New York: Holiday House, 1983.

Perl, Lila. *Don't Sing Before Breakfast, Don't Sleep in the Moonlight: Everyday Superstitions and How They Began*. New York: Clarion Books, 1988.

Robertson, Joanne. *Sea Witches*. New York: Dial Books for Young Readers, 1991.

Schwartz, Alvin. *Cross Your Fingers, Spit in Your Hat*. Philadelphia: J.B. Lippincott Co., 1974.

Stamaty, Mark Alan. *Minnie Maloney and Macaroni*. New York: Dial Press, 1976.

BOOK CLUB

Read Kathleen Herson's *The Half Child*.

INTRODUCTORY ACTIVITIES

DAY ONE

| *Objective:* | The students will discuss superstitions; what they are, why people practice them, and the impact of superstitious rituals on one's life. |

Display and discuss the quotes of the week. Ask the students to read the quotes. **Ask**: "What are Shaw, Burke, and Bacon trying to tell us about their opinions and definitions of the word *superstition*? Who do you think is closest to the truth? Why do you feel this way?

"Why are these quotes interesting to read? Write a quote of your own telling about your insights into superstition. Use your own style of speaking to concisely express your view, whether serious or comical."

DAY TWO

STORY LESSON

Follow the *Presenting the Story Lesson* instructions in the Introduction. Each story lesson follows the same procedure; however, say the following in step 4: "The title of the story we're reading today is *The Luck of the Chimney Sweep*. What do you think the story is about? What do you already know about chimney sweeps and the superstitions surrounding them? Where did you learn about these superstitions?"

EXTENSION ACTIVITIES

1. Make copies of the good luck chart on page 5. In the first column, ask the students to fill in superstitious rituals they, friends, or family members practice to bring good luck during a given week. In the second column, enter the number of times the ritual was performed. In the last column, record the number of times the ritual appeared to bring good luck. Using mathematics, calculate a percentage to illustrate each ritual's effectiveness.

2. Review the charts from Extension Activity 1. Look closely at the results. "Was the 'good luck' experienced after the superstitious ritual real or simply imagined? Would the good luck have occurred whether or not the ritual was completed? Why do you feel this way? If good luck rituals do not bring luck, then why do people continue to practice them?"

Good luck chart

Good Luck Ritual	Times Performed	Good Luck	Percentage

Name _____   Date _____

THE LUCK OF THE CHIMNEY SWEEP

Anyone who grew up watching the movie *Mary Poppins* knows that chimney sweeps are lucky. Where did the superstition come from? How could shaking the hand of a soot-covered man bring anyone luck?

Chimney sweeps began to organize in the 1400s when Germany required all homeowners to clean their chimney twice a year. Due to the dangerous nature of the occupation, chimney sweeps enacted strict guidelines to become sweeps. A young man began his career with a three-year apprenticeship. At the end of the term, a committee judged the future sweep on his ability to clean a tall, wide chimney.

In fourteenth-century England, chimney sweeps adopted the uniform of a black top hat and tails. Usually bought used from the local undertaker, the dark clothing hid the smudges of soot.

Throughout the world it has long been considered good luck to kiss a chimney sweep or shake his hand. One story from France tells about a young chimney sweep who fell from his perch on the roof. He slid down the incline until his tailcoat caught on a drain pipe where he hung upside down until a young woman inside the house pulled him in through an upper-story window, saving his life. The onlookers below cheered as the grateful sweep kissed the woman. When he reached the street everyone wanted to shake the hand of the lucky man who later married the lady who saved him.

Today the tradition continues as chimney sweeps wait outside wedding chapels. For good luck the bride kisses the sweep, the groom shakes his hand, and a coin passes to the sweep thanking him for his favor.

One story tells about King George III traveling on horseback in the 1700s. Startled by a rabbit, the King's horse bucked wildly. An alert chimney sweep ran to the rescue, taking the reins and calming the horse. The King tipped his hat and bowed three times in a show of gratitude. One by one his attendants each bowed three times. Many people continue to bow three times to a chimney sweep in acknowledgment of his lucky powers.

QUESTIONS FOR THE LUCK OF THE CHIMNEY SWEEP

Literal Questions:

THE FACTS:

1. When and where did chimney sweeps begin to organize?

_____

_____

_____

2. How did a young man become a chimney sweep?

_____

_____

_____

3. Why is it considered good luck to kiss a chimney sweep or shake his hand?

_____

_____

_____

4. How did a chimney sweep help King George III?

_____

_____

_____

SEQUENCE OF EVENTS:

5. What happened to a young chimney sweep after he finished his three-year apprenticeship?

_____

_____

_____

6. What happened to the French chimney sweep before he kissed the young woman?

_____

_____

_____

Name _____ **Date** _____

Interpretive Questions:

DRAWING CONCLUSIONS:

7. Why do brides continue to kiss a chimney sweep for good luck?

_____

_____

_____

_____

MAKING INFERENCES:

8. Do chimney sweeps enjoy the tradition of kissing a bride? Why do you think so?

_____

_____

_____

_____

MAKING PREDICTIONS:

9. Will people continue to consider chimney sweeps good luck in the future? Why do you think so?

_____

_____

_____

_____

IDENTIFICATION OF CAUSE:

10. Why do people practice superstitious acts even though they seem illogical?

_____

_____

_____

_____

IDENTIFICATION OF THE MAIN IDEA:

11. Write a title for the story. Use as few words as possible.

_____

_____

_____

Name _____   Date _____

COMPARISON:

12. How is believing a black cat crossing your path is bad luck similar to believing a kiss from a chimney sweep is good luck? How are they different?

_____

_____

_____

_____

SUMMARIZE:

13. In your own words, tell why people believe chimney sweeps are lucky?

_____

_____

_____

_____

EFFECT:

14. Although there is no proof that kissing a chimney sweep will bring a couple good luck, what effect might acting out the tradition have on the newlyweds' marriage?

_____

_____

_____

_____

FACT AND OPINION:

15. The story tells us the occupation of a chimney sweep is dangerous. Is this a fact or an opinion? How can you prove your answer?

_____

_____

_____

_____

ON YOUR OWN:

16. Write a question about the story for a teacher or another student to answer.

_____

_____

Name _____   **Date** _____

2. THE DUST BOWL
Reading Level = 7.00

ABOUT THE STORY

The story tells about the Dust Bowl of the 1930s. It discusses the drought, the dust storms, and the impact of this natural disaster on individual lives.

QUOTES OF THE WEEK

Quote 1:

"Out of the dust and the drought of the plain,
To sing with the silver hosannas of rain."[2] *(p. 852)*—ROY CAMPBELL, *THE PALM*

Quote 2:

"When the night came again it was black night, for the stars could not pierce the dust to get down, and the window lights could not even spread beyond their own yards. Now the dust was evenly mixed with the air, an emulsion of dust and air. Houses were shut tight, and cloth wedged around doors and windows, but dust came in so thinly that it could not be seen in the air, and it settled like pollen on chairs and tables, on the dishes."[10]
—JOHN STEINBECK, *THE GRAPES OF WRATH*, Chapter 1

INTERVIEW TOPIC

Interview a person who lived during the Dust Bowl era. Prepare a list of questions that includes literal and interpretive questions: "What was it like to live through the Dust Bowl?" If the person did not live in an area of the country directly affected by the drought, did the drought touch his or her personal life in any way such as reducing food supply or job opportunities?

PREVIEW WORDS

Dust Bowl	*Great Depression*
New England	*American Plains*

WORD-ORIGIN STUDY

disaster:	The word *disaster* is rooted in the practice of astrology. The base word, *aster*, found in words such as asterisk, means "star." Astrologers see future misfortunes, or disasters, in the reading of stars.
meteorology:	The prefix *meteor-* comes from a Greek word meaning "meteor or things in the air." Meteorology means the study of the atmosphere or atmospheric phenomena, or the study of things in the air.

---

[2] Refer to *Quotation Footnotes for Level 7* on page 132.
[10] Refer to *Quotation Footnotes for Level 7* on page 132.

List other words beginning with the prefix *meteor-*. Write the words and their definitions in your vocabulary notebook.

BOOKS TO READ

Andryszewski, Tricia. *Dust Bowl: Disaster on the Plains*. Brookfield, CT: Millbrook Press, 1994.

Farris, John. *Dust Bowl*. San Diego: Lucent Books, 1989.

Ganzel, Bill. *Dust Bowl Descent*. Lincoln: University of Nebraska Press, 1984.

Heinrichs, Ann. *America the Beautiful: Oklahoma*. Chicago: Children's Press, 1989.

Hesse, Karen. *Out of the Dust*. New York: Scholastic Press, 1997. (Newbery Book)

Hurt, R. Douglas. *The Dust Bowl: An Agricultural and Social History*. Chicago: Nelson-Hall, 1981.

King, David C. (ed.). *Dust Bowl*. Carlisle, MA: Discovery Entertainment Ltd., 1997.

Low, Ann M. *Dust Bowl Diary*. Lincoln: University of Nebraska Press, 1984.

Rossiter, Phyllis. *Moxie*. New York: Four Winds Press, 1990.

Shindo, Charles. *Dust Bowl Migrants of the American Imagination*. Lawrence: University Press of Kansas, 1996.

Stanley, Jerry. *Children of the Dust Bowl: The True Story of the School at Weedpatch Camp*. New York: Crown, 1992.

Steinbeck, John. *John Steinbeck's The Grapes of Wrath*. Broomall, PA: Chelsea House Publishers, 1996.

Worster, Donald. *Dust Bowl: The Southern Plains in the 1930s*. Cary, NC: Oxford University Press, 1982.

VIDEO

The Grapes of Wrath (Twentieth Century Fox Film Corporation, 1940). Livonia, MI: CBS/Fox Company, 1988.

CDs, RECORDS, AND CASSETTES

Guthrie, Woody. *Dust Bowl Ballads* (Cassette). Cambridge, MA: Rounder Records, 1988, © 1940.

Steinbeck, John. *The Grapes of Wrath* (Cassette). Petaluma, CA: The Mind's Eye, 1980.

BOOK CLUB

Read *Out of the Dust* by Karen Hesse. (Newbery Book)

INTRODUCTORY ACTIVITIES

Note: Lessons for Day One and Day Two call for a guest meteorologist to visit your class. Contact your local television news organizations or the weather service to find a meteorologist who will visit your class. Tell the meteorologist you are looking for someone with knowledge of the Dust Bowl and the weather system that caused the drought.

DAY ONE

Objective: The students will discuss what a drought is and compile a list of questions (literal and interpretive) to ask a meteorologist about droughts.

Introduce the subject of drought to the students. What is a drought? How long can a drought last? Has anyone experienced a drought or felt the effects of a drought that occurred somewhere else in the world?

Prepare a list of questions to present to the guest speaker, a meteorologist. Make the following chart:

Literal Questions	Interpretive Questions
1.	1.
2.	2.

Help the students phrase literal and interpretive questions. For example:

■ *Literal question*, "What causes a drought?"

■ *Interpretive question*, "Is a drought a weather phenomenon we should fear? Why do you feel this way?"

Note: Students who write literal and interpretive questions understand how to approach similar questions when they encounter them on standardized tests.

After the lesson, contact your guest meteorologist. Give the speaker the questions so he or she can prepare for the discussion.

DAY TWO

Objective: The students will listen to a meteorologist describe a drought and introduce the topic of the Dust Bowl. They will participate in a discussion about droughts and the Dust Bowl.

Display the question chart in front of the class. Introduce the speaker, and tell the students that the speaker will present information about droughts and the American Dust Bowl.

During the lecture, note on a chart special vocabulary words used by the meteorologist. Display the chart throughout the week, and encourage the students to use these words often. The students should enter the words into their vocabulary notebooks. After the discussion, hold a question-and-answer session.

DAY THREE

STORY LESSON

Follow the *Presenting the Story Lesson* instructions in the Introduction. Each story lesson follows the same procedure; however, say the following in step 4: "The title of the story we're reading today is *The Dust Bowl*. What do you think the story is about? What do you already know about the Dust Bowl?"

EXTENSION ACTIVITIES

1. Read the story *Children of the Dust Bowl: The True Story of the School at Weedpatch Camp* to the class. Ask the students to list unfamiliar words in their vocabulary notebooks. Although this book is found in the children's section of the library, it gives a detailed and interesting first-hand account of life during the Dust Bowl era.

2. Have the students write an entry into an imaginary journal or diary in the voice of a person their own age living through the Dust Bowl. They should use as many of the vocabulary words they learned throughout the week as they can in their entries. Give a set length for the entry based on the ability of the student.

3. Watch the movie *The Grapes of Wrath* (see Video). Discuss the impact of the Dust Bowl on the characters in the film. How would a similar drought affect the lives of the students?

THE DUST BOWL

Anyone who lives in the American desert southwest can tell you about dust storms. March winds begin to blow, and fine desert dust rises in the air turning the turquoise blue sky to a dirty grey. Dust pellets blast your skin with a burning tingle, and the grit coats your teeth and grinds as you speak. You can feel the sand as you inhale. As uncomfortable as today's dust storms are, they cannot compare to the horror of the savage storms that created the Dust Bowl.

It was 1931 when the drought hit. Already stricken by the effects of the Great Depression, the people of the American plains faced a natural disaster that would destroy the lives of hundreds of farmers. By 1936, there had been only scant precipitation, and for five hideous years the land laid scorched in the sun.

Then the wind began to blow, and it blew for four consecutive years. The wind stirred the red, dry dirt carrying it high into the air until it looked like a bloody thunder cloud rising up from the Earth. It tore apart the farm land. It tore apart the crops. It tore apart the lives of the people living on the land.

Witnesses tell of standing on the open fields when they saw a huge wall of swirling dust moving across the plains. Hordes of jackrabbits frantically scurried in front of the storm hoping to outrun the sand as the farmers scrambled to get the livestock to shelter, then sped to their homes. Inside, they would do their best to seal up cracks with wet rags. Then the storm hit, pelting the house with sizzling sand strong enough to sandblast the paint off exterior walls.

Children slept with wet towels and sponges over their faces to filter out the dirt. In the morning, everyone cleaned the house before the next blast. Sand buried anything from fences to livestock and the chores of children included cleaning the sand out of the nostrils of the cows several times a day.

The dust clouds rose up into the atmosphere and blew eastward. People along the eastern coast reported smelling dust. In February 1934 brown snow fell in New England. Chemists analyzed the snow and found dirt from Oklahoma, Texas, and Kansas.

QUESTIONS FOR THE DUST BOWL

Literal Questions:

THE FACTS:

1. When did the drought that led to the Dust Bowl begin?

_____

_____

_____

2. What did people witness just before a dust storm hit?

_____

_____

_____

3. How did children try to keep the dust out of their faces as they slept?

_____

_____

_____

4. In what year did brown snow fall in New England?

_____

_____

_____

SEQUENCE OF EVENTS:

5. What happened after the American plains experienced drought for five years?

_____

_____

_____

6. What did people do after a sand storm was over?

_____

_____

_____

Name _____   Date _____

Interpretive Questions:

DRAWING CONCLUSIONS:

7. Why was the Dust Bowl harder on farmers than any other people in the American plains?

_____

_____

_____

_____

MAKING INFERENCES:

8. How did the children feel during a sand storm?

_____

_____

_____

_____

MAKING PREDICTIONS:

9. Do you believe America will experience a severe drought and sand storm in the future? Why do you think so?

_____

_____

_____

_____

IDENTIFICATION OF CAUSE:

10. What caused the brown snow of 1934 in New England?

_____

_____

_____

_____

IDENTIFICATION OF THE MAIN IDEA:

11. Write a title for the story. Use as few words as possible.

_____

_____

_____

Name _____   **Date** _____

COMPARISON:

12. How is a severe drought similar to a devastating flood? How is it different?

_____

_____

_____

_____

SUMMARIZE:

13. In your own words, describe what it would be like to experience a sand storm during the Dust Bowl.

_____

_____

_____

_____

EFFECT:

14. What effect might the Dust Bowl have had on the children who experienced it?

_____

_____

_____

_____

FACT AND OPINION:

15. The story tells us the drought that led to the Dust Bowl began in 1931. Is this a fact or someone's opinion? How can you prove your answer?

_____

_____

_____

_____

ON YOUR OWN:

16. Write a question about the story for a teacher or another student to answer.

_____

_____

Name _____ **Date** _____

3. MYSTERY OF THE DEEP
Reading Level = 7.40

ABOUT THE STORY

Although carcasses of giant squid wash ashore from time to time, no one has seen a live giant squid in its natural habitat. Clyde Roper of the Smithsonian perseveres in his quest to become the first human to witness the life-habits of the giant squid.

QUOTES OF THE WEEK

Quote 1:

"There is, one knows not what sweet mystery about this sea, whose gently awful stirrings seem to speak of some hidden soul beneath; like those fabled undulations of the Ephesian sod over the buried Evangelist St. John."[2] *(page 571)*—HERMAN MELVILLE, *MOBY DICK*

Quote 2:

"So is this great and wide sea, wherein are things creeping innumerable, both small and great beasts.

"There go the ships: there is that leviathan, whom thou hast made to play therein."[2] *(page 21)*—*THE HOLY BIBLE*, PSALMS 104:19–27

Quote 3:

"Great works are performed not by strength but by perseverance."[3]
(page 15)—SAMUEL JOHNSON

INTERVIEW TOPIC

Interview someone between the ages of 30-50 about perseverance in a task or quest that interests him or her. Incorporate literal and interpretive questions in your prepared interview list. Such questions might include: "Why are you steadfast in your pursuit? Why is the quest important? How is your attitude toward life affected by the quest?"

PREVIEW WORDS

carcasses   *leviathans*   *colossal*

WORD-ORIGIN STUDY

leviathan: *Leviathan* is a large aquatic animal described in the Bible's Book of Job. The term encompasses "anything huge of its kind."

---

[2] Refer to *Quotation Footnotes for Level 7* on page 132.

[3] Refer to *Quotation Footnotes for Level 7* on page 132.

colossal: The word *colossal* originated from the name of a giant statue of Apollo called the Colossus of Rhodes. It was 120 feet tall, and was made by a man named Chares around 280 B.C. In ancient times it was included in a list called *The Seven Wonders of the World*. The word *Colossus* and terms derived from the name, such as colossal, refer to anything of enormous size.

persevere: The prefix *per-* means "thoroughly or completely." The base word *severe* is from the Latin *severus* (serious, strict). Therefore, to *persevere* is to be completely serious, strict, or steadfast in purpose.

List other words beginning with the prefix *per-*. Write the words and their definitions in your vocabulary notebook.

BOOKS TO READ

Broad, William J. *The Universe Below: Discovering the Secrets of the Deep Sea*. New York: Simon & Schuster, 1997.

Carson, Rachel. *The Sea Around Us*. New York: Penguin Books, 1979.

Cousteau, Jacques Yves. *Octopus and Squid: The Soft Intelligence*. Garden City, NY: Doubleday, 1973.

Dipper, Frances. *Mysteries of the Ocean Deep*. Brookfield, CT: Copper Beech Books, 1996.

Fleisher, Paul. *Our Oceans: Experiments and Activities in Marine Science.* Brookfield, CT: Millbrook Press, 1995.

Melville, Herman. *Moby Dick or, The Whale.*

Melville, Herman. *Moby Dick as Adapted and Retold by Frank L. Beals*. San Antonio, TX: The Naylor Company, 1965. (adapted for younger readers)

O'Dell, Scott. *The Black Pearl*. Boston: Houghton Mifflin Company, 1967.

Reed, Don C. *The Kraken*. Honesdale, PA: Boyds Mill Press, 1995.

Thiele, Colin. *Shadow Shark*. New York: Harper & Row, 1985.

ARTICLES

Broad, William J. "Biologist Closing on Hidden Lair of Giant Squid; A Submersible Dive Is Planned to 3,000 Feet." *The New York Times*, February 13, 1996, B7, C1.

_____. "Squid Keeps Its Secrets." *The New York Times*, June 24, 1997, B11.

Coniff, Richard. "Clyde Roper Can't Wait to Be Attacked by the Giant Squid." *Smithsonian*, May 1996, p126.

Conley-Early, Andrea. "The Hunt for a Giant Squid." *Sea Frontiers*, Fall 1995, 48.

Fisher, Arthur. "The Hunt for Giant Squid: A High-Tech Search Is on for the Sea's Most Elusive Creature." *Popular Science*, March 1997, 74.

Young, Catherine. "Scientists Use Crittercam to Search for Sea's Most Elusive Creature." *Insight on the News*, May 5, 1997, 39.

VIDEOS

Jones, Hardy and Julia Whitty. *Challenge of the Seas: Silent Skies: Florida Everglades.* Falls Church, VA: Landmark Films, 1990.

_____. *Challenge of the Seas: Tribes in the Sea.* Anaheim, CA: Diamond Entertainment Corp., 1994.

Scholz, Julie (producer). *Discovering Great Minds of Science.* San Ramon, CA: International Video Network, 1995.

Time-Life Films. *The Living Planet: Oceans.* New York: Time-Life Video, 1984.

BOOK CLUB

Read *Moby Dick* by Herman Melville. Alternate books: *The Kraken* by Don C. Reed; *The Black Pearl* by Scott O'Dell; or *Shadow Shark* by Colin Thiele.

INTRODUCTORY ACTIVITIES

DAY ONE

Objective: The students will make a list of life goals they would like to achieve.

Discuss famous people who have or are currently pursuing a life's dream. A goal that takes perseverance to complete or reach is also called a "quest." For example, Carl Sagan was on a quest to find intelligent life in the universe. Habitat for Humanity is a group of people on a quest to eradicate homelessness.

Each student will look through his or her list to find goals that could become their life's quest. Students write a short essay describing the life quest: Why you would like to achieve your goal, what means you would follow to achieve your goal (i.e., get a college degree), and why your quest is important to you and others. Will the quest be important even if the attempt is made, but the goal is never realized in your lifetime?

DAY TWO

STORY LESSON

Follow the *Presenting the Story Lesson* instructions in the Introduction. Each story lesson follows the same procedure; however, say the following in step 4: "Yesterday we talked about quests. Today we will read about a man named Clyde Roper. He is on a quest to find a giant squid."

EXTENSION ACTIVITIES

1. Students look for people who are on a quest. They may be either someone no one knows about or someone famous. Students write a short story about the person and his or her quest. Students also design a poster telling about the person and his or her quest. Display the poster and story together. Students set up an exhibit of the posters, working together to give the collection a title.

2. Review the essays written on Day One. "What have you learned from the people you studied in Extension Activity 1 that would help you achieve your goals? What did you learn about perseverance from these people?"

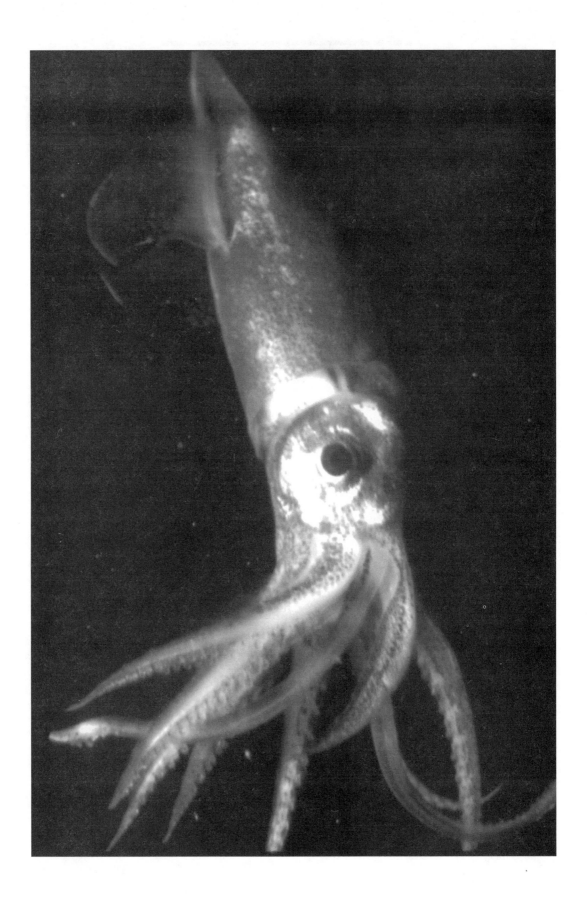

MYSTERY OF THE DEEP

There is a mystery in the deep ocean abyss. Creatures never seen alive dwell in the unexplored darkness. Folklore tells us of colossal monsters rising from the deep attacking ships as they cross the sea. Many of these tales originated from the imaginations of weary sailors. However, concrete evidence points to the existence of an awesome creature, the giant squid.

Reports of giant squid carcasses washing ashore are almost common events. Jules Verne based scenes from his novel 20,000 *Leagues Under the Sea* on factual reports of furious attacks on ships. Nevertheless, no human has seen a living giant squid in its natural habitat.

Scientists estimate the size of an adult giant squid between 60 and 75 feet, weighing in at more than a ton. Its eyes are the size of hub caps. Two elongated feeding tentacles containing toothed suckers snare its prey. Dragging the helpless animal to a sharp beak and tongue, the squid tears its dinner into edible bits.

Clyde Roper of the Smithsonian Institution is on a quest to find and study the giant squid. He looks in the feeding grounds of the squid's natural enemy, the sperm whale.

Fully grown, an adult sperm whale is about 80 feet long and weighs 70 tons. It is the largest of the toothed whales. The sperm whale diet includes large portions of giant squid. Researchers have found many indigestible giant squid beaks and nearly 30,000 small squid in the stomachs of sperm whales.

Roper and his team of scientists created a high-tech search party to scout the feeding grounds of the sperm whale. They hope to be the first to witness a meeting of these two leviathans of the deep.

Questions for Mystery of the Deep

Literal Questions:

THE FACTS:

1. What is the estimated size of an adult giant squid?

_____

_____

_____

2. How much does a giant squid weigh?

_____

_____

_____

3. Where is Clyde Roper looking for giant squids?

_____

_____

_____

4. What have researchers found in the stomachs of sperm whales?

_____

_____

_____

SEQUENCE OF EVENTS:

5. What does a giant squid do to its prey before it tears it into edible bits?

_____

_____

_____

6. What does Clyde Roper intend to do after he finds the giant squid?

_____

_____

_____

Name _____ **Date** _____

Interpretive Questions:

DRAWING CONCLUSIONS:

7. What one word best describes Clyde Roper?

_____

_____

_____

_____

MAKING INFERENCES:

8. How have sailors felt about giant squids in the past? Why do you feel this way?

_____

_____

_____

_____

MAKING PREDICTIONS:

9. Do you think Clyde Roper will find a live giant squid? Why do you think so?

_____

_____

_____

_____

IDENTIFICATION OF CAUSE:

10. Why is Clyde Roper looking for a live giant squid?

_____

_____

_____

_____

IDENTIFICATION OF MAIN IDEA:

11. Write a title for the story. Use as few words as possible.

_____

_____

_____

Name _____   Date _____

COMPARISON:

12. How are giant squid and sperm whales alike? How are they different?

_____

_____

_____

_____

SUMMARIZE:

13. In your own words, describe a giant squid and its eating behaviors.

_____

_____

_____

_____

EFFECT:

14. What effect might finding a live giant squid have on Clyde Roper's life? Why do you think so?

_____

_____

_____

_____

FACT AND OPINION:

15. The story said, "Its (the giant squid's) eyes are the size of hub caps." Is this a fact or someone's opinion? How can you prove your answer?

_____

_____

_____

_____

ON YOUR OWN:

16. Write a question about the story for a teacher or another student to answer.

_____

_____

Name _____   **Date** _____

4. BUYING YOUR FIRST CAR
Reading Level = 7.42

ABOUT THE STORY

The article explains various sources for buying used cars and the precautions every buyer should take to avoid losing money.

QUOTES OF THE WEEK

Quote 1:

"No other manmade device since the shield and lances of the knights quite fulfills a man's ego like an automobile."[3] *(page 338)*—WILLIAM ROOTES

Quote 2:

"This is the only country that ever went to the poorhouse in an automobile."[3] *(page 339)*—WILL ROGERS

INTERVIEW TOPIC

Interview a parent, grandparent, or friend who can tell about his or her experiences in buying a first car. Prepare a question list including literal and interpretive questions: "Where did you buy your first car? How old were you? What was the make, model, and year of the car? Why did you choose that particular car?" If possible, obtain a photograph of the car or a copy of the photograph to mount next to your interview.

PREVIEW WORDS

enthusiastically   *monstrosity*   *exorbitant*

WORD-ORIGIN STUDY

exorbitant:	The prefix *ex-* means "out" and the base word *orbit* means "track." *Exorbitance* is "to go out of the track," or to go far beyond the limits of reasonable prices. To be *exorbitant* is to go beyond what is reasonable or usual.
automobile:	The prefix *auto-* comes from the Greek word *autos,* meaning "self." When combined with mobile, or movable, the word *automobile* means "self-moving."

List other words beginning with the prefix *auto-.* Write the words and their definitions in your vocabulary notebook.

---

[3] Refer to *Quotation Footnotes for Level 7* on page 132.

BOOKS TO READ

Bunting, Eve. *Such Nice Kids*. New York: Clarion Books, 1990.

Donovan, Stacey. *Dive*. New York: Dutton Children's Books, 1994.

Draper, Sharon M. *Tears of a Tiger*. New York: Maxwell Macmillan International, 1994.

Gillis, Jack. *The Used Car Book, 1994-1995: The Definitive Guide to Buying a Safe, Reliable, and Economical Used Car*. New York: Harper Perennial, 1994.

Kerr, M.E. *Fell Down*. New York: HarperCollins Publishers, 1991.

The Merritt Editors. *How to Insure Your Car: A Step by Step Guide to Buying the Coverage You Need at Prices You Can Afford*. Santa Monica, CA: Merritt Publishers, 1996.

Myers, Edward. *Climb or Die*. New York: Hyperion Books for Children, 1994.

Naughton, Jim. *My Brother Stealing Second*. New York: Harper & Row, 1989.

Paulsen, Gary. *The Car*. San Diego: Harcourt Brace, 1994.

CDS, RECORDS, AND CASSETTES

Lathen, Emma (pseud.). *Brewing Up a Storm* (Cassette). Santa Fe, NM: Sunset Productions, 1996.

BOOK CLUB

Read *The Car* by Gary Paulsen.

INTRODUCTORY ACTIVITIES

DAY ONE

Objective: The students will write a story telling about buying their first car.

Tell the students they will spend a week learning about buying cars. Discuss what they believe they will do when they buy their first car. *DO NOT CORRECT THEM ON THEIR ESTIMATES OF COST.* (See Extension Activity 4.)

The students will write a story telling about how they plan to buy their first car. What type of car will they buy? How much will it cost? Where will they look for their car? Etc.

DAY TWO

STORY LESSON

Follow the *Presenting the Story Lesson* instructions in the Introduction. Each story lesson follows the same procedure; however, say the following in step 4: "The title of the story we're reading today is *Buying Your First Car*. What do you think the story is about? What do you already know about buying cars?"

EXTENSION ACTIVITIES

1. Each day of the week invite one of the following speakers to your class or visit them at their place of business.

   ■ Representative from the Better Business Bureau

   ■ Banker (loan officer)

   ■ Insurance salesperson;

   ■ Car salesperson.

   Before each session, help the students prepare literal and interpretive questions about each specialty. During the interview, the students take notes including terminology of the trade with definitions.

2. The students make charts or graphs to illustrate the complete cost of a car including the price paid, taxes, interest on a loan, insurance, maintenance, etc. Each student calculates the percentage of the cost each of these areas represent. They can use bar graphs, pie graphs, pictographs, line graphs, etc.

3. The students write a "how-to" guide for buying a car using the vocabulary words they learned throughout the week. Incorporate the graphs from Activity 2 into the guide.

4. The students compare the stories written on Day One to the "how-to" guide written in Activity 3. Were any of their expectations unrealistic? Why do they feel this way?

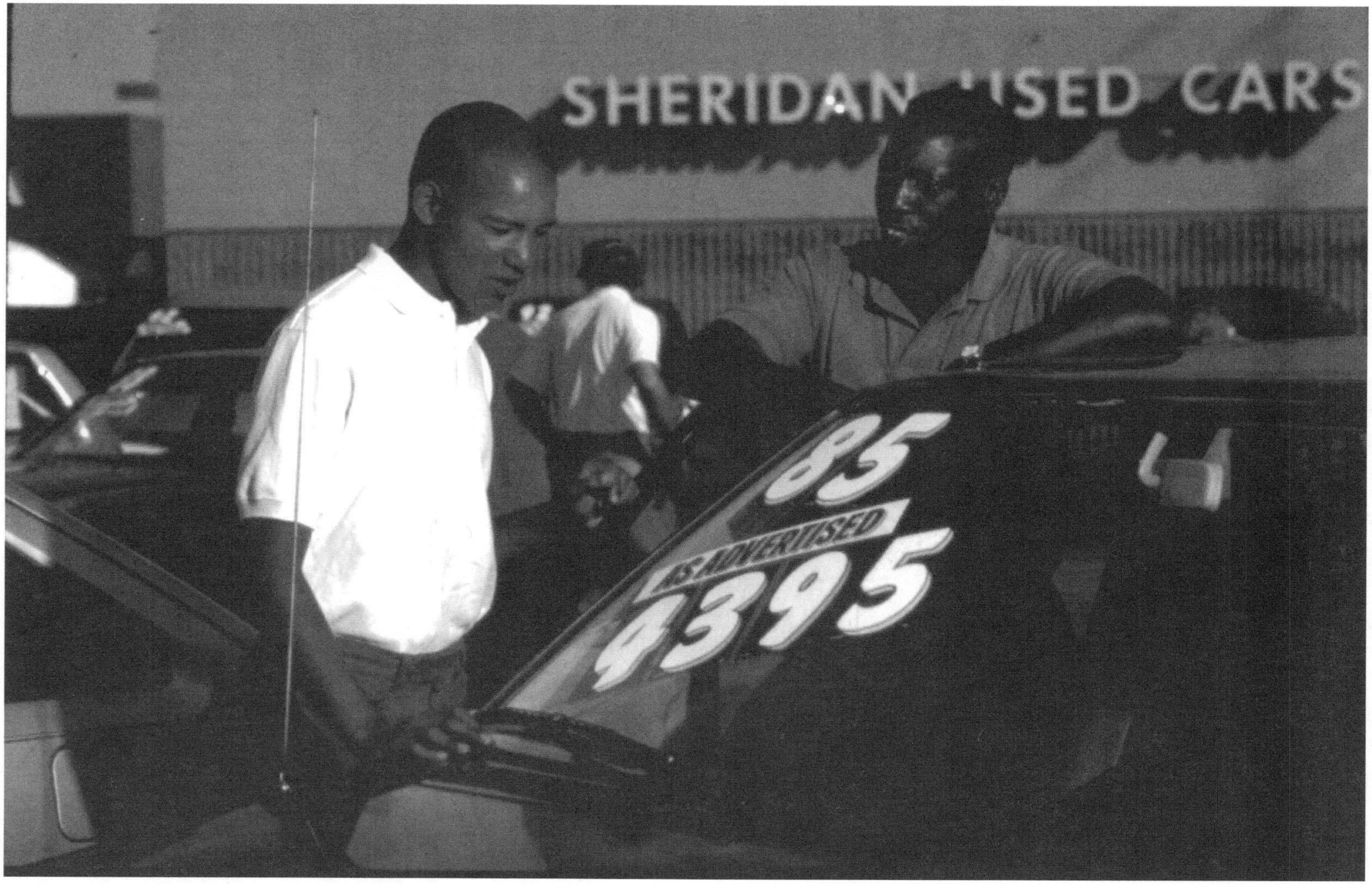
SHERIDAN USED CARS
85
AS ADVERTISED
4395

BUYING YOUR FIRST CAR

Year after year high school students begin the rituals considered to many as "rites of passage." Driver's Education leads to the driving test. The driving test leads to the purchase of the first car.

Teenagers, as well as adults, enthusiastically buy the car of their dreams at first sight. Yet thousands of these young people discover their shiny new automobile is a horrible monstrosity. That beautiful car on the outside becomes a huge expensive repair job on the inside.

How can you safeguard yourself and still find the ideal car? Educate yourself before you even glance at a car. There are several informative sources found as close as your local library.

Begin your education with a thorough reading of the latest consumer guides. Consumer guides tell you how much to pay for a used car based on condition and years of age. Learn about the good points and bad points of the model you want. What type of engine is available in the model? Does the model require expensive repairs? What is the recall history of the model year?

Next, look carefully at the individual selling the car. You can't rely on the information given by a stranger advertising the car in a newspaper. Used-car dealers might offer warranties that will give you peace of mind. Ask for the car's history and scrutinize it carefully. Is the car sold "as is"? In other words, who is responsible for the cost of repair if problems arise? Remember, always call your local Better Business Bureau before you step onto any used-car lot.

Buying your first car is an exciting adventure. Arm yourself with good, current information and you'll avoid an exorbitant nightmare.

QUESTIONS FOR BUYING YOUR FIRST CAR

Literal Questions:

THE FACTS:

1. How can you safeguard yourself and still find the ideal car?

_____

_____

_____

2. Where can you find several informative sources?

_____

_____

_____

3. Name three things you should look for in a consumer guide before you buy your first car.

_____

_____

_____

4. Who should you call before you step onto any used-car lot?

_____

_____

_____

SEQUENCE OF EVENTS:

5. Which source of information does the story list first?

_____

_____

_____

6. Which source of information does the story list last?

_____

_____

_____

Name _____   Date _____

Interpretive Questions:

DRAWING CONCLUSIONS:

7. Is it wise to buy a car without educating yourself first? Why do you feel this way?

_____

_____

_____

_____

MAKING INFERENCES:

8. Does the author of the story feel that it is safer to buy from an individual or a used-car dealer? What did the author say that led you to your answer?

_____

_____

_____

_____

MAKING PREDICTIONS:

9. Will you educate yourself before buying a car? Why do you think so?

_____

_____

_____

_____

IDENTIFICATION OF CAUSE:

10. Why do teenagers, as well as adults, buy cars on impulse?

_____

_____

_____

_____

IDENTIFICATION OF THE MAIN IDEA:

11. Write a title for the story. Use as few words as possible.

_____

_____

_____

Name _____   **Date** _____

COMPARISON:

12. How is buying a used-car from an individual like buying from a used car dealer? How is it different?

_____

_____

_____

_____

SUMMARIZE:

13. In your own words, tell a friend what to do when buying his or her first car.

_____

_____

_____

_____

EFFECT:

14. How might using a consumer guide affect the price you pay for a used car?

_____

_____

_____

_____

FACT AND OPINION:

15. The story stated, "You can't rely on the information given by a stranger advertising the car in a newspaper." Is this a fact or the author's opinion? How can you prove your answer?

_____

_____

_____

_____

ON YOUR OWN:

16. Write a question about the story for a teacher or another student to answer.

_____

_____

Name _____ **Date** _____

5. LIFE IS SWEET:
THE STORY OF MILTON HERSHEY
Reading Level = 7.52

ABOUT THE STORY

The story is a biography about Milton Hershey, the founder of the Hershey's® candy corporation. Milton Hershey made several failed attempts to start a business before developing his successful chocolate company.

QUOTES OF THE WEEK

Quote 1:

"To be a success in business, be daring, be first, be different."[1] *(page 88)* —MARCHANT

Quote 2:

"From a very early age, go into business with your children. Don't give allowances—make joint ventures instead. Turn every chore into a business. Breed entrepreneurs."[6] *(page 166)*—WILSON HARRELL

INTERVIEW TOPIC

Interview an entrepreneur in your area. Examples of entrepreneurs are owners of family-owned restaurants, home-based businesses, family-run specialty stores, etc. Prepare a question list including literal and interpretive questions: "Why did you start your business? Why did you think your business would be successful? What risks are involved in starting a business?" Make a list of unique terms used by the entrepreneur, and enter them into your vocabulary notebook.

PREVIEW WORDS

apprenticeship   *confectionery*   *the Great Depression*

WORD-ORIGIN STUDY

entrepreneur:	The word *entrepreneur* comes from the French verb *entrepredre*, "to undertake." An *entrepreneur* undertakes a business, assuming the financial risk for the possibility of profit.
confection:	*Confection* is derived from the Latin word *confectus*. *Con-*, meaning "with," and *facere*, "to make," mean to prepare or mix together. Today a *confection* is anything made or preserved with sugar such as candy or ice cream.
confectionery:	A place where confections are made.

---

[1] Refer to *Quotation Footnotes for Level 7* on page 132.

[6] Refer to *Quotation Footnotes for Level 7* on page 132.

List other words beginning with the prefix *con-*. Write the words and their definitions in your vocabulary notebook.

BOOKS TO READ

Be the Boss: The Must Have Book for Anyone Starting Their Own Business. Coral Gables, FL: S.T.A.R.T., 1994.

Harrell, Wilson. *For Entrepreneurs Only: Success Strategies for Anyone Starting or Growing a Business*. Hawthorne, NJ: Career Press, 1994.

Malone, Mary. *Milton Hershey: Chocolate King*. Champaign, IL: Garrard Publishing Company, 1971.

Nicholas, Ted. *The Ted Nicholas Small Business Course: A Step-by-Step Guide to Starting and Running Your Own Business*. Chicago: Enterprise Dearborn, 1994.

Riolo, Al. *The New-Idea Success Book: Starting a Money-Making Business*. Blue Ridge Summit, PA: Liberty House, 1989.

Shippen, Katherine Binney. *Milton S. Hershey*. New York: Random House, 1959.

Taylor, T.M. *Secrets to a Successful Greenhouse Business: A Complete Guide to Starting and Operating a High-Profit Business That's Beneficial to the Environment*. Melbourne, FL: T.M. Taylor Co., 1991.

Williams-Garcia, Rita. *Fast Talk on a Slow Track*. New York: Dutton, 1991.

BOOK CLUB

Read *Fast Talk on a Slow Track* by Rita Williams-Garcia.

INTRODUCTORY ACTIVITIES

DAY ONE

Objective: The students will discuss jobs they do to earn money.

Ask the students if they work small jobs to earn money. For example, do they mow neighbors' yards, clean cars, or baby sit? Why do they earn money this way? How do they determine the price they charge? What are their expenses? How do they find their customers? If they work in this way, they are entrepreneurs.

The students will brainstorm and list jobs they can do to earn extra money. Write the list on the board. Then break the students into groups. Each group will choose a business from the list and work together throughout the week to plan a business. In the end each group will determine if the business is financially feasible.

DAY TWO

STORY LESSON

Follow the *Presenting the Story Lesson* instructions in the Introduction. Each story lesson follows the same procedure; however, say the following in step 4: "The title of the story we're reading today is *Life Is Sweet: The Story of Milton Hershey*. What do you think the story is about? What do you already know about Hershey?"

EXTENSION ACTIVITIES

1. Invite members of the Junior Chamber of Commerce to come to your class. After reviewing the story *Life Is Sweet: The Story of Milton Hershey*, ask the members to give their opinions on why Milton Hershey's first attempts at business failed. Why do they think Hershey kept trying to start his own business?

2. Match each Junior Chamber of Commerce member (as a consultant) with a group set up on Day One. The students work together to set up a business plan, and prepare a start-up plan based on the advice of their consultant. They should prepare charts and graphs to illustrate their financial plans.

3. Each group makes creative advertising posters that it believes will attract customers to its imaginary business.

4. On the final day, the groups present their business plans and posters to the class.

LIFE IS SWEET:
THE STORY OF MILTON HERSHEY

Born in September 1857, in the heart of Pennsylvania Dutch country, Milton Hershey began life thinking about candy. His first job was an apprenticeship to the local printer who shortly dismissed him. His mother suggested that candy was the trade for Milton, and sent him to learn about the confectionery business. Later, Milton moved to Philadelphia where he founded his first candy shop. Yet with all his hard work the business failed.

Milton moved to Denver. He found work with a candy manufacturer. He learned about fine-quality caramels made with fresh milk. Fresh milk, Milton learned, allowed the candies to stay sweet and fresh.

After borrowing money from his mother's family, Milton moved on to New York City to open a new candy shop. Again the business failed. This time his creditors also lost money. Milton vowed he would pay his remaining debt.

One more time Milton opened a confectionery business. This time he made fine caramels. By focusing on a specialty item, Milton's business quickly grew. He paid back his creditors, and later sold the business for one million dollars.

Milton Hershey still dreamed of making chocolate. In 1894, he started the Hershey Chocolate Company in Lancaster, Pennsylvania, as a subsidiary of the Lancaster Caramel Company. Later, he set up business in the small town later known as Hershey, Pennsylvania. He built a large factory and housing for his workers close to dairy farms. His greatest pride was Hershey Industrial School for orphan boys.

During the Great Depression he added buildings to his town at a time when money was scarce. No man went without wages.

When World War II erupted, Hershey developed a chocolate bar for soldiers to carry as emergency food. The U.S. government honored Hershey for his contribution.

Milton Hershey died in 1945 at the age of 88. The town of Hershey continues not only as a world-class manufacturing town, but also as a tourist attraction. The pride of Milton Hershey also lives on as the Milton Hershey School educates thousands of children.

QUESTIONS FOR LIFE IS SWEET: THE STORY OF MILTON HERSHEY

Literal Questions:

THE FACTS:

1. When and where was Milton Hershey born?

_____

_____

_____

2. Who suggested that Hershey should enter the candy trade?

_____

_____

_____

3. Where did Hershey set up his chocolate business?

_____

_____

_____

4. What did Hershey develop during World War II?

_____

_____

_____

SEQUENCE OF EVENTS:

5. List the following events of Hershey's life in chronological order: Hershey added buildings to his town during the Great Depression; Hershey moved to Denver and found work with a candy manufacturer; Hershey sold his confectionery business for one million dollars.

_____

_____

_____

6. What did the U.S. government do after Hershey developed a chocolate bar for soldiers to carry as emergency food?

_____

_____

_____

Name _____   Date _____

Interpretive Questions:

DRAWING CONCLUSIONS:

7. What one word best describes Milton Hershey?

_____

_____

_____

_____

MAKING INFERENCES:

8. How did Milton feel about his workers? What facts in the story support your answer?

_____

_____

_____

_____

MAKING PREDICTIONS:

9. Will Hershey's® chocolates continue to be a popular snack? Why do you feel this way?

_____

_____

_____

_____

IDENTIFICATION OF CAUSE:

10. Hershey dedicated himself to the repayment of his creditors after his New York candy shop failed. Why do you think he was so determined to pay back his debt?

_____

_____

_____

_____

IDENTIFICATION OF THE MAIN IDEA:

11. Write a title for the story. Use as few words as possible.

_____

_____

_____

Name _____   **Date** _____

COMPARISON:

12. How was Hershey's fine caramel confectionery business like his chocolate business? How was it different?

_____

_____

_____

_____

SUMMARIZE:

13. In your own words, describe Hershey's struggle to create a successful candy business.

_____

_____

_____

_____

EFFECT:

14. What effect did Hershey's dedication to his workers have on his employees during the Great Depression?

_____

_____

_____

_____

FACT AND OPINION:

15. The story said, "His (Hershey's) greatest pride was Hershey Industrial School for orphan boys." Is this statement a fact or an opinion? Why do you feel this way?

_____

_____

_____

_____

ON YOUR OWN:

16. Write a question about the story for a teacher or another student to answer.

_____

_____

Name _____ **Date** _____

6. MINA DEL PADRE, THE LOST PADRE MINE

Reading Level = 7.59

ABOUT THE STORY

The Lost Padre Mine, Mina del Padre, is a legend of lost treasure over 300 years old. This popular piece of folklore tells about a mysterious mine hidden in the Franklin Mountains in El Paso, Texas.

QUOTES OF THE WEEK

Quote 1:

"Something hidden. Go and find it. Go and look behind the Ranges— Something lost behind the Ranges. Lost and waiting for you. Go!"[2] *(page 710)*—RUDYARD KIPLING, *THE EXPLORER*, stanza

Quote 2:

"For where your treasure is, there will your heart be also."[11] *(page 1129)*—THE HOLY BIBLE, Matthew 6:21

Quote 3:

"The human heart has hidden treasures, In secret kept, in silence sealed."[2] *(page 555)*—CHARLOTTE BRONTË, *EVENING SOLACE*, Stanza 1

INTERVIEW TOPIC

Interview a long-standing member of the community well versed in local folklore. Ask the person to tell about a local legend. Prepare a question list including literal and interpretive questions: "What is the legend? Is it based on historically accurate events? Do you believe in the legend? Why do you feel this way?" Make a list of unique terms used by the subject, and enter the words in your vocabulary notebook with their definitions.

PREVIEW WORDS

Jesuit	*Juan de Onate*	*Juarez*
cache	*ingot*	

WORD-ORIGIN STUDY

treasure: *Treasure* comes from the Latin word *thesaurus*. A thesaurus is a store or treasure. Today a thesaurus is a book, such as a dictionary or a book of synonyms and antonyms, which contains a store of words.

---

[2] Refer to *Quotation Footnotes for Level 7* on page 132.

[11] Refer to *Quotation Footnotes for Level 7* on page 132.

Jesuit: A person belonging to the Society of Jesus founded in 1534 as a Roman Catholic religious order.

jesuit: Spelled using a lower-case letter, *jesuit* is a "crafty schemer." This derogatory form of the word was used by anti-Jesuits.

List words that are synonyms of the word *treasure*. Write the words, their definitions, and origins in your vocabulary notebook. (See Introductory Activities, Day One.)

BOOKS TO READ

Burgess, Robert Forrest. *The Found Treasure*. New York: Dodd, Mead, 1977.

Cussler, Clive. *Treasure: A Novel*. New York: Simon & Schuster, 1988.

Daley, Robert. *Treasure*. New York: Random House, 1977.

Earle, Peter. *The Treasure of the Conceptcion: The Wreck of the Almirata*. New York: Viking Press, 1980.

Groushko, Michael. *Lost Treasures of the World*. London, England: Multimedia Books, 1993.

Mangan, Frank J.*Bordertown: The Life and Times of El Paso del Norte*. El Paso, TX: C. Hertzog, 1964.

_____. *Bordertown Revisited*. El Paso, TX: Guynes Press, 1973.

Manushkin, Fran. *Annie and the Desert Treasure*. New York: Random House, 1982.

Moore, Robin. *Treasure Hunter*. Englewood Cliffs, NJ: Prentice-Hall, Inc., 1974.

Paulsen, Gary. *Canyons*. New York: Delacorte Press, 1990.

Pickford, Nigel. *The Atlas of Shipwrecks and Treasure: The History, Location, and Treasures of Ships Lost at Sea*. New York: Dorling Kindersley, 1994.

Sachar, Louis. *Holes*. New York: Frances Foster Books/Farrar, Straus and Giroux, 1998.

Smith, Wilbur A. *The Eye of the Tiger*. New York: Doubleday, 1976.

Strasser, Todd. *Beyond the Reef*. New York: Dell Publishers, 1989.

Sullivan, George. *Treasure Hunt: The Sixteen-Year Search for the Lost Treasure Ship, Atocha*. New York: Henry Holt & Co., 1987.

Svidine, Nicholas. *Cossack Gold: The Secret of the White Army Treasure*. Boston: Little, Brown & Co., 1975.

Titler, Dale Milton. *Haunted Treasures*. Englewood Cliffs, NJ: Prentice-Hall, Inc., 1976.

Williams, Brad. *Lost Treasures of the West*. New York: Holt, Rinehart & Winston, 1975.

Yenne, Bill. *Hidden Treasure: Where to Find It, How to Get It*. New York: Avon Books, 1997.

BOOK CLUB

Read *Holes* by Louis Sachar.

INTRODUCTORY ACTIVITIES

DAY ONE

Objective: The students will discuss hidden treasures both fictional and nonfictional.

To insure that the students understand that a hidden treasure can be located anywhere, ask the following questions:

1. What is a hidden treasure?
2. Where can you find a treasure? (in the ocean, on deserted islands, etc.)
3. Can you give examples of what you might find in a treasure?
4. Have you heard of any recently found treasures?
5. Name hidden treasures both fictional and nonfictional.

Prepare the students to go on a hunt for lost treasures. Make a list of words that mean treasure, such as cache, store, deposit, hoard, etc. Use a thesaurus for other similar terms. Enter the words into the vocabulary notebooks.

Make a list of possible places the students can find information about lost treasures. Include encyclopedias, the Internet, magazine articles, their interview subject, etc.

Break the students into groups. Send them on a hunt to find a lost treasure they would like to investigate further. Each group needs to make note of where it found the information, and prepare to vote as a group on which hidden treasure it would like to learn more about.

DAY TWO

STORY LESSON

Follow the *Presenting the Story Lesson* instructions in the Introduction. Each story lesson follows the same procedure; however, say the following in step 4: "The title of the story we're reading today is *Mina del Padre, The Lost Padre Mine*. It is an example of a legend about lost or hidden treasure. What do you think the story will tell you? What do you already know about hidden treasures?"

EXTENSION ACTIVITIES

Throughout the week students will work in groups to investigate a hidden or lost treasure. On the last day they will give oral reports about their findings. Encourage students to use as many visuals, charts, pictures, and maps as possible. Their projects must include:

1. A brief history of the hidden treasure including the circumstances behind the loss or hiding of the treasure.

2. A description of what the treasure might contain and its value.

3. Information about attempts to find the treasure.

4. Varied vocabulary must be used that expand the students' ability to employ a wide variety of words.

5. A map of the location of the treasure including a scale and legend.

6. A bibliography of the references used including Internet sites.

Note: The students should enter any unique or unknown terms with their definitions into the vocabulary notebooks.

MINA DEL PADRE, THE LOST PADRE MINE

Over 300 years ago, Jesuit priests came to a rich river valley. The wide flowing river soon earned its name, Rio Grande. Surrounded by high mountains, the Rio Grande cut open a pass between the south and north of the North American continent. The valley offered safe and easy passage amid a dry, hostile desert. Travellers soon called the breezeway El Paso del Norte, the Pass of the North.

As the Jesuit priests settled into their new home, they toiled in rich mines in the mountains just north of the Rio Grande. Day after day they buried their treasure at the bottom of a shaft. According to legend, the padres hid nearly 300 burro loads of silver bullion. In 1680, the Pueblo Indian Rebellion drove the priests out of their river valley, leaving the hidden treasure behind.

Juan de Onate, founder of the province of New Mexico, discovered the padres' shaft. Juan de Onate added treasures stolen from the Aztecs of Mexico to the cache. His hoard included 4,000 gold ingots; 5,000 bars of silver; nine burro loads of jewels; and ancient church manuscripts. He hid his riches, then left the mine now lost in history and folklore.

Where is the Lost Padre Mine? Myth tells us, in various forms, that you must stand in the bell tower of the old Juarez Mission. Look northeast on exactly the right day of the year and exactly as the sun rises in the east. The sun will shine on the face of the Franklin Mountains revealing the shadowy entrance of the ghostly shaft.

Over the centuries hundreds of people have stood in the tower. Each carefully drew a map to the mine. As the seekers of treasure leave the tower and methodically make their way up the mountain, the entrance to the Mina del Padre mysteriously disappears.

QUESTIONS FOR MINA DEL PADRE, THE LOST PADRE MINE

Literal Questions:

THE FACTS:

1. When did the Jesuit priests move to the Rio Grande valley?

_____

_____

_____

2. Where did the Jesuit priests bury their treasure?

_____

_____

_____

3. Who was Juan de Onate?

_____

_____

_____

4. What did Juan de Onate hide in the padres' shaft?

_____

_____

_____

SEQUENCE OF EVENTS:

5. Who put their treasure into the mine first: the Jesuit priests or Juan de Onate?

_____

_____

_____

6. What happens to the Mina del Padre after a treasure seeker leaves the Juarez Mission tower and begins to look for the shaft?

_____

_____

_____

Name _____   Date _____

Interpretive Questions:

DRAWING CONCLUSIONS:

7. Does the Lost Padre Mine truly exist? Why do you feel this way?

_____

_____

_____

_____

MAKING INFERENCES:

8. Was the Padre Mine a safe place to hide a treasure? Why do you feel this way?

_____

_____

_____

_____

MAKING PREDICTIONS:

9. Do you believe anyone will find the treasure of the Lost Padre Mine? Why do you feel this way?

_____

_____

_____

_____

IDENTIFICATION OF CAUSE:

10. Why were Jesuit priests mining for silver and hiding it in a shaft?

_____

_____

_____

_____

IDENTIFICATION OF THE MAIN IDEA:

11. Write a title for the story. Use as few words as possible.

_____

_____

_____

Name _____ **Date** _____

COMPARISON:

12. How are the treasures of the Jesuit priests and Juan de Onate alike? How are they different?

_____

_____

_____

_____

SUMMARIZE:

13. In your own words, tell what you must do to find the entrance to Mina del Padre.

_____

_____

_____

_____

EFFECT:

14. What effect might the story of the Lost Padre Mine have on tourism in the El Paso area? Why do you feel this way?

_____

_____

_____

_____

FACT OR OPINION:

15. Is the story about Juan de Onate's treasure a fact? How can you prove your answer?

_____

_____

_____

_____

ON YOUR OWN:

16. Write a question about the story for a teacher or another student to answer.

_____

_____

Name _____ Date _____

7. PO CHIENG MA'S CODED PENCILS
Reading Level = 7.65

ABOUT THE STORY

Po Chieng Ma operated a scam involving illegal college entrance exams. Po Chieng Ma offered a "unique" test-taking approach that centered around encoded pencils. Not only was Po Chieng Ma sentenced to jail time, his former clients face expulsion from college.

QUOTES OF THE WEEK

Quote 1:

"It is as impossible for a man to be cheated by anyone but himself, as for a thing to be, and not to be, at the same time."[2] *(page 497)*—RALPH WALDO EMERSON, *ESSAYS: FIRST SERIES. COMPENSATION*

Quote 2:

"Gamesmanship: The Art of Winning Games Without Actually Cheating."[2] *(page 848)*—STEPHEN POTTER (BOOK TITLE)

INTERVIEW TOPIC

Discuss the topic of cheating with a person of any age or background. Prepare a question list including literal and interpretive questions: "What is your opinion of cheating? Have you cheated in the past? If yes, what were the circumstances surrounding the incident? Do you believe there are situations in which cheating is acceptable? Why do you feel this way?" Include the person's age and background.

PREVIEW WORDS

Po Chieng Ma   *eligibility*   *scam*   *expulsion*   *cohort*

WORD-ORIGIN STUDY

scam: Scam apparently stems from the word *scheme*, "a plan or plot." The word *scam* indicates a confidence game. A confidence game is a "swindle for which first you must get the victim's confidence."

expulsion: *Expulsion* comes from a Latin word meaning "to drive out."

List six words based on the root words *expel* and *expulse*. Write their definitions in your vocabulary notebook.

---

[2] Refer to *Quotation Footnotes for Level 7* on page 132.

BOOKS TO READ

Bates, Auline. *Final Exam*. New York: Scholastic, 1990.

Berry, Joy Wilt. *Let's Talk About Cheating*. Chicago: Children's Press, 1985.

Boyd, Candy Dawson. *Breadsticks and Blessing Places*. New York: Macmillan, 1985.

Bromberg, Murray. *601 Words You Need to Know to Pass Your Exam*. Hauppauge, NY: Barron's Educational Series, 1997.

Reed, Teresa. *Keisha, the Fairy Snow Queen*. Portland, ME: Magic Attic Press, 1995.

Ryan, Mary E. *The Trouble with Perfect*. New York: Simon & Schuster Books for Young Readers, 1995.

William, Kate. *Cheating to Win*. New York: Bantam, 1991.

VIDEOS

Claman, Cathy. *Look Inside the SAT I: Test Prep from the Test Makers*. New York: College Entrance Examination Board, 1994.

BOOK CLUB

Read *The Trouble With Perfect* by Mary E. Ryan (a Junior Library Guild selection).

INTRODUCTORY ACTIVITIES

DAY ONE

Objective: The students will discuss what they believe cheating is, and begin a schoolwide cheating survey.

Discuss what the students think the meaning of cheating is. Do they consider cheating inappropriate? Why do they feel this way? Does cheating become more or less improper according to the circumstances? For example, is it all right to cheat in a card game with a younger person, but not all right to cheat on an exam?

Begin a schoolwide survey on opinions of cheating. Copy the survey and set up survey tables around the school. Be sure to include adults in the survey. Try to collect at least 100 completed questionnaires. The surveys allow for confidential responses. At the end of the week the students make graphs and charts based on the information they collect in the survey. (See Extension Activities.)

Cheating survey

Age: _____

Sex: Male _____   Female _____

Grade level or occupation: _____

Where do you look for ethical guidance?

     parents/family _____   teachers _____   religion _____

     friends _____   other (describe)_____

Do you believe cheating is wrong?

     Yes _____   No _____

Are there circumstances in which cheating is appropriate?

     Yes _____   No _____

If yes, please give an example.

_____

_____

_____

_____

Name _____   **Date** _____

DAY TWO

STORY LESSON

Follow the *Presenting the Story Lesson* instructions in the Introduction. Each story lesson follows the same procedure; however, say the following in step 4: "The title of the story we're reading today is *Po Chieng Ma's Coded Pencils*. What do you think the story is about? What do you already know about cheating?"

EXTENSION ACTIVITIES

1. Invite a police officer to the school to talk about scams directed at teen victims. Ask the officer to describe some of the scams as well as ways to avoid being taken in by a confidence game. What are the current scams? Who are the most likely victims? Do victims report these types of crimes? Are scam artists difficult to prosecute?

2. Collect the survey questionnaires from Day One. Using a variety of criteria, students make several graphs including bar graphs, pictographs, and pie graphs showing the percentage of people responding to the questions. For example, make a pie graph showing the percent of males who consider cheating appropriate compared to the percent of females who consider cheating appropriate. Make a bar graph showing the occurrence of cheating according to age, etc. Break the class into groups. Give each group a graph to enlarge onto posterboard. Display the posters in a grouping in the classroom.

3. Make math problems based on the graphs. For example, if 30 out of 120 students find cheating acceptable, based on this information, what is a reasonable estimate of the number of students who would find cheating acceptable in a sampling of 200 students?

PO CHIENG MA'S CODED PENCILS

Do you feel pressure to pass your college entrance exam? Perhaps you are depending on a scholarship in order to even think about higher education. Maybe you're one of thousands of athletes who must meet the NCAA required freshman eligibility scores. Whatever the reason, college entrance exams cause anxiety among graduating high school seniors.

What chances would you take to avoid the pressure? What price would you pay? Would you cheat?

Recently, federal agents broke up a college entrance exam scam engineered by a man named Po Chieng Ma. Ma snared his clients with tempting advertisements for a "unique" approach that guaranteed high scores on entrance exams. The cost was $6,000 and a trip to Los Angeles.

Federal investigators planted an undercover postal inspector into Ma's program. According to the inspector, there were no study courses required. Test takers simply arrived at the Los Angeles airport. Ma collected his clients and chauffeured them to various test sites around the city to avoid detection. In New York, on an earlier time zone, Ma's accomplices took the scheduled exam. As the clients waited, Ma received a phone call from his cohort with the answers to the test. Ma then supplied each student with a special "coded pencil." By reading the code, the client learned the answers to the test.

Federal agents charged Ma with two counts of mail and wire fraud. If found guilty, Ma could serve up to ten years in prison and be given a heavy fine.

Perhaps the people who should worry the most are Ma's former clients. According to the Educational Testing Service that oversees the exams, the false scores will be nullified and the colleges alerted. In other words, students who cheated to enter college face the possibility of expulsion. Po Chieng Ma's former clients cheated themselves by destroying their dreams of a future based on a college degree.

QUESTIONS FOR PO CHIENG MA'S CODED PENCILS

Literal Questions:

THE FACTS:

1. Who engineered a college entrance exam scam?

_____

_____

_____

2. How much did Ma's clients pay for the answers to college entrance exams?

_____

_____

_____

3. What did federal agents charge Ma with?

_____

_____

_____

4. What will happen to those who used Ma's scam to cheat on college entrance exams?

_____

_____

_____

SEQUENCE OF EVENTS:

5. Write the following events in chronological order: Ma supplied clients with a special coded pencil; Ma picked up his clients at the Los Angeles airport; Ma received a phone call with the answers to the test.

_____

_____

_____

6. What did Ma's accomplice in New York do before calling Ma with the answers to the test?

_____

_____

_____

Name _____ **Date** _____

Interpretive Questions:

DRAWING CONCLUSIONS:

7. What one word best describes Po Chieng Ma's scam?

_____

_____

_____

_____

MAKING INFERENCES:

8. Describe a person most likely to become one of Ma's clients.

_____

_____

_____

_____

MAKING PREDICTIONS:

9. Will people continue to look for ways to cheat on college entrance exams? Why do you feel this way?

_____

_____

_____

_____

IDENTIFICATION OF CAUSE:

10. What factors might have motivated Ma to help people illegally cheat on entrance exams?

_____

_____

_____

_____

IDENTIFICATION OF MAIN IDEA:

11. Write a title for the story. Use as few words as possible.

_____

_____

_____

Name _____   Date _____

COMPARISON:

12. Compare the motives for Ma's involvement in the entrance exam scam to those of his clients. How are they alike? How are they different?

_____

_____

_____

_____

SUMMARIZE:

13. In your own words, tell how federal agents broke up Po Chieng Ma's college entrance exam scam.

_____

_____

_____

_____

EFFECT:

14. What effect might the apprehension of Ma and the disclosure of his scam have on the way colleges administer entrance exams?

_____

_____

_____

_____

FACT AND OPINION:

15. The story said, ". . . college entrance exams cause anxiety among graduating high school seniors." Is this a fact or someone's opinion? How can you prove your answer?

_____

_____

_____

_____

ON YOUR OWN:

16. Write a question about the story for a teacher or another student to answer.

_____

_____

Name _____ **Date** _____

8. LOWE'S <u>INTREPID</u>
Reading Level = 7.69

ABOUT THE STORY

Professor Thadeus Lowe (1832-1913) was a scientist studying air currents. During the Civil War he put his knowledge of balloon flight to use as a spy for the North. His silk balloon, the *Intrepid*, hovered over the battlefield just out of gun range. From his perch in the sky, Lowe sent telegraph messages giving Northern generals immediate information about troop size and location.

QUOTES OF THE WEEK

Quote 1:

"Duty is the sublimest word in our language. Do your duty in all things. You cannot do more. You should never wish to do less."[2] *(page 509)*—ROBERT E. LEE, *HALL OF FAME INSCRIPTION*

Quote 2:

"The art of war is simple enough. Find out where your enemy is. Get at him as soon as you can. Strike at him as hard as you can and as often as you can, and keep moving on."[2] *(page 589)*—ULYSSES S. GRANT, *DESCRIBING THE ART OF WAR*

INTERVIEW TOPIC

Interview the oldest person you know on the topic of the Civil War. Such a person might be found in a retirement center or nursing home. Ask the person what he or she believes was the most interesting aspect of the Civil War. Prepare a question list including literal and interpretive questions: "Did you know anyone who lived during the Civil War? What did this person tell you about life during the war? What are the lingering effects of the Civil War on the United States?"

PREVIEW WORDS

Thadeus Lowe	*hydrogen gas*
ensconced	*aeronautic*

WORD-ORIGIN STUDY

ensconced: A *sconce* is a small fortification. With *en-*, meaning "in or into," *ensconced* means to be in a small fort or defensive trench.

aeronautic: An *aeronaut* is a sailor of the air (*aero-* means "air" and *-naut* means "sailor"). *Aeronautics* is the study of making flying ships.

---

[2] Refer to *Quotation Footnotes for Level 7* on page 132.

List other words beginning with *aero-* or containing *-naut*. Write the words and their definitions in your vocabulary notebook.

BOOKS TO READ

Armstrong, Jennifer. *Mary Mehan Awake*. New York: Knopf, 1997.

Campbell, R. Thomas. *Southern Thunder: Exploits of the Confederate States' Navy*. Shippensburg, PA: Burd Street Press, 1996.

Crane, Stephen. *The Red Badge of Courage*.

Colman, Penny. *Spies! Women in the Civil War*. Cincinnati, OH: Betterway Books, 1992.

Duey, Kathleen. *Emma Eileen Grove: Mississippi, 1865*. New York: Aladdin Paperbacks, 1996.

Forrester, Sandra. *My Home Is Over Jordan*. New York: Lodestar Books/Dutton, 1997.

Morris, Gilbert. *The Battle of Lookout Mountain*. Chicago: Moody Press, 1996.

_____. *Blockade Runner*. Chicago: Moody Press, 1996.

_____. *Encounter a Cold Harbor*. Chicago: Moody Press, 1997.

_____. *The Gallant Boys of Gettysburg*. Chicago: Moody Press, 1996.

_____. *The Soldier Boy's Discovery*. Chicago: Moody Press, 1996.

Paulsen, Gary. *Nightjohn*. New York: Delacorte Press, 1993.

_____. *Sarny: A Life Remembered* (companion book to *Nightjohn*). New York: Delacorte Press, 1997.

Stern, Philip Van Doren. *Secret Missions of the Civil War*. New York: Bonanza Books, 1959.

CDs, RECORDS, AND CASSETTES

Ward, Geoffrey C. *Civil War*. New York: Random House Audio, 1991.

VIDEOS

Burns, Kenneth Lauren. *The Civil War* (two cassettes). Beverly Hills, CA: PBS Home Video, 1990.

BOOK CLUB

Read *Blockade Runner* by Gilbert Morris.

INTRODUCTORY ACTIVITIES

DAY ONE

Objective: The students will watch the video *The Civil War* by Ken Burns.

Show the video *The Civil War* by Ken Burns. As the students watch the movie, ask them to write down the names of people mentioned in the movie. The students will use these names in the Extension Activities.

After each episode, discuss what the students learned and how they felt about what they saw. Include a discussion on the presentation of the material. "Was it effective to have actors read actual letters from people living during the Civil War? Did the use of historic photographs have a greater impact than showing a reenactment of the war? Which person made the strongest impression on you? Why do you feel this way?"

DAY TWO

STORY LESSON

Follow the *Presenting the Story Lesson* instructions in the Introduction. Each story lesson follows the same procedure; however, say the following in step 4: "The title of the story we're reading today is *Lowe's Intrepid*. What do you think the story is about? What do you already know about the Civil War?"

EXTENSION ACTIVITIES

1. Using the list of names from Day One, students look for quotes attributed to each person. Your librarian can guide the students to reference books of quotes. These books might include:

   ■ Applewhite, Ashton, William R. Evans III, and Andrew Frothingham. *And I Quote: The Definitive Collection of Quotes, Sayings, and Jokes for the Contemporary Speechmaker*. New York: St. Martin's Press, 1992.

   ■ Bartlett, John. *Bartlett's Familiar Quotations*. Boston, MA: Little, Brown and Company, 1980.

   ■ *The Oxford Dictionary of Quotations, second ed.* London, England: Oxford University Press, 1966.

2. Collect photographs or drawings of the person who made the quote. There are several sources for photographs, including the Library of Congress. You can locate a sampling of the Library of Congress collection at the Internet site:

   http://lcweb.loc.gov/rr/print/

   If a photograph is not available, the students can make a drawing of their subject.

3. Lay a long piece of bulletin board paper lengthwise. Have the students mount all their pictures and quotes along the length of the paper. The students copy their quotes onto the paper in large letters, and mount the picture of the person to which the quote is attributed next to his or her words. Display the Wall of Quotes in a hallway or prominent wall.

4. Research secret codes of the Civil War. The students will make code books based on these codes. Civil War codes and ciphers include Morse Code, the Vigenère Tableau (or Vicksburg Code), and the Route Ciphers. Examples of these and other Civil War codes can be found in Philip Van Doren Stern's *Secret Missions of the Civil War*. The students choose a code, write it onto plain or lined paper, and include an explanation of how the code works. Students give the code book a title and bind the book with laminated construction paper.

LOWE'S <u>INTREPID</u>

Ensconced in trenches surrounding Richmond, Virginia, General Joe Johnston's troops prepared for a battle to save the capital of the Confederate states. The approaching Northern army could not see the men hidden below eye level. How many Southern troops lie concealed? Where were they located? Professor Thadeus Lowe (1832–1913) would soon supply the answers.

To General Johnston's astonishment a round, orange orb rose from the northern side. Dangling below the balloon was a basket holding two men— observation spies for the Union. Above the range of Confederate guns, Professor Lowe sent the first telegraph message from an aircraft in battle. "This would be a good time to attack," the message read. "They do not seem to expect anything. . . . Their forces are weakest just below the bend of the river." From Lowe's vantage point he witnessed the terror on the battlefield. Finally, he sent his last dispatch, "They're on the run!"

Professor Lowe began his interest in flight as a scientist studying air currents. He believed strong west winds could carry a balloon across the Atlantic. On a preparatory flight in 1861, Lowe flew from Ohio to South Carolina. An unfortunate landing placed him in Southern territory where the Confederacy mistakenly captured him as a Northern spy. Little did they know that the strange man in the balloon would return and assist the North in a battle that would capture their capital.

Professor Lowe made the skin of his spy balloon, the Intrepid, from silk cloth. A silken tube attached to the balloon served as a filling hose. Hydrogen gas made from sulfuric acid and iron filings gave the balloon lift. To descend, Lowe pulled a rope connected to a wooden valve sealed with beeswax. Pulling the rope opened the valve, slowly releasing the hydrogen. Without high-angle guns, the Southern troops could not destroy the high-flying Peeping Tom.

Transportation of Intrepid required an "aeronautic train" made up of four wagons. By 1862, the Union employed seven balloons in the Balloon Corps. Lowe's fleet became the first aircrafts to send telegraph messages and photographs to an active field of battle.

QUESTIONS FOR LOWE'S <u>INTREPID</u>

Literal Questions:

THE FACTS:

1. In what year was Professor Thadeus Lowe born?

_____

_____

_____

2. How did Professor Lowe send his messages from the balloon to the Northern troops?

_____

_____

_____

3. When did Professor Lowe begin his interest in flight?

_____

_____

_____

4. By 1862, how many balloons did the Union employ in the Balloon Corps?

_____

_____

_____

SEQUENCE OF EVENTS:

5. Which happened first: Lowe's preparatory flight from Ohio to South Carolina or the creation of the Balloon Corps?

_____

_____

_____

6. What did the Confederate army do after it captured Lowe as a Northern spy?

_____

_____

_____

Name _____ **Date** _____

Interpretive Questions:

DRAWING CONCLUSIONS:

7. Why did Lowe name his balloon the *Intrepid*?

_____

_____

_____

_____

MAKING INFERENCES:

8. What was the Northern army's opinion of the success of Lowe's first spy flight? Why do you feel this way?

_____

_____

_____

_____

MAKING PREDICTIONS:

9. Will aircraft continue to be an important part of military intelligence gathering? Why do you feel this way?

_____

_____

_____

_____

IDENTIFICATION OF CAUSE:

10. Why did Lowe construct the *Intrepid* out of silk?

_____

_____

_____

_____

IDENTIFICATION OF THE MAIN IDEA:

11. Write a title for the story. Use as few words as possible.

_____

_____

_____

Name _____   Date _____

COMPARISON:

12. How was Lowe's *Intrepid* like the spy satellites used by today's army? How was it different?

_____

_____

_____

_____

SUMMARIZE:

13. In your own words, tell about the *Intrepid's* flight over General Joe Johnston's troops.

_____

_____

_____

_____

EFFECT:

14. What effect, if any, did Lowe's Balloon Corps have on the outcome of the Civil War? Why do you feel this way?

_____

_____

_____

_____

FACT AND OPINION:

15. The story said, "By 1862, the Union employed seven balloons in the Balloon Corps." Is this a fact or the author's opinion? How can you prove your answer?

_____

_____

_____

_____

ON YOUR OWN:

16. Write a question about the story for a teacher or another student to answer.

_____

_____

Name _____   **Date** _____

9. THE NEVER-FADING POPULARITY OF LEVI'S® JEANS

Reading Level = 7.81

ABOUT THE STORY

This is a short biography about Levi Strauss. Strauss was a poor immigrant who came to America and became the founder of one of the largest corporations in the country.

QUOTES OF THE WEEK

Quote 1:

"I do not think large fortunes cause happiness to their owners, for immediately those who possess them become slaves to their wealth. They must devote their lives to caring for their possessions. I don't think money brings friends to its owner. In fact, often the result is quite the contrary."[5]
(page 61)—LEVI STRAUSS

Quote 2:

"Every generation laughs at the old fashions, but follows religiously the new."[3] *(page 341)*—HENRY DAVID THOREAU

INTERVIEW TOPIC

Interview three people, one from each of the following age groups: 15–24, 25–39, and 40–up. Ask them about the style of jeans they wore as teenagers. Prepare a question list including literal and interpretive questions: "Why were jeans popular among teens? What could you tell about a person by the jeans he or she wore?" If possible, obtain a photograph or a copy of a photograph of the person as a teenager wearing jeans. Mount the photograph next to each interview.

PREVIEW WORDS

trademark   *rivets*   *synonymous*

WORD-ORIGIN STUDY

denim:	A strong heavy twill cotton cloth originally produced in Nimes, France. Americans nicknamed the material "de Nimes" (of Nimes) which was later shortened to *denim*.[a]
jeans:	*Jeans* are sturdy pants made from denim. These pants were popular among sailors from Genoa, Italy. Americans shortened the name Genoa to *jeans*, and the name remains to this day.[a]

---

[5] Refer to *Quotation Footnotes for Level 7* on page 132.

[3] Refer to *Quotation Footnotes for Level 7* on page 132.

[a] Weidt, Maryann N. *Mr. Blue Jeans: A Story about Levi Strauss.* Minneapolis: Carolrhoda Books, Inc., 1990, page 40.

synonymous: The prefix *syn-* comes from the Greek word meaning with, together with, or at the same time. *Synonymous* means "expressing the same or nearly the same meaning."

List other words beginning with the prefix *syn-*. Write the words and their definitions in your vocabulary notebook.

BOOKS TO READ

Dolber, Rosly. *Opportunities in Fashion Careers*. Lincolnwood, IL: VGM Career Books, 1993.

Gaines, Steven S. *Obsession: The Lives and Times of Calvin Klein*. New York: Carol Publishing Group, 1994.

Harlow, Eve. *The Jeans Scene*. New York: Drake Publishers Inc., 1973.

L'Hommediew, Arthur John. *From Plant to Blue Jeans: A Photo Essay*. New York: Children's Press, 1997.

Martin, Richard (ed.). *Contemporary Fashion*. New York: St. James Press, 1995.

Mathis, Darlene. *Women of Color: The Multicultural Guide to Fashion and Beauty*. New York: Ballantine Books, 1994.

Weidt, Maryann N. *Mr. Blue Jeans: A Story About Levi Strauss*. Minneapolis: Carolrhoda Books, 1990.

BOOK CLUB

The students read a biography or autobiography of their choosing.

INTRODUCTORY ACTIVITIES

Note: Several days before the lesson, notify the students that they are to wear their favorite jeans to school on a given date. Ask them to bring examples of jeans from their family and friends. The more variety and uniqueness, the better. Tell them to be as creative as they want, even to bringing toys wearing jeans.

DAY ONE

Objective: The students will discuss the various styles of jeans people wear and the popularity of jeans in American society.

Begin the class with a discussion on the popularity of jeans. "Why do people like jeans? Why are Americans known for their jeans? What do jeans tell you about the person who is wearing them?"

Hold a jeans fashion show and/or Show and Tell. Ask each student to tell about the jeans he or she is wearing. Why do they like their jeans? The students display and report on the different types of jean items they brought to class.

DAY TWO

STORY LESSON

Follow the *Presenting the Story Lesson* instructions in the Introduction. Each story lesson follows the same procedure; however, say the following in step 4: "The title of the story we're reading today is *The Never-Fading Popularity of Levi's® Jeans*. What do you think the story is about? What do you already know about jeans?"

EXTENSION ACTIVITIES

1. Invite a clothing designer, a clothing (preferably a jeans) manufacturer, a teacher of design, and/or a teacher of sewing to class. Ask them to tell about the process involved in the design, sewing, and manufacturing of clothing. What information can they share about the design elements and requirements of jeans? Enter the students into a question-and-answer session.

2. The students design jeans of the future. Ask the students to imagine living 20 to 50 years in the future. They are to design a pair of jeans that might be popular at that time. Students create a poster advertising the jeans and write an essay explaining for what year the jeans are designed. "Why will your jeans be popular during this time period? What are the unique features of your jeans? Who will want to wear your jeans?"

3. Using the interviews, photographs collected during the interviews, and the posters, make a timeline of jean fashion along a wall showing the progression of jean fashion from the past to the future. Ask the students to give the timeline a title.

THE NEVER-FADING POPULARITY OF LEVI'S® JEANS

Fashion trends come and go, but nothing in fashion has lasted like Levi Strauss's jeans. Strauss was born on February 26, 1829, in the small village of Buttenheim, Bavaria. The Jewish boy's birth name was Loeb Strauss. His father worked as a peddler of dry goods. Loeb's parents had both passed away by 1845. His stepbrothers had already migrated to America and wrote about the abundant opportunities. Jews were even allowed to vote! Loeb and several of his siblings moved to New York.

Loeb worked with his stepbrothers at their dry goods company, "J. Strauss Brother & Co." Loeb (now known as Levi) went west when the Gold Rush hit California. He was not searching for gold, but starting a dry goods company for the growing population.

Mr. Strauss founded Levi Strauss & Co. in 1853. The new company grew into a thriving business by 1866. The new headquarters had all the modern conveniences including gaslight chandeliers and a freight elevator.

It was not until 1872 that a tailor named Jacob Davis contacted Levi. Davis developed an innovative technique to strengthen pants. He improved durability by adding metal rivets at the pocket corners and the base of the button fly. The two men received a patent in 1873. The demand for Levi's riveted "waist overalls," or jeans, boomed. Levi Strauss & Co. appointed the lot number 501® to the now-famous denim jeans in 1890.

Levi Strauss died in 1902. The San Francisco Board of Trade described Mr. Strauss as a man having "a broad and generous love for and sympathy with humanity."

The Levi Strauss & Co. headquarters suffered complete destruction during the San Francisco earthquake of 1906. However, the company continued to pay its employees and extended credit to other merchants struggling to rebuild. Levi Strauss & Co. rose from the devastation. The popularity of Levi's quality jeans spread around the world to become synonymous with the freedom and strength of America.

QUESTIONS FOR THE NEVER-FADING POPULARITY OF LEVI'S® JEANS

Literal Questions:

THE FACTS:

1. When was Loeb Strauss born?

_____

_____

_____

2. When did Mr. Strauss found Levi Strauss & Co.?

_____

_____

_____

3. What was the appointed name of the riveted pants made by Levi Strauss & Co.?

_____

_____

_____

4. When did Levi Strauss die?

_____

_____

_____

SEQUENCE OF EVENTS:

5. Where did Levi Strauss live before he moved to America?

_____

_____

_____

6. What did Levi Strauss & Co. do after the San Francisco earthquake of 1906?

_____

_____

_____

Name _____   Date _____

Interpretive Questions:

DRAWING CONCLUSIONS:

7. What one word best describes Levi Strauss?

_____

_____

_____

_____

MAKING INFERENCES:

8. Why did Levi Strauss enter the dry goods business?

_____

_____

_____

_____

MAKING PREDICTIONS:

9. Will 501® jeans continue to be popular? Why do you feel this way?

_____

_____

_____

_____

IDENTIFICATION OF CAUSE:

10. Why did Mr. Davis and Mr. Strauss patent the riveted "waist overall" design?

_____

_____

_____

_____

IDENTIFICATION OF MAIN IDEA:

11. Write a title for the story. Use as few words as possible.

_____

_____

_____

Name _____   Date _____

COMPARISON:

12. How was the first pair of 501® jeans like jeans sold today? How was it different?

_____

_____

_____

_____

SUMMARIZE:

13. In your own words, tell the history of Levi Strauss & Co.

_____

_____

_____

_____

EFFECT:

14. What effect did Levi Strauss & Co.'s actions toward their employees and other suffering businesses have on the San Francisco economy after the 1906 earthquake?

_____

_____

_____

_____

FACT AND OPINION:

15. The story said, "The popularity of Levi's quality jeans spread around the world to become synonymous with the freedom and strength of America." Is this a fact or the author's opinion? How can you prove your answer?

_____

_____

_____

_____

ON YOUR OWN:

16. Write a question about the story for a teacher or another student to answer.

_____

_____

Name _____ **Date** _____

10. A LETTER HOME
Reading Level = 7.83

About the Story

Based on a historical event, the story is a fictional letter from a soldier in South Dakota describing the fear among the white people of a Native American religious ceremony called Ghost Dancing. The gossip leads to the massacre of 200 innocent Sioux at Wounded Knee Creek.

Quotes of the Week

Quote 1:

"My people are few. They resemble the scattering trees of a storm-swept plain... There was a time when our people covered the land as the waves of a wind-ruffled sea cover its shell-paved floor, but that time long since passed away with the greatness of tribes that are now but a mournful memory."[2] *(page 455)*—CHIEF SEATTLE AT THE SURRENDERING OF TRIBAL LANDS (1855)

Quote 2:

"There is not among these three hundred bands of Indians (in the United States) one which has not suffered cruelly at the hands either of the Government or of white settlers. The poorer, the more insignificant, the more helpless the band, the more certain the cruelty and outrage to which they have been subjected."[7] *(page 491)*—HELEN HUNT JACKSON OF COLORADO SPRINGS, *A CENTURY OF DISHONOR* (1881)

Interview Topic

Interview any person about his or her viewpoint on Native American history in relationship to the white man. Note the age of the subject, ethnic background, and where the person obtained the information on which his or her opinions were formed (i.e., textbooks, movies, documentaries, personal experience). Prepare a question list including literal and interpretive questions: "In your opinion, on what was the conflict between Native Americans and the white man based? Is your interpretation of this conflict like that of your parents and grandparents? If not, how and why is your opinion different?"

Preview Words

Wowoka	*Wounded Knee Creek*	*reservation*
Ghost Dancing	*Paiute*	*cataclysm*
paranoid	*insurrection*	

---

[2] Refer to *Quotation Footnotes for Level 7* on page 132.

[7] Refer to *Quotation Footnotes for Level 7* on page 132.

WORD-ORIGIN STUDY

reservation: *Reservation* comes from the Latin word *reservare*, "to keep back." In this case, the prefix *re-* means "back" and *servare* means "to keep." A *reservation* is land kept back, or set aside, for a special purpose such as an Indian reservation or a military reservation.

The prefix *re-* can also mean "again." List other words beginning with the prefix *re-*. Enter the words and their definitions into your vocabulary notebook.

cataclysm: The prefix *cata-* means down, or regression. The Greek word *klyzein*, or *-clysm*, means to wash. A *cataclysm* is a large, violent washing away or erasure of a landscape or civilization, such as that caused by a flood, earthquake, or war.

List other words beginning with the prefix *cata-*. Enter the words and their definitions into your vocabulary notebook.

BOOKS TO READ

Ackerman, Ned. *Spirit Horse*. New York: Scholastic Press, 1998.

Belting, Natalia Maree. *Whirlwind Is a Ghost Dancing*. New York: E.P. Dutton & Co., Inc., 1974.

Brooks, Marth. *Bone Dance*. New York: Orchard Books, 1977.

Brown, Dee Alexander. *Bury My Heart at Wounded Knee: An Indian History of the American West*. New York: Henry Holt & Co., 1991.

Burks, Brian. *Walks Alone*. San Diego: Harcourt, Brace & Company, 1998.

Caduto, Michael J. *Keepers of the Night: Native American Stories and Nocturnal Activities for Children*. Golden, CO: Fulcrum Pub., 1994.

Caduto, Michael J. and Joseph Bruchac. *Keepers of Life: Discovering Plants Through Native American Stories and Earth Activities for Children*. Golden, CO: Fulcrum Pub., 1994.

Ehrlich, Amy. *Wounded Knee: An Indian History of the American West*. New York: Henry Holt & Co., 1993.

Frank, Lois Ellen. *Native American Cooking: Foods of the Southwest Indian Nations*. New York: Wings Books, 1995.

Greene, Carl. *Black Elk: A Man With a Vision*. Chicago: Children's Press, 1990.

Hobbs, Will. *Ghost Canoe*. New York: Morrow Junior Books, 1997.

Jones, Douglass. *A Creek Called Wounded Knee*. New York: Scribner, 1978.

Paulsen, Gary. *Canyons*. New York: Delacorte Press, 1990.

Smith, Rex Alan. *Moon of Popping Trees*. Pleasantville: Reader's Digest Press, 1975.

Stein, R. Conrad. *The Story of Wounded Knee*. Chicago: Children's Press, 1983.

Waldman, Carl. *Word Dance: The Language of Native American Culture*. New York: Facts On File, 1994.

Wood, Ted. *A Boy Becomes a Man at Wounded Knee*. New York: Walker, 1992.

BOOK CLUB

Read *Canyons* by Gary Paulsen or *Walks Alone* by Brian Burks.

INTRODUCTORY ACTIVITIES

DAY ONE

Objective: The students will discuss their interpretation of the relationship between Native Americans and western settlers (American government) both in the past and the present.

Without giving the students any information to influence their present opinions, discuss their viewpoints on the relationship between Native Americans and western settlers (American government) both in the past and the present. "What do you believe was the cause of the conflict? On what information did you base your opinion? Where did you get this information (movies, textbooks, documentaries, etc.)?"

Are the students' opinions and viewpoints different from their parents' and grandparents'? If they are, why are these opinions different?

Guide the students through the series of events and battles leading up to Wounded Knee, including the Battle of Little Bighorn (1876).

DAY TWO

STORY LESSON

Follow the *Presenting the Story Lesson* instructions in the Introduction. Each story lesson follows the same procedure; however, say the following in step 4: "The title of the story we're reading today is *A Letter Home*. It is a fictional letter telling about the true massacre of a band of Sioux at a creek called Wounded Knee."

EXTENSION ACTIVITIES

1. The students work in groups to choose a Native American tribe to study. Working together, the students investigate the following information:

   a. Where was the location of the tribe's original homeland?

   b. When did the tribe surrender?

   c. What were the circumstances surrounding the surrender?

   d. Can you find quotes from the tribal members?

e. Where was the tribe relocated and why was the reservation established at this site?

2. Each group makes a scene box showing its tribe in its original homeland. To make the scene box, students will need: a printing paper box; scissors; and various materials such as clay, toy people, papier-mâché, etc. to create the scene.

a. Set the box upright on a table with the opening pointing up without the lid.

b. Cut a 3-inch by 5-inch hole in the center of the short end of the box. This is the view hole.

c. Using their imagination and creativity, the students make a small model of the tribe in their homeland in the bottom of the box. Include the tribe's housing and scenes from everyday life.

To view the scene, set the box on a tall table and look through the view hole.

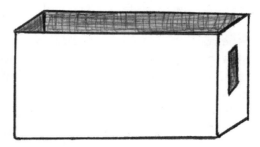

3. Students make a map showing the original site of the tribal homeland and the location of the reservation. Mark each site clearly. Include a legend and scale with the map.

4. Display the maps and scene boxes around the room.

Note: Michael J. Caduto and Joseph Bruchac wrote a wonderful series of books containing many stories from several Native American tribes along with activities based on tribal traditions. These books include *Keepers of Life: Discovering Plants Through Native American Stories and Earth Activities for Children* and *Keepers of the Night: Native American Stories and Nocturnal Activities for Children.*

Burial of the Dead at the Battle of Wounded Knee S.D.

NorthWestern Photo Co Chadron Neb

A LETTER HOME

Dear Sara,

I have not written for several months, and I hope you have not worried needlessly. I am in good health, although my spirits are low.

We arrived at the Pine Ridge Agency in South Dakota safely. Several other troops preceded our arrival along with inexperienced Indian agents appointed by the Democratic Administration to manage the reservation. The agents are to keep order, and we, the troops, the peace. At first glance all appeared tranquil and calm.

Recently, I watched the Indians perform a frenzied ritual dance. Their singular costumes, songs, and rhythms were hypnotic; however, I became alarmed when rumors spread about this new cult.

The Indians base this cult, called Ghost Dancing, on the fantastic vision of a Paiute Indian named Wowoka. According to his vision a great cataclysm will sweep over our country. In the end all white men will disappear, the buffalo will return, and the Indian dead will rise from their graves to join their surviving brothers and sisters. Soon gossip of insurrection spread like wild fire. These baseless rumors convinced everyone that the Indians intended to massacre our wives, children, mothers, and fathers.

At the same time about 356 ill-fated Sioux surrendered peacefully to our troops. Orders instructed us to escort the Indians to the reservation, yet the soldiers took the group as far as Wounded Knee Creek just northeast of Pine Ridge. Without any verifiable provocation, the troops attacked the gathering. Over 200 Sioux, including women and children, died. Sixty U.S. cavalrymen also lost their lives.

Sara, I fear a wave of paranoid rumor took hold of our reason. A young Sioux brave spoke to me after hearing of the massacre. He interpreted Wowoka's vision as the depiction of a natural cataclysm brought about by the hand of their god, not by the hand of the Indians. The Ghost Dancers had no intention of attacking the white man. Our unjustified panic lead only to the deaths of innocents. What have we done?

Your loving friend,

Michael

Michael

QUESTIONS FOR A LETTER HOME

Literal Questions:

THE FACTS:

1. Where was the author of the letter stationed?

_____

_____

_____

2. Who managed the reservation?

_____

_____

_____

3. Who was Wowoka?

_____

_____

_____

4. How many Sioux died at Wounded Knee Creek?

_____

_____

_____

SEQUENCE OF EVENTS:

5. According to Wowoka's vision, what will happen after a great cataclysm sweeps over the country?

_____

_____

_____

6. Which event happened first: Wowoka's vision or the massacre at Wounded Knee Creek?

_____

_____

_____

Name _____   Date _____

Interpretive Questions:

DRAWING CONCLUSIONS:

7. How did Michael, the author of the letter, feel about the incident at Wounded Knee? Which of his statements led you to your conclusion?

_____

_____

_____

_____

MAKING INFERENCES:

8. How did the white men feel about Wowoka's predictions and the Ghost Dancing cult? Why do you feel this way?

_____

_____

_____

_____

MAKING PREDICTIONS:

9. Could an incident like the massacre at Wounded Knee happen again? If you said yes, what could be done to prevent it? If you said no, on what specific reason do you base your answer?

_____

_____

_____

_____

IDENTIFICATION OF CAUSE:

10. Why did the Ghost Dancing cult become so widely accepted by Native Americans?

_____

_____

_____

_____

IDENTIFICATION OF MAIN IDEA:

11. Write a title for the story. Use as few words as possible.

_____

_____

Name _____ **Date** _____

COMPARISON:

12. Compare the Native Americans' motives and emotions surrounding the belief of Wowoka's vision to the motives and emotions of the soldiers. How were the roots of their feelings alike? How were they different?

_____

_____

_____

_____

SUMMARIZE:

13. In your own words, tell about the events that led to the massacre at Wounded Knee.

_____

_____

_____

_____

EFFECT:

14. What effect, if any, did the inexperience of the Indian agents have on the outcome at Wounded Knee?

_____

_____

_____

_____

FACT AND OPINION:

15. Michael, the author of the letter, said, ". . . I fear a wave of paranoid rumor took hold of our reason." Is this a fact or Michael's opinion? How can you prove your answer?

_____

_____

_____

_____

ON YOUR OWN:

16. Write a question about the story for a teacher or another student to answer.

_____

_____

Name _____   **Date** _____

11. QUANAH PARKER: COMANCHE CHIEF

Reading Level = 7.84

ABOUT THE STORY

The biography of Quanah Parker begins as his mother is abducted as a child from her family at Fort Parker, Texas. She later married a Comanche and gave birth to Quanah. Quanah became the last Comanche chief to lead his people outside a reservation.

QUOTES OF THE WEEK

Quote 1:

"I am related to both the white and the red people. I realize it as so, and for that reason will not do anything bad, but looking for the good road, a suppliant for the red people, so when Washington hears he will help us."[8]
(page 31)—QUANAH PARKER

Quote 2:

"It (Arizona) is my land, my home, my father's land, to which I now ask to be allowed to return. I want to spend my last days there, and be buried among those mountains. If this could be I might die in peace, feeling that my people, placed in their native homes, would increase in numbers, rather than diminish as at present, and that our name would not become extinct."[2]
(page 603)—GERONIMO IN A LETTER TO PRESIDENT GRANT AFTER SURRENDERING (1877)

INTERVIEW TOPIC

Through the Internet or the writing of a letter, contact a member of a Native American tribe. If you are Native American, talk to an elder. Your local library can provide listings of tribal addresses along with names of tribal leaders. Ask about the last chief to lead the tribe before the tribe entered the reservation. Prepare a question list including literal and interpretive questions: "Who was the chief? If you could tell someone about this chief, what would you say? What should his people and people outside the tribe remember about the chief?"

PREVIEW WORDS

Quanah Parker   encroaching   Naudah

WORD-ORIGIN STUDY

siege:	The word *siege* originates from a term meaning "to sit." It went on to mean "the sitting down before a town." A *siege* is the attempt to take, or sit down before, a fortified area by armed forces.

---

[8] Refer to *Quotation Footnotes for Level 7* on page 132.

[2] Refer to *Quotation Footnotes for Level 7* on page 132.

encroach: The prefix *en-* means "in." The base, *croach* (croc), means "a hook." To *encroach* on someone else's property is to snare it in your hook, or intrude upon the rights or property of others.

List other words beginning with the prefix *en-*. Write the words and their definitions in your vocabulary notebook.

BOOKS TO READ

Anderson, LaVere. *Quanah Parker: Indian Warrior for Peace.* Champaign, IL: Garrard, 1970.

Berger, Thomas. *Little Big Man.* New York: Dell Publishing, 1989.

_____. *The Return of Little Big Man.* Boston: Little, Brown and Company, 1999.

Foreman, Paul. *Quanah. The Serpent Eagle.* Flagstaff, AZ: Northland Press, 1983.

Frank, Lois Ellen. *Native American Cooking: Foods of the Southwest Indian Nations.* New York: Wings Books, 1995.

Hagan, William Thomas. *Quanah Parker, Comanche Chief.* Norman: University of Oklahoma Press, 1993.

Hobbs, Will. *Kokopelli's Flute.* New York: Atheneum Books for Young Readers, 1995.

Kavasch, E. Barrie. *A Student's Guide to Native American Genealogy.* Phoenix, AZ: Oryx Press, 1996.

Kissinger, Rosemary K. *Quanah Parker: Comanche Chief.* Gretna, LA: Pelican Publishing Co., 1991.

May, Julian. *Quanah, Leader of the Comanche.* Mankato, MN: Creative Educational Society, 1973.

Reader's Digest Association. *Through Indian Eyes: The Untold Story of Native American Peoples.* Pleasantville, NY: Reader's Digest Association, Inc., 1995.

Trafzer, Clifford E. (ed.). *Blue Dawn, Red Earth: New Native American Storytellers.* New York: Anchor Books, 1996.

Weems, John Edward. *Death Song: The Last of the Indian Wars.* New York: Doubleday, 1976.

VIDEOS

Foulkrod, Patricia and Micahel Grant (producers). *The Natives of the Southwest: Artists, Innovators and Rebels.* Atlanta: Turner Home Entertainment, 1994.

_____. *The People of the Great Plains: Part 1: Buffalo People and Dog Days.* Atlanta: Turner Home Entertainment, 1994.

_____. *The People of the Great Plains: Part 2: The Coming of the Horse, the White Man and the Rifle.* Atlanta: Turner Home Entertainment, 1994.

_____. *The Tribal People of the Northwest: Living in Harmony With the Land.* Atlanta: Turner Home Entertainment, 1994.Foulkrod, Patricia and Michael Grant (producers).

_____. *The Tribes of the Southeast: Persistent Cultures of Resilient People.* Atlanta: Turner Home Entertainment, 1994.

How the West Was Lost: Volumes 1-3. Bethesda, MD: Discovery Enterprises, 1993.

Little Big Man. New York: CBS/Fox Video, 1989.

Lixey, Bruce and Robert Hercules (producers). *America's Great Indian Leaders*. Chicago: Questar Video, 1994. (Includes Geronimo, Quanah Parker, Crazy Horse, and Chief Joseph)

_____. *America's Great Indian Nations*. Chicago: Questar Video, 1995.

Purvis, Stephen (producer and director). *Great Chiefs at the Crossroads*. Stamford, CT: Capital Cities/ABC Video Publishing, 1994.

Wavelength Video; Simitar Entertainment, Inc. (compilers). *The Legend of Custer*. Plymouth, MN: Simitar Entertainment, 1992.

BOOK CLUB (VIDEO CRITIQUE)

Watch two documentaries about Native Americans and critique their presentation and content.

INTRODUCTORY ACTIVITIES

DAY ONE

Objective: The students will list names of famous Native American leaders. They will listen to stories written by Native Americans.

Ask the students to list famous Native American leaders both past and present. Write the names on the board next to the name of their tribes. Why are these people important to American history? What contributions did they make to their people and the country?

Go on a hunt for the names and tribes of Native American leaders. Collect their names, tribe, dates of birth and death, major contributions to their people and the country, and quotes attributed to the leader.

Read stories from the book *Blue Dawn, Red Earth: New Native American Storytellers* edited by Clifford E. Trafzer.

DAY TWO

STORY LESSON

Follow the *Presenting the Story Lesson* instructions in the Introduction. Each story lesson follows the same procedure; however, say the following in step 4:

"The title of the story we're reading today is *Quanah Parker: Comanche Chief*. What do you think the story is about? What do you already know about Quanah Parker? What do you know about the Comanche tribe?"

EXTENSION ACTIVITIES

1. Watch the film *America's Great Indian Leaders* produced by Bruce Lixey and Robert Hercules.

2. Students write to current tribal chiefs through e-mail or regular post. Addresses are available at your local library. Prepare a question list including literal and interpretive questions. "What are some of your duties as chief? What are your tribe's long-term goals? What do you hope the future will hold for your tribe? What is the most important lesson you'd like your children to learn from your tribal history?" If a student is Native American, he or she can contact the leader of another tribe and ask the same questions.

3. Based on the information gathered on Native American leaders, students make posters that tell a brief biography of each leader including quotes attributed to the subject.

4. Using Native American cookbooks (see examples in the Books to Read), students prepare Native American dishes either in the classroom or as a home assignment.

5. Take the box scenes from *A Letter Home*, samples of Native American food, and the posters of Native American leaders to a local elementary school. The students conduct a presentation telling what they learned about tribal history, leaders, and the future of America's Native American tribes.

QUANAH PARKER: COMANCHE CHIEF

Over 160 years ago, Fort Parker in East-Central Texas shielded the Parker family. The family of pioneers moved to Texas to find a new life. In the same land of promise, the native Comanches vowed to protect their land and food supply, the buffalo, from the encroaching white man.

In May 1836, the Comanche attacked Fort Parker. By the end of the siege several members of the Parker family laid dead or injured. Lucy Parker witnessed the abduction of two of her children, including nine-year-old Cynthia Ann.

The Comanches adopted Cynthia Ann and changed her name to Naudah. Naudah became a Comanche at heart while she learned the customs and lifestyle of her adopted family. As an adult, Naudah married and gave birth to a son named Quanah.

Quanah grew up to be a strong young man while he watched as the white man moved into his native land, building fences and slaughtering the buffalo. When he became chief he swore to fight for the land and traditions of his people.

As time passed and the buffalo herds dwindled, other tribes entered the reservations. Quanah continued his fight until the anguish of his people forced him to become the last chief to surrender.

Quanah realized his people had to prepare for life among the white men. He encouraged his tribe to seek out an education and to learn to trade with the ranchers. He met with and befriended five Presidents of the United States including Theodore Roosevelt.

Soldiers recaptured Cynthia Ann Parker and returned her to her birth-family. Unable to adjust to her new life, she died of a broken heart. Quanah later met the Parkers who treated him with kindness. Out of respect he took the name Quanah Parker.

Quanah Parker earned the admiration of both his people and the white man. On his death in 1911, the entire nation mourned as Congress erected a tall granite obelisk over Quanah Parker's grave. The monument reads: "Resting here until the day breaks and the shadows fall and darkness disappears is Quanah Parker, the last chief of the Comanches."

QUESTIONS FOR QUANAH PARKER: COMANCHE CHIEF

Literal Questions:

THE FACTS:

1. What happened in May 1836?

_____

_____

_____

2. Who did the Comanches abduct from Fort Parker?

_____

_____

_____

3. Why did Quanah eventually surrender?

_____

_____

_____

4. What did Congress write on the monument erected in the memory of Quanah Parker?

_____

_____

_____

SEQUENCE OF EVENTS:

5. What did Quanah swear to do after he became chief?

_____

_____

_____

6. What happened to Cynthia Parker after she was recaptured?

_____

_____

_____

Name _____ Date _____

Interpretive Questions:

DRAWING CONCLUSIONS:

7. What one word best describes the life of Cynthia Parker?

_____

_____

_____

_____

MAKING INFERENCES:

8. How did Quanah Parker feel about Comanche traditions?

_____

_____

_____

_____

MAKING PREDICTIONS:

9. Will Quanah Parker's contributions to the Comanche tribe last throughout many generations? Why do you feel this way?

_____

_____

_____

_____

IDENTIFICATION OF CAUSE:

10. Why did five Presidents befriend Quanah Parker?

_____

_____

_____

_____

IDENTIFICATION OF THE MAIN IDEA:

11. Write a title for the story. Use as few words as possible.

_____

_____

_____

Name _____ **Date** _____

COMPARISON:

12. How was Quanah's devotion to the Comanches like that of his mother, Naudah? How was it different?

_____

_____

_____

_____

SUMMARIZE:

13. In your own words, tell about the contributions Quanah Parker made to the Comanche people.

_____

_____

_____

_____

EFFECT:

14. What effect did meeting his mother's family have on Quanah Parker?

_____

_____

_____

_____

FACT AND OPINION:

15. The story said, "He (Quanah Parker) encouraged his tribe to seek out an education and to learn to trade with the ranchers." Is this a fact or someone's opinion? How can you prove your answer?

_____

_____

_____

_____

ON YOUR OWN:

16. Write a question about the story for a teacher or another student to answer.

_____

_____

Name _____ **Date** _____

12. MARTIN LUTHER KING, JR. RECEIVES THE NOBEL PEACE PRIZE

Reading Level = 7.86

ABOUT THE STORY

This story is based on one in a series called *Moments in Time*. The article takes the students back to the moment when Martin Luther King, Jr. received the Nobel Peace Prize.

QUOTES OF THE WEEK

Quote 1:

"Some few spectators, who had not been trained in the discipline of nonviolence, reacted to the brutality of the policemen by throwing rocks and bottles. But the demonstrators remained nonviolent. In the face of this resolution and bravery, the moral conscience of the nation was deeply stirred . . . ."[9] *(page 45)*—MARTIN LUTHER KING, JR. (MAY 4, 1963)

QUOTE 2:

"Even the most casual observer can see that the South has marvelous possibilities. It is rich in natural resources, blessed with the beauties of nature and endowed with a native warmth of spirit. Yet in spite of these assets, it is retarded by a blight that debilitates not only the Negro but also the white man. . . . Segregation has placed the whole South socially, educationally, and economically behind the rest of the nation."[9] *(page 47)*—MARTIN LUTHER KING, JR.

INTERVIEW TOPIC

Interview a person who lived during Martin Luther King's civil rights movement. What was his or her reaction to the nonviolent protests led by Reverend King? Even if the person was a child at the time, he or she can give unique insight into the era.

PREVIEW WORDS

Nobel Peace Prize   *Oslo, Norway*   *Mahatma Gandhi*

WORD-ORIGIN STUDY

undaunted: The original meaning of the word *daunt* was "to tame or subdue." The prefix *un-* means "not." If you are *undaunted* in your beliefs, your opinion cannot be changed, tamed, or subdued.

---

[9] Refer to *Quotation Footnotes for Level 7* on page 132.

nonviolent: The prefix *non-* means "not." If you practice *nonviolence,*
                                 you resolve your disputes through avenues that are not
                                 injurious or violent.

List other words beginning with the prefixes *un-* and *non-*. Write the words and
their definitions in your vocabulary notebook.

BOOKS TO READ

Darby, Jean. *Martin Luther King, Jr.* Minneapolis: Lerner Publications Co., 1990.

Davidson, Margaret. *I Have a Dream: The Story of Martin Luther King.* New York:
    Scholastic, 1986.

Davis, Ossie. *Just Like Martin.* New York: Simon & Schuster, 1992.

Fairclough, Adam. *Martin Luther King, Jr.* Athens: University of Georgia Press, 1995.

Friedly, Michael. *Martin Luther King, Jr.: The FBI File.* New York: Carroll & Graf, 1993.

Jakoubek, Robert. *Martin Luther King, Jr.: Black Americans of Achievement Series.* New
    York: Chelsea, 1990.

Kallen, Stuart A. *Martin Luther King, Jr.: A Man and His Dream.* Edina: Abdo &
    Daughters, 1993.

King, Martin Luther, Jr. *The Martin Luther King, Jr. Companion: Quotations from the Speeches,
    Essays, and Books of Martin Luther King, Jr.* New York: St. Martin's Press, 1993.

_____. *The Measure of Man.* Minneapolis: Augsburg Fortress, 1988.

_____. *Strength to Love.* Minneapolis: Augsburg Fortress, 1981.

_____. *Stride Toward Freedom: The Montgomery Story.* New York: Harper, 1989.

_____. *The Words of Martin Luther King, Jr.* New York: New Market, 1987.

Levine, Ellen. *If You Lived at the Time of Martin Luther King.* New York: Scholastic, 1990.

Lischer, Richard. *The Preacher King: Martin Luther King, Jr. and the Word That Moved
    America.* New York: Oxford University Press, 1995.

Moore, Yvette. *Freedom Songs.* New York: Orchard Books, 1991.

Patterson, Lillie. *Martin Luther King, Jr., and the Freedom Movement.* New York: Facts on
    File, 1989.

Ray, James Earl. *Who Killed Martin Luther King?: The True Story by the Alleged Assassin.*
    Washington, D.C.: National Press Books, 1992.

Shuker, Nancy F. *Martin Luther King Jr.: World Leaders—Past and Present Series.* New York:
    Chelsea, 1985.

VIDEOS

A Day to Remember: August 28, 1963. Arlington, VA: PAS Video, 1989.

Fabian, Rhonda. *African American Life.* Bala Cynwyd, PA: Schlessinger Video
    Productions, 1996.

Kaplan, Richard. *Legacy of a Dream.* Oak Forest, IL: MPI Home Video, 1990.

King, Montgomery to Memphis. Beverly Hills, CA: Pacific Arts Video, 1988.

Martin Luther King: Commemorative Collection. Oak Forest, IL: MPI Home Video, 1988.

CDs, Records, and Cassettes

Copage, Eric V. *Black Pearls: Daily Meditations* (Cassette). New York: Harper Audio, 1994.

Great Speeches of the 20th Century (Cassette). Santa Monica, CA: Rhino Word Beat, 1991.

INTRODUCTORY ACTIVITIES

Day One

> *Objective:* The students will listen to Martin Luther King's "I Have a Dream" speech. They will discuss the content and meaning of the speech.

Display and discuss the quotes of the week. Continue to display the quotes in a prominent location throughout the week.

Before showing the video, discuss recent protests the students observed locally, nationally, and internationally. Were the protests violent or nonviolent? How effective were the protests? Do the students think the protestors will get what they want? Why do they feel this way?

Show the video *A Day to Remember: August 28, 1963* or listen to the audio cassette *Great Speeches of the 20th Century*, paying close attention to the "I Have a Dream" speech. Discuss the text of the speech. Finally, guide the students as they look for the meaning within the words.

Day Two

> *Objective:* The students will gain insight to Reverend King's civil rights movement from someone involved in, or a witness to, the movement.

Invite a witness to Reverend King's civil rights movement to class. Before the speaker arrives, help the students prepare interview questions. Include literal and interpretive questions. Write the questions on chart paper and display the chart at the front of the room. Give the speaker a list of the questions so that he or she can prepare. After the discussion encourage the students to ask impromptu questions.

Day Three

STORY LESSON

Follow the *Presenting the Story Lesson* instructions in the Introduction. Each story lesson follows the same procedure; however, say the following in step 4: "The title of the story we're reading today is *Martin Luther King, Jr. Receives the Nobel Peace Prize*. This is a *Moments in Time* article. As you read the article, try to visualize the time in which the event occurred. What do you think the story is about? What do you already know about Martin Luther King, Jr.?"

EXTENSION ACTIVITIES

1. Students review Quote 2 from the Quotes of the Week. "What did Martin Luther King mean when he said, 'Yet in spite of these assets, it (the South) is retarded by a blight that debilitates not only the Negro but also the white man. . . .'? How does segregation retard the marvelous possibilities of those being denied access as well as those prohibiting access to others?"

   Discuss the current trend of "self-segregation." Although all races work together in the classroom, do students tend to group with their own race during lunch? Why does this happen? Why does it not happen at your school? Are the students and the school enriched by this behavior or, as Reverend King stated, are all students' and the school's "marvelous possibilities" retarded by this behavior?

2. Ask each student to bring in an article or write a summary of an article dealing with self-segregation. Review the articles using Quote 2 as a guide for the discussion.

3. Ask the students to voluntarily mix with other racial groups during lunch breaks for one week. Pair black students with white, Asians with Hispanics, and so on. What did the students learn from the experience? How did they feel at the beginning of the week? How did they feel at the end?

December 10, 1964

MARTIN LUTHER KING, JR. RECEIVES THE NOBEL PEACE PRIZE

The Nobel committee awarded Martin Luther King, Jr. the Nobel Peace Prize today in Oslo, Norway. Reverend King, a father of four children, became the youngest person to receive the prize.

According to set requirements, the recipient of the Peace Prize must play a key role in "the furtherance of brotherhood among men . . . the abolishment or reduction of standing armies and . . . the extension of these purposes." No other man of our time so clearly stands for these ideals than Reverend King.

The prize citation goes on to praise King as the "undaunted champion of peace." Reverend King is "the first person in the Western world to have shown us that a struggle can be waged without violence."

The Nobel board described King as "the man who has never abandoned his faith in the unarmed struggle he is waging, who has suffered for his faith, been imprisoned on many occasions, whose home has been subjected to bomb attacks, whose life and those of his family have been threatened, and who nevertheless has never faltered." King called the teachings of Christ and Mahatma Gandhi his guidepost.

While accepting the Nobel Peace Prize Reverend King vowed, "We will return good for evil. Christ showed us the way and Mahatma Gandhi showed us it could work." He dedicated his prize to the "humble children" of the civil rights movement. These courageous marchers carry on their crusade through the practice of nonviolence.

QUESTIONS FOR MARTIN LUTHER KING, JR. RECEIVES THE NOBEL PEACE PRIZE

Literal Questions:

THE FACTS:

1. On what day did Martin Luther King, Jr. receive the Nobel Peace Prize?

_____

_____

_____

2. Where did Reverend King accept the Nobel Peace Prize?

_____

_____

_____

3. What are the requirements a Peace Prize recipient must meet?

_____

_____

_____

4. To whom did Reverend King dedicate his prize?

_____

_____

_____

SEQUENCE OF EVENTS:

5. Was Reverend King's home subjected to bomb attacks before or after he received the Nobel Peace Prize?

_____

_____

_____

6. Which two men came before Martin Luther King and "showed us the way"?

_____

_____

_____

Name _____   Date _____

Interpretive Questions:

DRAWING CONCLUSIONS:

7. The citation described King as the "undaunted champion of peace." Why did the Nobel committee choose these words to describe Reverend King?

_____

_____

_____

_____

MAKING INFERENCES:

8. Why did people threaten Martin Luther King's life and bomb his home?

_____

_____

_____

_____

MAKING PREDICTIONS:

9. Think about recent protests you have seen or read about in the news. Were they violent or nonviolent protests? Would protests be more productive if they were nonviolent? Why do you feel this way?

_____

_____

_____

_____

IDENTIFICATION OF CAUSE:

10. Why did Martin Luther King choose nonviolent protests over violence?

_____

_____

_____

_____

IDENTIFICATION OF THE MAIN IDEA:

11. Write a title for the story. Use as few words as possible.

_____

_____

Name _____ **Date** _____

COMPARISON:

12. Read a biography about the life of Mahatma Gandhi. How was Gandhi's philosophy like Martin Luther King's? How was it different?

_____

_____

_____

_____

SUMMARIZE:

13. In your own words, summarize the prize citation given to Reverend King.

_____

_____

_____

_____

EFFECT:

14. What effect, if any, do you believe the presentation of the Nobel Peace Prize had on Martin Luther King's civil rights movement? Why do you feel this way?

_____

_____

_____

_____

FACT AND OPINION:

15. The Nobel Peace Prize citation described King as the "undaunted champion of peace." Is this a fact or the committee's opinion? How can you prove your answer?

_____

_____

_____

_____

ON YOUR OWN:

16. Write a question about the story for a teacher or another student to answer.

_____

_____

Name _____   Date _____

13. WALKING STONES OF DEATH VALLEY

Reading Level = 7.86

ABOUT THE STORY

This story tells about the mysterious walking stones found in what is called the Racetrack, a playa in the northern region of Death Valley. Scientists Robert Sharp and Dwight Carey studied the rocks to determine what causes the movement of these massive stones.

QUOTES OF THE WEEK

Quote 1:

"Stones have been known to move and trees to speak."[2] *(page 239)*
—SHAKESPEARE, *MACBETH*, III, iv, 122

Quote 2:

"Trees and stones will teach you that which you can never learn from masters."[2] *(page 136)*—ST. BERNARD (1091-1153), *EPISTLE* 106

INTERVIEW TOPIC

It is best to interview a person over 50, although it is not necessary. Prepare a question list that includes literal and interpretive questions based on the question, "What is the most amazing thing you have ever seen?" Don't limit the person's responses, but you might want to give the person a few days to consider his or her answers. Ask the person: "Why were you amazed by this experience or object? How did it make you feel? Why did you feel this way?"

PREVIEW WORDS

Death Valley   *hypothesized*
ambling   *meandered*

WORD-ORIGIN STUDY

meander: The word *meander* comes from a river in Phrygia called the Meander. It was known for its twisting and winding course. To *meander* is to travel in a winding, aimless manner. It is also used to describe a type of design, such as Greek keys, in which a solid line twists and turns to create the pattern.

hypothesis: The prefix *hypo-* means "under, beneath, or below." *Hypothesis* is the groundwork, or foundation, on which a person builds a theory; a supposition.

List other words beginning with the prefix *hypo-*. Write the words and their definitions in your vocabulary notebook.

---

[2] Refer to *Quotation Footnotes for Level 7* on page 132.

BOOKS TO READ

American Geological Institute. *Dictionary of Geological Terms*. Garden City, NY: Doubleday (Anchor Press), 1976.

Clark, William D. *Death Valley*. Las Vegas: KC Publications, 1995.

Duey, Kathleen and K.A. Bale, *Death Valley, California, 1849*. New York: Aladdin Paperbacks, 1998.

Heller, Robert E. *Geology and Earth Science Sourcebook for Elementary and Secondary Schools*. New York: Holt, Rinehart and Winston, 1970.

Hildreth, Wes. *Death Valley Geology*. Death Valley: Death Valley Natural History Association, 1976.

Kirk, Ruth. *Exploring Death Valley, 3rd ed., rev.* Stanford, CT: Stanford University Press, 1977.

Lambert, David. *The Field Guide to Geology*. New York: Facts on File, 1988.

MacFarlane, Ruth B. *Making Your Own Nature Museum*. New York: Franklin Watts, 1989.

Moss, Marissa. *Amelia Hits the Road*. Berkeley, CA: Tricycle Press, 1997.

Smith, Bruce G. and David McKay. *Geology Projects for Young Scientists*. New York: Franklin Watts, 1992.

ARTICLES

Findley, Rowe. "Death Valley, the Land and the Legend." *National Geographic*, January, 1970.

PERIODICALS

Earth Science, American Geological Institute, 4220 King St., Alexandria, VA 22303-1507.

VIDEOS

Death Valley: Life Against the Land. Whittier, CA: Finley–Holiday Film Corp., 1989.

Faye, Ted (director). *Death Valley Memories*. New York: Carousel Film and Video, 1995.

ORGANIZATIONS

American Institute of Professional Geologists, 7828 Vance Drive, Arvado, CO 80003.

Association for Women Geoscientists, P.O. Box 1005, Menlo Park, CA 94026.

BOOK CLUB

Read *Death Valley, California, 1849* by Kathleen Duey and K.A. Bale.

INTRODUCTORY ACTIVITIES

DAY ONE

Objective: The students will watch a video about Death Valley. They will make a list of geological sites in Death Valley.

Show the video *Death Valley: Life Against the Land*. Before the film, locate Death Valley on a map. The students will make a list of the geological sites as they watch the video.

After the movie, discuss the geological formations. Which site did they find most interesting? Why do they feel this way?

The students should begin listing unknown terms in their vocabulary notebooks.

DAY TWO

STORY LESSON

Follow the *Presenting the Story Lesson* instructions in the Introduction. Each story lesson follows the same procedure; however, say the following in step 4: "The title of the story we're reading today is *Walking Stones of Death Valley*. What do you think the story is about? What do you already know about Death Valley?"

EXTENSION ACTIVITIES

1. During a week-long activity, break the students into small groups of three. Display a list of sites found within Death Valley. For example:

Furnace Creek	Black Mountains	Hanaupah Canyon
Telescope Peak	Mosaic Canyon	Devil's Golf Course
Funeral Mountains	Stovepipe Wells	Zabriskie Point
Racetrack Playa	Mushroom Rock	Sand Dunes
Natural Bridge	Ubehebe Crater	

    Each group chooses a different site. The group prepares a presentation about the site using as many interesting vocabulary words as possible. Every presentation must include:

    - a map of Death Valley with the chosen site highlighted

    - a geological explanation of how the formation was made

    - a discussion of the origin of the name of the site

    - a model of the formation (Students can use books such as *Geology Projects for Young Scientists* by Bruce Smith and David McKay [see Books to Read] to find ideas on how to create their model.)

    Encourage the students to find creative ways to make their presentations.

2. Display the models, maps, etc., in a high-traffic location, such as the library. Ask the students to devise a title for the exhibit.

WALKING STONES OF DEATH VALLEY

For centuries Native Americans observed the boulders silently march across arid lake beds in California and Nevada. In 1978 researchers returned to Death Valley to investigate this seemingly inexplicable movement of stones.

These walking stones mystified scientists as large boulders self-propelled themselves across the sand. Stones weighing less than one pound to more than a third of a ton left tracks many hundreds of miles long. Most researchers hypothesized that sheets of winter ice slide the stones across the lake beds until Robert Sharp of Caltech and Dwight Carey of UCLA conducted experiments to discover the true forces behind the ambling stones.

Sharp and Carey marked 30 stones known to have left tracks. Next, they erected metal stakes around each stone. The stones could move between the stakes; however, the poles obstructed the movement of ice. This prevented ice flows from transporting the stones.

After several years of observation, the scientists recorded the motility of 28 of the 30 marked stones. Due to the careful placement of the stakes, Sharp and Carey realized that ice flows could not have moved the boulders. Therefore, what caused the stones to "walk?"

The majority of the movement occurred during three winter months. A half-pound stone, affectionately nicknamed Nancy, meandered more than 600 feet. Sharp and Carey theorized that rain and mud lubricated the surface of the lake beds allowing strong gusts of wind to propel Nancy across the slick desert floor.

How fast could a wind-blown stone move? Sharp and Carey calculated velocities of up to 200 feet per minute.

QUESTIONS FOR WALKING STONES OF DEATH VALLEY

Literal Questions:

THE FACTS:

1. Where are the walking rocks found?

_____

_____

_____

2. In what year did researchers return to investigate the movement of the stones?

_____

_____

_____

3. Name the researchers who studied the walking stones.

_____

_____

_____

4. What conclusions were drawn by the researchers after they studied the walking stones?

_____

_____

_____

SEQUENCE OF EVENTS:

5. Who were the first people to observe the walking boulders in California and Nevada?

_____

_____

_____

6. Which theory was postulated first: ice flows moved the stones, or wind propelled the stones over rain-lubricated surfaces?

_____

_____

_____

Name _____   Date _____

Interpretive Questions:

DRAWING CONCLUSIONS:

7. Do you think Sharp and Carey chose the best procedure in their experiment on the walking stones? Why do you feel this way?

_____

_____

_____

_____

MAKING INFERENCES:

8. Did Sharp and Carey show concrete proof that the stones were moved by wind? Why do you feel this way?

_____

_____

_____

_____

MAKING PREDICTIONS:

9. How can people use the research conducted by Sharp and Carey in other areas?

_____

_____

_____

_____

IDENTIFICATION OF CAUSE:

10. Why did Robert Sharp and Dwight Carey study the walking stones of Death Valley?

_____

_____

_____

_____

IDENTIFICATION OF THE MAIN IDEA:

11. Write a title for the story. Use as few words as possible.

_____

_____

_____

Name _____ **Date** _____

COMPARISON:

12. Compare the two theories on how the stones moved as presented in the story. How are they alike? How are they different?

_____

_____

_____

_____

SUMMARIZE:

13. In your own words, tell about Sharp and Carey's hypothesis concerning the movement of the walking stones.

_____

_____

_____

_____

EFFECT:

14. What effect might learning the true reason for the movement of the stones have on local folklore?

_____

_____

_____

_____

FACT AND OPINION:

15. The story stated, "Sharp and Carey theorized that rain and mud lubricated the surface of the lake beds allowing strong gusts of wind to propel Nancy (a stone) across the slick desert floor." Is this a fact or the researchers' opinion? How can you prove your answer?

_____

_____

_____

_____

ON YOUR OWN:

16. Write a question about the story for a teacher or another student to answer.

_____

_____

Name _____   Date _____

14. CAN SAND SING?

Reading Level = 7.90

ABOUT THE STORY

Throughout history, travelers reported hearing sounds emitted from sand dunes. Some describe the sound as pounding hoofs while others compare it to a foghorn. Scientists Marcel Leach and Douglas Goldsack investigated the cause of the "singing sand," and discovered a surprising, yet simple, explanation.

QUOTES OF THE WEEK

Quote 1:

"The most beautiful thing we can experience is the mysterious. It is the source of all true art and science."[2] *(page 763)*—ALBERT EINSTEIN, *WHAT I BELIEVE*

Quote 2:

"We must never make experiments to confirm our ideas, but simply to control them."[2] *(page 552)*—CLAUDE BERNARD, *FROM BULLETIN OF NEW YORK ACADEMY OF MEDICINE, VOL. IV*, page 997

INTERVIEW TOPIC

Interview a scientist. Students can try contacting their favorite scientist—such as Nobel Prize winners—by mail, phone, or e-mail if he or she lives out of town. The local librarian can help students locate addresses. Ask the scientist about conducting experiments. Prepare a question list including literal and interpretive questions: "Why do scientists conduct experiments? Are there set requirements a scientist must follow to obtain the most accurate results possible? Do you enjoy making hypotheses and checking them with experiments? Why do you feel this way? Is experimentation a legitimate form of scientific investigation? Why do you feel this way?"

PREVIEW WORDS

Marcel Leach	*Douglas Goldsack*
Laurentian University	*Sudbury, Ontario*
silica	*coalesced*

WORD-ORIGIN STUDY

silica: *Silica* comes from a Latin word meaning "flint." *Silica* is silicon dioxide which is a hard, glossy mineral found in quartz, sand, opal, etc.

---

[2] Refer to *Quotation Footnotes for Level 7* on page 132.

coalesce:	The prefix *co-* means "together," while *alescere* means "to grow up." To *coalesce* is to grow together or unite.

List other words beginning with the prefix *co-*. Write the words and their definitions in your vocabulary notebook.

BOOKS TO READ

Christian, Spencer and Antonia Felix. *Can It Really Rain Frogs?: The World's Strangest Weather Events.* New York: Wiley, 1997.

National Geographic Society, the Special Publications Division. *Nature's World of Wonders.* Washington, D.C.: The National Geographic Society, 1983.

Paulsen, Gary. *The Island.* New York: Orchard Books, 1988.

Rinard, Judith E. *Wonders of the Desert World.* Washington, D.C.: National Geographic Society, 1976.

Robins, Joyce. *Natural Wonders of the World.* Secaucus, NJ: Chartwell Books, 1992.

Rowland-Entwistle, Theodore. *Natural Wonders of the World.* London, England: Octopus Books, 1980.

Yenne, Bill. *100 Natural Wonders of the World.* San Francisco: Bluewood Books, 1995.

VIDEOS

Jones, Doug. *World's Amazing Wonders.* San Ramon, CA: International Video Network, 1992.

The Seven Wonders of the Ancient World. Chicago: Questar Video, 1990.

ARTICLES

Editorial Staff. "Break Throughs in Science, Technology, and Medicine: Singing Sand." *Discover,* August 1997, 14(2).

BOOK CLUB

Read Gary Paulsen's *The Island.*

INTRODUCTORY ACTIVITIES

DAY ONE

Objective:	The students will review Story 13, *Walking Stones of Death Valley.* They will categorize unusual events under natural occurrences, man-made occurrences, and folklore.

Review what the students learned in *Walking Stones of Death Valley*. "What amazing things did you learn about nature and geology in the lesson? Do you know of any other astonishing facts about nature? What are they? Where do they occur? How do they make you feel?"

Make a list of all the things the students mention even if they are fictitious. Make a large chart as follows:

True Wonders of Nature	Man-Made Wonders	Legends or Folklore

The students write the things they listed under the appropriate category.

DAY TWO

STORY LESSON

Follow the *Presenting the Story Lesson* instructions in the Introduction. Each story lesson follows the same procedure; however, say the following in step 4: "The title of the story we're reading today is *Can Sand Sing*? What do you think the story is about? Do you think sand can really sing or make noises? Will the story tell about a man-made phenomena? Will the story be a folktale? Why do you feel this way?"

EXTENSION ACTIVITIES

1. Invite a local geologist or geology teacher to the class to talk about the geology of the region. If the region is mountainous, what formed the mountains? If the region is near the sea, how does the sea affect the land? Are there any fault lines in the area?

   Ask the geologist to share information about any unusual natural formations in the area. Many times Native Americans have stories surrounding the land. What is unique about your area?

2. Break the students into groups. Assign each group a local geological feature. Using reference books, the students make models and topographic maps of their particular feature.

3. The students present the models and maps to the class. Set up a display area in the classroom.

CAN SAND SING?

For centuries, people around the world reported hearing singing sand. Lord Curzon, the British viceroy of India, told stories of the strange sounds rising from the sands. Even Marco Polo in his historic travels heard sand sing. From beaches to sand dunes, eerie sounds fill the air, and can be heard miles away. Some compare the sound to the pounding hoofs of cavalry horses. Others liken it to the blare of a foghorn. What causes these bizarre noises in the sand?

For several years, a physicist named Marcel Leach from Laurentian University in Sudbury, Ontario studied the mystery. After several years without a breakthrough, Leach turned to a chemist, Douglas Goldsack. Perhaps, Goldsack suggested, Leach should analyze the composition of singing sand.

What the two men found was that singing sand contained an unexpectedly high silica content. Normally, sand contains only fifty-percent silica. Singing sand contained ninety-percent silica. These sand particles also held higher amounts of moisture. Could high levels of silica and moisture cause grains of sand to sing?

When Goldsack examined individual grains of singing sand, he noticed they had a pearl-like appearance. By analyzing the sand under an infrared spectrometer, the pair discovered that the water and silica coalesced to form a silica gel. This set the singing sand samples apart from non-singing varieties.

Silica gel is a common substance. Electronic manufacturers use silica gel in packaging to absorb moisture. Silica gel protects products susceptible to moisture damage by acting as a drying agent.

This made the next step in the experiment simple and inexpensive. Goldsack filled a glass jar with pure silica gel and closed the lid. When he shook the jar, the gel emitted a "thrumming sound."

The investigators reached the conclusion that silica gel causes sand to sing. The gel acts as a gum bonding the grains of sand together. When the wind blows, it vibrates the entire sand dune turning it into a giant tuning fork. The vibration of the sand transmits these vibrations to the air, causing the sand to sing.

QUESTIONS FOR CAN SAND SING?

Literal Questions:

THE FACTS:

1. How do people describe the sound of the singing sand?

_____

_____

_____

2. Name the two men who studied the singing sand.

_____

_____

_____

3. What two things does singing sand contain in high amounts?

_____

_____

_____

4. According to the investigators, what causes sand to sing?

_____

_____

_____

SEQUENCE OF EVENTS:

5. Which occurred first: Lord Curzon told stories of the strange sounds rising from the sands, or Douglas Goldsack and Marcel Leach analyzed the composition of singing sand?

_____

_____

_____

6. What happened to the silica gel after Goldsack shook it in a jar?

_____

_____

_____

Name _____   Date _____

Interpretive Questions:

DRAWING CONCLUSIONS:

7. What one word best describes Marcel Leach?

_____

_____

_____

_____

MAKING INFERENCES:

8. How might people feel if they hear the sand sing and not know why?

_____

_____

_____

_____

MAKING PREDICTIONS:

9. Will other scientists try to duplicate Goldsack's experiment in the future? Why do you feel this way?

_____

_____

_____

_____

IDENTIFICATION OF CAUSE:

10. Why did Leach and Goldsack investigate the cause of singing sand?

_____

_____

_____

_____

IDENTIFICATION OF THE MAIN IDEA:

11. Write a title for the story. Use as few words as possible.

_____

_____

_____

Name _____ **Date** _____

COMPARISON:

12. In what way are Leach and Goldsack alike? How are they different?

_____

_____

_____

_____

SUMMARIZE:

13. In your own words, tell how Leach and Goldsack discovered the cause of singing sand.

_____

_____

_____

_____

EFFECT:

14. What effect will Leach and Goldsack's findings have on the scientific community? What effect will their study have on people who live near singing sand?

_____

_____

_____

_____

FACT AND OPINION:

15. The story said, "What the two men (Leach and Goldsack) found was that singing sand contained an unexpectedly high silica content." Is this a fact, or Leach and Goldsack's opinion? How can you prove your answer?

_____

_____

_____

_____

ON YOUR OWN:

16. Write a question about the story for a teacher or another student to answer.

_____

_____

Name _____   **Date** _____

15. <u>THOMAS FLYER</u> ARRIVES IN PARIS
Reading Level = 7.98

ABOUT THE STORY

This is a *Moments in Time* story telling about an automobile race in 1908. The race, featuring America's *Thomas Flyer*, ran from New York to Paris.

QUOTES OF THE WEEK

Quote 1:

"Ride on! Rough-shod if need be, smooth-shod if that will do, but ride on! Ride on over all obstacles, and win the race!"[2] *(page 549)*—CHARLES DICKENS, *DAVID COPPERFIELD*

Quote 2:

"It were not best that we should all think alike; it is difference of opinion that makes horse races."[2] *(page 624)*—MARK TWAIN, *PUDD'NHEAD WILSON'S CALENDAR*

INTERVIEW TOPIC

Interview any person about his or her viewpoints on winning. Prepare a question list including literal and interpretive questions: "Is winning important? Why do you feel this way? Have you won a contest that was important to you? What was it? Did you spend time preparing for the contest? If so, what did you have to do to prepare yourself?"

PREVIEW WORDS

entourage	*St. Chaffray*	*Vladivostok*
Lt. Koeppen	*Grand Duke Vladimir*	

WORD-ORIGIN STUDY

enthusiasm: The word *enthusiasm* comes from a combination of two words: *en* meaning "in" and *theos* meaning "god." Therefore, the original interpretation of enthusiasm was to be possessed by a god, or in God's powers. The word *enthusiasm* had the supernatural implications of an inspiration from a god, such as a prophet. Today, *enthusiasm* refers to an intense zeal or interest.

entourage: *Entourage* comes from the French phrase *en tour*, "around or to surround." An *entourage* is a group of people, or attendants, surrounding the event. It is also the surroundings or environment.

---

[2] Refer to *Quotation Footnotes for Level 7* on page 132.

List other words derived from French terms (examples: *valet, tête à tête,* or *carte blanche*). Look them up in the dictionary, and write their definitions in your vocabulary notebooks.

BOOKS TO READ

Butterworth, W.E. *High Wind: The Story of NASCAR Racing.* New York: Grosset & Dunlap, Inc., 1971.

_____. *Redline 7100.* New York: Grosset & Dunlap, Inc., 1968.

_____. *Road Racer.* New York: Grosset & Dunlap, Inc., 1967.

_____. *Team Racer.* New York: Grosset & Dunlap, Inc., 1972.

Calvert, Patricia. *The Hour of the Wolf.* New York: Signet, 1983.

Cutter, Robert Arthur. *The Encyclopedia of Auto Racing Greats.* Englewood Cliffs, NJ: Prentice-Hall, 1973.

Karl, Herb. *The Toom County Mud Race.* New York: Doubleday, 1992.

Lerner, Mark. *Careers in Auto Racing.* Minneapolis: Lerner Publication Co., 1980.

Olney, Ross Robert. *Super-Champions of Auto Racing.* New York: Clarion Books, 1984.

VIDEOS

The Great Race. Burbank, CA: Warner Home Video, 1991.

BOOK CLUB

Read Herb Karl's *The Toom County Mud Race.*

INTRODUCTORY ACTIVITIES

DAY ONE

Objective: The students will watch a movie and discuss whether the story is based on fact or fiction.

Discuss how movie scripts can find their story lines in both factual and fictional plots. Watch the movie *The Great Race.* After the movie, hold a vote on whether the story is based on fact or fiction. Record the results to use in the Extension Activities.

Note: The plot of the movie *The Great Race* is based on the automobile race described in the story lesson. Do not tell the students about this information until the discussion in the Extension Activities.

Day Two

STORY LESSON

Follow the *Presenting the Story Lesson* instructions in the Introduction. Each story lesson follows the same procedure; however, say the following in step 4: "The title of the story we're reading today is *Thomas Flyer Arrives in Paris*. What do you think the story is about? What do you already know about the *Thomas Flyer*?"

EXTENSION ACTIVITIES

1. Discuss the results from the votes taken at the end of Introductory Activity, Day One. Did many students think the story was based on fiction? Why did they feel this way? How was the story like the real race in 1908? How was it different?

2. Break the students into groups. Assign each student a movie based on factual events or a biography (for example, *Pocahontas*; *Malcom X*; *JFK*; *Schindler's List*; or *Annie Get Your Gun*. First, each group researches the facts about the event or person's life. Next, they watch the movie together. Using their research as a guide, they write a compare/contrast report detailing how the movie and the true story are alike and how they are different. The report should include a bibliography of at least five references, an outline, and a cover page.

3. The students present oral reports on their research from Extension Activity 1. Encourage the students to use visuals, timelines, or charts to help illustrate their findings.

July 26, 1908

THOMAS FLYER ARRIVES IN PARIS

It all began 170 days ago, February 12, at Times Square, New York. Almost a quarter of a million people cheered as six cars (three French, one German, one Italian, and one American) began a race to the other side of the world. The trek would take these stouthearted men over the frozen north of America, across the Pacific, through Siberia, and finally to Paris.

Each car carried a three-man crew: two drivers and a mechanic. At 11:15 A.M., along an eight-mile stretch of cheers and band music, a 200-car entourage led the racers down the streets of New York. The spirited send-off foretold of the warmhearted greetings every contestant experienced along the route across the United States.

It appeared the Americans had the upper hand as they reached the west coast. A ship met the *Thomas Flyer*, sailing the car and crew to the next leg of the trip across the Bering Strait. Unfortunately, the ice of the strait was not solid. Embarrassed committee members granted the *Thomas Flyer* a 15-day allowance to make up for the lost time, and sailed them back to Seattle.

In the meantime, race officials granted Germany's trailing *Protos* railroad passage to meet the other cars in Seattle for the trip across the Pacific. The *Protos* crew accepted a 15-day penalty rather than disqualification.

As the cars reached Vladivostok in Siberia, St. Chaffray of France withdrew due to the poor condition of his car. Yet American dreams of winning ebbed as reports came in. Lost in mountain terrain, the *Thomas Flyer* lost 2 days. The back-up driver dropped out, and the *Thomas Flyer* required major repairs after sinking in a Siberian swamp. All the while the *Protos* moved farther into the lead.

On July 20, the *Protos* arrived in Paris winning the Grand Duke Vladimir of Russia Trophy and the $1,000 prize. The *Thomas Flyer* crossed the finish line on July 30. After calculating the 30-day penalty, race officials declared America's *Thomas Flyer* the winner. Lt. Koeppen of the German team told reporters, "I wish the roads in America were as nice as the people. Altogether, the trip has been a great success."

QUESTIONS FOR <u>THOMAS FLYER</u> ARRIVES IN PARIS

Literal Questions:

THE FACTS:

1. On what day did the story take place?

_____

_____

_____

2. Where and when did the race begin?

_____

_____

_____

3. How many cars were in the race?

_____

_____

_____

4. How many men were in each crew?

_____

_____

_____

SEQUENCE OF EVENTS:

5. Write these events in chronological order: The *Protos* crew accepted a 15-day penalty rather than disqualification; the *Thomas Flyer* crossed the finish line; the *Protos* arrived in Paris.

_____

_____

_____

6. What happened to the *Thomas Flyer* after it became lost in mountain terrain?

_____

_____

_____

Name _____   Date _____

Interpretive Questions:

DRAWING CONCLUSIONS:

7. What one word best describes the race from New York to Paris?

_____

_____

_____

_____

MAKING INFERENCES:

8. How did the general population feel about the race to the other side of the world?

_____

_____

_____

_____

MAKING PREDICTIONS:

9. Will drivers participate in a race from New York to Paris in the future? Why do you feel this way?

_____

_____

_____

_____

IDENTIFICATION OF CAUSE:

10. The race of 1908 drew attention and interest to the newly invented automobile. If a similar race took place today, what purpose might it serve?

_____

_____

_____

_____

IDENTIFICATION OF THE MAIN IDEA:

11. Write a title for the story. Use as few words as possible.

_____

_____

Name _____ **Date** _____

COMPARISON:

12. How would a race along the same route today be similar to the race of 1908? How would it be different?

_____

_____

_____

_____

SUMMARIZE:

13. In your own words, tell about the 1908 race from New York to Paris.

_____

_____

_____

_____

EFFECT:

14. What effect might the race of 1908 have had on the automobile industry?

_____

_____

_____

_____

FACT AND OPINION:

15. According to the story, Lt. Koeppen of the German team said, "I wish the roads in America were as nice as the people." Is this a fact or Lt. Koeppen's opinion? Why do you feel this way?

_____

_____

_____

_____

ON YOUR OWN:

16. Write a question about the story for a teacher or another student to answer.

_____

_____

Name _____   **Date** _____

REFERENCES FOR LEVEL 7

THE LUCK OF THE CHIMNEY SWEEP

Giblin, James Cross. *Chimney Sweeps Yesterday and Today*. New York: Thomas Crowell, 1982, pp. 9-13.

Zolar Staff. *Encyclopedia of Signs, Omens, and Superstitions*. Secaucus, NJ: Carol Publishing Group, 1995, p. 75.

THE DUST BOWL

Beauchamp, Wilbur L., John C. Mayfield and Joe Young West. "How the Earth's Surface Changes." *Our Wonderful World Encyclopedia* (1962), 1, 13.

"Breakthroughs in Science, Technology, and Medicine: Environment: The Once and Future Dust Bowl." *Discover*, 18, no. 4 (April 1997), 16.

Stanley, Jerry. *Children of the Dust Bowl: The True Story of the School at Weedpatch Camp*. New York: Crown Publishers, Inc., 1992, pp. 3-7.

MYSTERY OF THE DEEP

Conley-Early, Andrea. "The Hunt for a Giant Squid." *Sea Frontiers*, 41, no. 3 (Fall 1995), 48(4).

Conniff, Richard. "Clyde Roper Can't Wait to Be Attacked by the Giant Squid." *Smithsonian*, 27, no. 2 (May 1996), 126(9).

Fisher, Arthur. "The Hunt for Giant Squid: A High-Tech Search Is on for the Sea's Most Elusive Creature: Two Expeditions in the Kaikoura Peninsula." *Popular Science*, 250, no. 3 (March 1997), 74(4).

Young, Catherine. "Scientists Use Crittercam to Search for Sea's Most Elusive Creature: Giant Squid Filmed on an Underwater Video Camera." *Insight on the News*, 13, no. 16 (May 5, 1997), 39.

BUYING YOUR FIRST CAR

Bohr, Peter. "Certified Used Cars: Everything But the New-Car Smell." *Road & Track*, May 1997, pp. 136-140.

Consumer Guide. *Complete Guide to Used Cars: 1997 Edition*. Lincolnwood, IL: Publications International, Ltd., 1997.

LIFE IS SWEET: THE STORY OF MILTON HERSHEY

Hershey Archives, 170 W. Hersheypark Dr., Hershey, PA 17033.

Malone, Mary. *Milton Hershey: Chocolate King*. Champaign, IL: Garrard Publishing Company, 1971.

Shippen, Katherine Binney. *Milton S. Hershey*. New York: Random House, 1959.

MINA DEL PADRE, THE LOST PADRE MINE

Mangan, Frank J. *Bordertown*. El Paso, TX: C. Hertzog, 1964.

Yenne, Bill. *Hidden Treasure: Where to Find It, How to Get It*. New York: Avon Books, 1997.

Po Chieng Ma's Coded Pencils

"Education: For $6,000, You Get a Pencil With the Answers Included: Federal Agents Break Up a Cheating Ring Charged with Beating Graduate-School Entrance Exams." *Newsweek*, 128, no. 20 (November 11, 1996), 69.

Lowe's Intrepid

Catton, Bruce. *The Centennial History of the Civil War—Volume Two: Terrible Swift Sword.* Garden City, NY: Doubleday & Company, Inc., 1963, pp. 274-275.

————. *The Civil War.* New York: American Heritage Press, 1971, p. 66.

Davis, Burke. *Runaway Balloon: The Last Flight of Confederate Air Force One.* New York: Coward, McCann & Geoghegan, Inc., 1976, pp. 5-8.

Lossing, Benson J. *Matthew Brady's Illustrated History of the Civil War (1861-64) and the Causes That Led Up to the Great Conflict.* New York: The Fairfax Press, 1912 (Crown Publishing, 1977), p. 252.

"Lowe, Thaddeus S.C." *Pictorial Encyclopedia: People Who Made America, vol. 10.* Skokie, IL: United States History Society, Inc., 1973, p. 773.

The Never-Fading Popularity of Levi's® Jeans

"Strauss, Levi." *Pictorial Encyclopedia: People Who Made America, vol. 7.* Skokie, IL: United States History Society, Inc., 1973, p. 1337.

Weidt, Maryann N. *Mr. Blue Jeans: A Story About Levi Strauss.* Minneapolis: Carolrhoda Books, Inc., 1990.

Special thanks to Lynn Downey, Historian, Levi Strauss & Co.

Web site: www.levistrauss.com

A Letter Home

Linton, Calvin D. (ed.) *The Bicentennial Almanac: 200 Years of America.* Nashville, TN: Thomas Nelson Inc., Publishers, 1975, p. 235.

Owen, Roger C., James J.F. Deetz and Anthony D. Fisher. *The North American Indians: A Sourcebook.* London, England: Macmillan Company, Collier-Macmillan Limited, 1967, p. 107.

Quanah Parker: Comanche Chief

Anderson, LaVere. *Quanah Parker: Indian Warrior for Peace.* Champaign, IL: Garrard Publishing Company, 1970.

Kissinger, Rosemary K. *Quanah Parker: Comanche Chief.* Gretna, LA: Pelican Publishing Company, 1991.

May, Julian. *Quanah: Leader of the Comanche.* Mankato, MN: Creative Educational Society, Inc., 1973.

Martin Luther King, Jr. Receives the Nobel Peace Prize

Editorial Staff. "Nobel Prizes." *The Americana Annual: 1965,* 524.

King, Martin Luther, Jr. *The Martin Luther King, Jr. Companion: Quotations From the Speeches, Essays, and Books of Martin Luther King, Jr.* New York: St. Martin's Press, 1993.

WALKING STONES OF DEATH VALLEY

"Sailing Stones." *Nature/Science Annual* (1978). Alexandria, VA: Time-Life Books, 1977, p. 177.

CAN SAND SING?

"Breakthroughs in Science, Technology, and Medicine: Geology: Singing Sand." *Discover*, 18, no. 8 (August 1997), 14(2).

THOMAS FLYER ARRIVES IN PARIS

Daniel, Clifton (ed.) *Chronicle of the Twentieth Century*. Mount Kisco, NY: Chronicle Publications, 1987, pp. 109, 110, 111, 113.

Reader's Digest Staff. *Strange Stories, Amazing Facts: Stories That Are Bizarre Unusual, Odd, Astonishing and Often Incredible*. Pleasantville, NY: Reader's Digest Association, Inc., 1976, pp. 232-233.

QUOTATION FOOTNOTES FOR LEVEL 7

[1] Peter, Laurance J. Dr., *Peter's Quotations: Ideas of Our Times*. New York: William Morrow and Company, Inc., 1977.

[2] Bartlett, John. *Bartlett's Familiar Quotations*. Boston: Little, Brown and Company, 1980.

[3] Applewhite, Ashton, William R. Evans III and Andrew Frothingham. *And I Quote: The Definitive Collection of Quotes, Sayings, and Jokes for the Contemporary Speechmaker*. New York: St. Martin's Press, 1992.

[4] Rowes, Barbara. *The Book of Quotes*. New York: E.P. Dutton, 1979.

[5] Weidt, Maryann N. *Mr. Blue Jeans: A Story of Levi Strauss*. Minneapolis: Carolrhoda Books, Inc., 1990.

[6] Harrell, Wilson. *For Entrepreneurs Only: Success Strategies for Anyone Starting or Growing a Business*. Hawthorne, NJ: Career Press, 1994.

[7] Current, Richard N., T. Harry Williams and Frank Freidel. *American History: A Survey*. New York: Alfred A. Knopf, 1975.

[8] Hagan, William T. *Quanah Parker, Comanche Chief*. Norman, OK: University of Oklahoma Press, 1993.

[9] King, Martin Luther, Jr. *The Martin Luther King, Jr. Companion: Quotations From the Speeches, Essays, and Books of Martin Luther King, Jr.* New York: St. Martin's Press, 1993.

[10] Steinbeck, John. *The Grapes of Wrath*. New York: Book-of-the-Month Club, Inc., 1995.

[11] The Holy Bible: Authorized (King James) Version. Philadelphia: The National Bible Press, 1944.

WORD-ORIGIN STUDY REFERENCE FOR LEVEL 7

Unless otherwise noted:

Webster, Noah. *Webster's New Twentieth Century Dictionary of the English Language*. New York: The World Publishing Company, 1964.

READING LEVEL 8

STORY TITLE	READING LEVEL	PAGE
1. Is Anyone Awake Out There?	8.04	**134**
2. Ferris and His Wheel	8.05	**143**
3. Where Does All the Money Go?	8.16	**153**
4. The Hale House of Harlem	8.17	**163**
5. Sir Walter Raleigh's Lost Colony	8.19	**171**
6. Lewis Wickes Hine	8.21	**179**
7. Mysterious Crash of Airship *Akron:* 73 Feared Dead	8.45	**188**
8. The True Pooh	8.45	**197**
9. Scott Joplin: Ragtime King	8.53	**205**
10. Betty Ford: A True First Lady	8.54	**213**
11. Rachel Carson: The Coming of a Silent Spring	8.58	**223**
12. The Return of Supersonic Flight	8.61	**232**
13. The Guest Star	8.70	**241**
14. There Lives a Monster in the Loch	8.76	**250**
15. "D.B. Cooper—Where Are You?"	8.76	**259**
References for Level 8		**269**
Quotation Footnotes for Level 8		**272**
Word-Origin Study Reference for Level 8		**272**

1. IS ANYONE AWAKE OUT THERE?

Reading Level = 8.04

ABOUT THE STORY

Teens often have difficulty going to sleep at night and waking early in the morning. The story investigates the causes and possible solutions for sleepy students.

QUOTES OF THE WEEK

Quote 1:

"Now blessings light on him that first invented this same sleep! It covers a man all over, thoughts and all, like a cloak; 'tis meat for the hungry, drink for the thirsty, heat for the cold, and cold for the hot."[1] *(page 171)*—MIGUEL DE CERVANTES, *DON QUIXOTE DE LA MANCHA.* (Based on a quote from Sancho Panza in *Tristram Shandy* by Laurence Sterne)

Quote 2:

"Oh sleep! it is a gentle thing,
Beloved from pole to pole."[1] *(page 434)*—SAMUEL TAYLOR COLERIDGE, *THE ANCIENT MARINER*

INTERVIEW TOPIC

Interview a teenager on his or her sleeping habits. Prepare a question list including literal and interpretive questions: "Did your sleeping patterns change after you entered your teenage years? If so, how did they change? If you had no schedule to follow, when would you naturally go to sleep? When would you get up? Do you have trouble concentrating in class because you are tired? If so, why do you feel tired?"

PREVIEW WORDS

psychological	*Kari Poikolainen*
melatonin	*psychosomatic*

WORD-ORIGIN STUDY

psychological:	The prefix *psycho-* comes from a Greek word meaning "soul or mind." The suffix *-logy,* from which we base *-logical,* means "to speak." *Psychological* means to refer to or speak of things concerning the mind.

---

[1] Refer to *Quotation Footnotes for Level 8* on page 272.

psychosomatic: *Somatic* can stand alone as a word. It means corporeal, or dealing with the body distinctly separate from the mind or soul. *Psychosomatic* refers to a physical disorder of the body that is aggravated by the mind or emotions of the individual. This does not mean that the symptoms or illness are imaginary.

List other words beginning with the prefix *psycho-* and/or ending with the suffix *-logy*. Write the words and their definitions in your vocabulary notebook.

BOOKS TO READ

Borbely, Alexander A. *Secrets of Sleep*. New York: Basic Books, 1986.

Bstan-'dzin-rgya-mtsho, Dalai Lama XIV. *Sleeping, Dreaming, and Dying: An Exploration of Consciousness with the Dalai Lama*. Boston: Wisdom, 1997.

Dement, William C. *The Sleepwatchers*. Stanford: Stanford Alumni Association, 1992.

Dunkell, Samuel. *Sleep Positions: The Night Language of the Body*. New York: Morrow, 1977.

Ferber, Richard. *Solve Your Child's Sleep Problems*. New York: Simon & Schuster, 1985.

Fritz, Roger. *Sleep Disorders: America's Hidden Nightmare*. Naperville, IL: National Sleep Alert, 1993.

Garber, Richard. *How to Get a Good Night's Sleep: More Than 100 Ways You Can Improve Your Sleep*. Minneapolis: Chronimed Publishers, 1995.

Hartmann, Ernest. *The Nightmare: The Psychology and Biology of Terrifying Dreams*. New York: Basic Books, 1984.

Poortvliet, Rien. *The Book of the Sandman and the Alphabet of Sleep*. New York: Harry N. Abrams, Inc., Publishers, 1988.

Sykes, Shelley. *For Mike*. New York: Delacorte Press, 1998.

Wood, Audrey. *Moonflute*. San Diego: Harcourt Brace Jovanovich, Publishers, 1986.

BOOK CLUB

Read *For Mike* by Shelley Sykes.

INTRODUCTORY ACTIVITIES

DAY ONE

Objective: The students will discuss their sleeping habits and how these habits affect their alertness during the day.

Conduct a discussion on the students' sleeping habits. How does the amount of sleep they get at night affect their performance at school, their enjoyment of extracurricular activities, and their relationships? Have their sleeping habits changed since they became teenagers? If so, how have they changed? What time do they go to bed? What time do they usually fall asleep? When do they get up in the morning? Do they feel well rested in the morning?

Make a chart showing the times the students go to bed, go to sleep, and when they get up. Note whether they feel rested in the morning. Continue the chart showing what time they would feel most comfortable going to bed and getting up if they had no schedule to follow. Here is an example of such a chart:

	School Day				Without a Schedule	
	TIME IN BED	**TIME ASLEEP**	**TIME AWAKING**	**ALERT?**	**TIME IN BED**	**TIME AWAKING**
1. Bob	10:30 P.M.	11:30 P.M.	5:30 A.M.	no	11:30 P.M.	8:00 A.M.
2. Jane	11:00 P.M.	1:00 A.M.	6:30 A.M.	no	midnight	9:00 A.M.
3. Sam	10:00 P.M.	10:30 P.M.	6:00 A.M.	yes	10:30 P.M.	6:00 A.M.

Display the chart for reference throughout the lesson week.

DAY TWO

STORY LESSON

Follow the *Presenting the Story Lesson* instructions in the Introduction. Each story lesson follows the same procedure; however, say the following in step 4: "The title of the story we're reading today is *Is Anyone Awake Out There?* What do you think the story is about?"

EXTENSION ACTIVITIES

1. Referring to a book about sleep (see Books to Read), the class will list several ways to enhance sleep naturally through behavior changes. These might include not watching television in bed, not exercising several hours before bedtime, or not eating large snacks before bedtime. Discuss how simple changes in routine or behavior can affect one's quality of sleep.

2. Divide the class into groups. Assign one behavior change listed in Extension Activity 1 to each group. The students keep a sleep diary for two weeks to determine if the change in behavior improves sleep. Follow these steps:

■ Make a sleep diary made up of 14 copies of the chart below.

Date: _____

Behavior Change: _____

Time I Went to Bed: _____

Time I Fell Asleep: _____

Time I Awoke: _____

Quality of Sleep:

___ **poor** ___ **good** ___ **nightmares** ___ **good dreams**

Did I Feel Alert All Day? _____

■ On the first day of the diary, the students make no behavior changes as a pretest of their sleep habits. They enter the information in their diary.

■ Every morning for the following two weeks the students fill in their sleep diary. At the end of two weeks compare the results with other students in the same group. Next, compare the results with other groups implementing different behavior changes. Finally, compare the students' diaries to the chart made on Day One of the Introductory Activities.

3. Using mathematics, determine what percent of each group experienced improved sleep compared with those who did not. Determine which behavior change produced the greatest percent of improved sleep. Make graphs and charts illustrating the results.

4. Discuss the footnote format of the story references. "Why did the author choose this format to site references? Did the footnotes interfere with the story line? Why do you feel this way?" Students write a three-page article about teenage sleeping habits using footnotes to site their references.

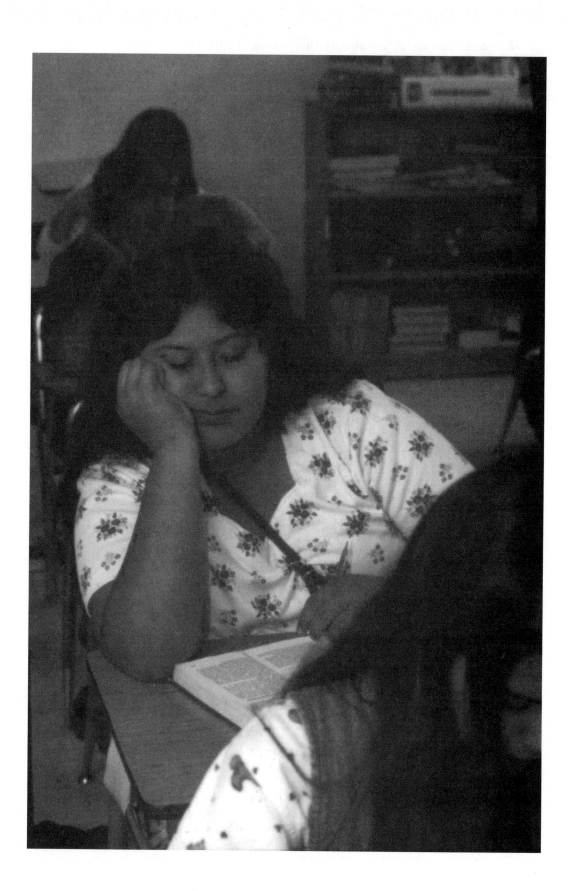

IS ANYONE AWAKE OUT THERE?

Do you find it difficult to get up in the morning? Are your grades in your afternoon classes higher than those in the morning? If so, you're not alone.

According to Jet Magazine[1], teenagers need 9.2 hours of sleep per night. Students who get plenty of sleep earn higher grades, and have fewer health and psychological problems. Yet, nearly 26% of high school students sleep only 6-1/2 hours on week nights.

Many factors can influence your ability to sleep. Kari Poikolainen, et. al.[2], point to stress as one source of sleeplessness. Adolescents become vulnerable to psychosomatic symptoms, such as sleep disorders and nightmares, when faced with life-crises. These include family problems, poor school performance, or even the loss of a boy- or girlfriend. Certain teens are more likely to experience these symptoms. These students display "low self-esteem, immature defense mechanisms, high anxiety, smoking, drug and alcohol use. . . ."

Most teenagers show a natural inclination to sleep late. Cate Martin[3] notes that teens have a "biological tendency" to go to bed late, and sleep later in the morning. Melatonin, a hormone secreted by the pineal gland, might influence this sleep pattern. Research links high levels of melatonin to drowsiness, and fluctuations in melatonin levels can affect the sleep cycle. Based on this information, some doctors advise school districts to modify high school hours.

In the meantime, there are changes you can make to improve your sleep. Deborah L. Cohn[4] recommends balanced meals and exercise to reduce stress, increase alertness, and enrich sleep. Simple changes in your lifestyle can lead to improvement in your overall life both in and out of school.

---

[1] "Teenagers in High School Need Proper Amount of Sleep to Excel in School, Study Reveals." *Jet*, Feb. 10, 1997, vol. 91, no. 12, p. 62(1).

[2] Poikolainen, Kari, Riitta Kanerva, and Jouko Lonnqvist. "Life Events and Other Risk Factors for Somatic Symptoms in Adolescence." *Pediatrics*, July 1995, vol. 96, no. 1, p. 59(5).

[3] Martin, Cate. "Dozing at Your Desk? Doctors Say Teens Need More Sleep and School Should Start Later!" *Science World*, March 8, 1996, vol. 52, no. 11, p. 9(3).

[4] Cohn, Deborah L. "Walk or Run (Benefits of Exercise)." *Current Health*. April 1994, vol. 20, no. 8, p.25(3).

QUESTIONS FOR IS ANYONE AWAKE OUT THERE?

Literal Questions:

THE FACTS:

1. According to *Jet* Magazine, how many hours of sleep do teenagers need per night?

_____

_____

_____

2. What percentage of high school students sleep only $6\frac{1}{2}$ hours on week nights?

_____

_____

_____

3. What hormone influences a person's sleep pattern?

_____

_____

_____

4. List four things you can do to improve your night's sleep.

_____

_____

_____

SEQUENCE OF EVENTS:

5. List the following information in the order in which it appeared in the article: Stress is one source of sleeplessness; Deborah L. Cohn recommends balanced meals and exercise to reduce stress; Most teenagers show a natural inclination to sleep late.

_____

_____

_____

6. What happens to students' grades and health after they develop good sleeping habits?

_____

_____

_____

Name _____   **Date** _____

Interpretive Questions:

DRAWING CONCLUSIONS:

7. What is the author's purpose in writing this article?

_____

_____

_____

_____

MAKING INFERENCES:

8. Some doctors advise school districts to modify high school hours. In what ways should school administrators modify school hours based on the information presented in the article?

_____

_____

_____

_____

MAKING PREDICTIONS:

9. Will high school hours change nationally over the next several years? Why do you feel this way?

_____

_____

_____

_____

IDENTIFICATION OF CAUSE:

10. Why don't teenagers get the recommended hours of sleep per night?

_____

_____

_____

_____

IDENTIFICATION OF THE MAIN IDEA:

11. Write a title for the story. Use as few words as possible.

_____

_____

_____

Name _____ Date _____

COMPARISON:

12. Compare the life experiences of a student getting 9.2 hours of sleep per night to those with only 6.5 hours of sleep or less?

_____

_____

_____

_____

SUMMARIZE:

13. In your own words, describe in detail one factor that can influence a person's ability to sleep.

_____

_____

_____

_____

EFFECT:

14. Referring to question 13, what effect will this one factor have on a person's lifestyle and experiences?

_____

_____

_____

_____

FACT AND OPINION:

15. The article said, "Simple changes in your lifestyle can lead to improvement in your overall life both in and out of school." Is this statement a fact or the author's opinion? How can you prove your answer?

_____

_____

_____

_____

ON YOUR OWN:

16. Write a question about the story for a teacher or another student to answer.

_____

_____

Name _____ **Date** _____

2. FERRIS AND HIS WHEEL
Reading Level = 8.05

ABOUT THE STORY

George Ferris was an architect specializing in structural steel and bridge design. In 1893, he designed the original Ferris wheel for the World's Columbian Exposition in Chicago. The first Ferris wheel stood on 140-foot high legs, and could accommodate over 1,000 passengers.

QUOTES OF THE WEEK

Quote 1:

"No matter what accomplishments you make, somebody helps you."[3]
(page 4)—ALTHEA GIBSON DARBEN

Quote 2:

"The only way to enjoy anything in this life is to earn it first."[3] *(page 4)*
—GINGER ROGERS

Quote 3:

"How many cares one loses when one decides not to be something but to be someone."[3] *(page 5)*—GABRIELLE (COCO) CHANEL

INTERVIEW TOPIC

Interview a person over the age of 40. Prepare a questions list of literal and interpretive questions based on the topic, "What is the most amazing human achievement?" This includes structures, such as buildings or monuments; art work; and inventions or discoveries. "Why do you find this achievement amazing? What one word best describes the achievement? How is your personal life touched by this achievement? What do you believe inspired the person or group of people to work toward their goal? How did this person or group of people find the fortitude to achieve such an accomplishment?"

PREVIEW WORDS

Daniel H. Burnham	*Eiffel Tower*
Rensselaer Polytechnic Institute	*tuberculosis*

WORD-ORIGIN STUDY

achievement: The original meaning of the word *achieve* was "to finish or end a task." An *achievement* is characterized not only by the completion of a goal, but also performing the heroic deed with valor and bravery.

---

[3] Refer to *Quotation Footnotes for Level 8* on page 272.

exposition: *Exposition* is based on the word *expose* which means "to set forth, narrate, or to display." An exposition, such as the 1893 World's Columbian Exposition in Chicago, set forth to narrate or display the progress achieved in the New World since the landing of Columbus 400 years earlier.

List other words based on the word expose including *exposé, exposedness, exposer, expositive, expositor, expository,* and *exposure.* Write their definitions in your vocabulary notebook.

BOOKS TO READ

Appelbaum, Stanley. *The Chicago World's Fair of 1893.* New York: Dover Publications, 1980.

Ash, Russell. *The Top Ten of Everything: 1997.* New York: DK Publishing, 1996.

Asimov, Isaac. *Isaac Asimov's Book of Facts.* New York: Grosset & Dunlap, 1979.

Burg, David F. *Chicago's White City of 1893.* Lexington: University of Kentucky Press, 1976.

Felton, Bruce. *The Best, Worst and Most Unusual: Noteworthy Achievements, Events, Feats, and Blunders of Every Conceivable Kind.* New York: Galahad Books, 1994.

Flinn, John J. (compiler). *Official Guide to the World's Columbian Exhibition.* Chicago: Columbian Guide Co., 1893.

The Guinness Book of World Records: 1999. Stamford, CT: Guinness Publishing, Inc., 1998.

Hoobler, Dorothy, Thomas Hoobler, and Carey–Greenberg Associates. *The Summer of Dreams: The Story of a World's Fair Girl.* Morristown, NJ: Silver Burdett Press, 1993.

Karwatka, Dennis. *Technology's Past: America's Industrial Revolution and the People Who Delivered the Goods.* Ann Arbor, MI: Prakken Publications, Inc., 1997.

Sanders, Dennis. *The First of Everything.* New York: Dell Press, 1981.

Spencer, J. *Tidbits: Treasury of Trivia: A Compendium of Miscellany: Odd and Obscure; Amazing and Amusing; Facts, Stories and Statistics.* Helena, MT: Jess Press, 1995.

VIDEOS

Jones, Doug. *World's Amazing Wonders.* San Ramon, CA: International Video Network, 1992.

WEB SITES

Detailed facts and photographs of the 1893 World's Columbian Exposition in Chicago can be found at the web site:

http://users.vnet.net/shulman/Columbian/columbian.html#TOP

BOOK CLUB

Read *The Summer of Dreams: The Story of a World's Fair Girl.* This book is at a lower reading level; however, the authors describe the *World's Columbian Exposition* of 1893—including the original Ferris wheel—through the eyes of the main character.

INTRODUCTORY ACTIVITIES

DAY ONE

Objective: The students will list goals they wish to achieve during their lifetime. The class will discuss how these achievements can be realized.

Review the Quotes of the Week. Discuss achievements the students wish to accomplish during their lifetime. These may be personal or community-wide goals. "Why are these goals important to you? How would achieving these goals affect people beyond yourself? What must you do to prepare yourself for pursuing these goals?"

Hand out copies of the achievements form for the students to fill out. Students list each goal in the first column, then list what must be done to prepare to meet these goals in the second column.

Encourage the students to put the list away where they can look at it when they are older. Perhaps they can put it in a yearbook or photo album. In this way they can see whether they completed their goals, or developed and worked toward other achievements in their lives.

Tell the students: "Tomorrow you will read about a man who prepared himself for an achievement that in itself was amazing. However, he never reaped financial success from the achievement. Does this make the achievement any less amazing? Why do you feel this way?"

DAY TWO

STORY LESSON

Follow the *Presenting the Story Lesson* instructions in the Introduction. Each story lesson follows the same procedure; however, say the following in step 4: "The title of the story we're reading today is *Ferris and His Wheel*. What do you think the story is about? What do you already know about the Ferris wheel?"

MY FUTURE ACHIEVEMENTS

Goals	How to Achieve the Goals
1.	
2.	
3.	
4.	
5.	

Name _____ Date _____

EXTENSION ACTIVITIES

1. Send the students on a research hunt for amazing achievements of individuals or a group of people. Examples:

The Colossus of Rhodes	Mount Rushmore
The Pyramids	The Great Wall of China
The Moon Landing	The Computer
The Polio Vaccination	Krak des Chevaliers
The Huge Desert Drawings of the Nazca Indians, Peru	

   Encourage the students to look for amazing achievements they did not know about before.

2. Have the students write a detailed report about the achievement they found in Extension Activity 1. They must tell how the person or people accomplished the feat, whether the deed could be completed without the help of others, and why the achievement is important. They need at least five references for the seven-page report. Information and photographs might be found on the Internet.

3. Have the students make a display of their choosing that would best illustrate their report. They might decide to make a model, a poster, a shadow box, etc.

4. Have the students present the reports in class. Ask the students why they found this achievement exciting. What did the research teach them about reaching their own goals? Display the reports and exhibits.

FERRIS AND HIS WHEEL

America celebrated the 400th anniversary of Christopher Columbus's voyage to the New World with a massive exposition in 1893. People from around the world came to Chicago to experience an entertainment event unlike any other.

Three years earlier, Daniel H. Burnham set out to look for a focal point of the fair. His search took him to a meeting of architects and engineers. Burnham challenged the engineers to design a structure that would outshine the Eiffel Tower.

Among those attending the conference was George Ferris. Ferris was born in 1859. As a young boy, Ferris dreamed of building bridges. He went on to graduate from the Rensselaer Polytechnic Institute with a degree in civil engineering.

Realizing that steel would soon replace iron, Ferris began a consulting firm and became an authority in structural steel. With his background in steel construction, Ferris took up Burnham's challenge.

Ferris proposed a giant wheel that would carry passengers around a central axle. The wheel stood on a foundation of eight 20-foot by 20-foot concrete footings. Weighing in at over 1,200 tons, the wheel turned around a 45-foot long hollow axle set on 140-foot-high legs. Although the wheel was a perfect circle, none of the parts curved.

Like a giant bicycle wheel, Ferris's creation turned with the power of two 1,000-horsepower steam engines buried in 4 foot pits. Passengers boarded one of 36 elongated cages each containing 40 upholstered swivel seats. The price of a ticket was fifty cents for a two-revolution, 20-minute ride. Costing $400,000 to construct, the wheel's earnings reached $726,805.50.

After the exposition, the wheel never made another profit. It later sold as scrap metal in 1903 for $1,800. Some believe the company buried the large axle in St. Louis's Franklin Park when no one could cut the axle into manageable pieces.

Ferris died in 1896 from tuberculosis without ever filing for a patent. However, his wheel was a steel marvel that heralded the end of the nineteenth century.

QUESTIONS FOR FERRIS AND HIS WHEEL

Literal Questions:

THE FACTS:

1. Who was looking for a focal point for the fair of 1893?

_____

_____

_____

2. What degree did George Ferris earn from the Rensselaer Polytechnic Institute?

_____

_____

_____

3. How much did Ferris's wheel weigh?

_____

_____

_____

4. How many seats were in each elongated cage?

_____

_____

_____

SEQUENCE OF EVENTS:

5. Where did Daniel H. Burnham search after he began looking for a focal point of the fair?

_____

_____

_____

6. What happened to the giant wheel after the exposition of 1893?

_____

_____

_____

Name _____   Date _____

Interpretive Questions:

DRAWING CONCLUSIONS:

7. What one word best describes George Ferris's wheel?

_____

_____

_____

_____

MAKING INFERENCES:

8. How many people could ride Ferris's wheel at one time?

_____

_____

_____

_____

MAKING PREDICTIONS:

9. Could a giant wheel built from Ferris's design be profitable today? Why do you feel this way?

_____

_____

_____

_____

IDENTIFICATION OF CAUSE:

10. Why do you think Daniel H. Burnham chose Ferris's wheel for the exposition?

_____

_____

_____

_____

IDENTIFICATION OF THE MAIN IDEA:

11. Write a title for the story. Use as few words as possible.

_____

_____

_____

Name _____ **Date** _____

COMPARISON:

12. How is the original Ferris wheel like those seen in amusement parks and fairs today? How is it different?

_____

_____

_____

_____

SUMMARIZE:

13. In your own words, describe the original Ferris wheel.

_____

_____

_____

_____

EFFECT:

14. What effect did Ferris's failure to file for a patent have on his family? Why do you feel this way?

_____

_____

_____

_____

FACT AND OPINION:

15. The story said, "Some believe the company buried the large axle in St. Louis's Franklin Park when no one could cut the axle into manageable pieces." Is this a fact or someone's opinion? How can you prove your answer?

_____

_____

_____

_____

ON YOUR OWN:

16. Write a question about the story for a teacher or another student to answer.

_____

_____

Name _____   **Date** _____

3. WHERE DOES ALL THE MONEY GO?

Reading Level = 8.16

ABOUT THE STORY

The majority of teens do not accurately assess how much money they will earn, how much it costs to pay for essentials, and the amount of money they need to save to prepare for a secure retirement. The story discusses ways to help teens become more financially aware.

QUOTES OF THE WEEK

Quote 1:

"Gives me some kind of content to remember how painful it is sometimes to keep money, as well as to get it."[1] *(page 310)*—SAMUEL PEPYS (DIARY, OCTOBER 11, 1667)

Quote 2:

"I finally know what distinguishes man from the other beasts: financial worries."[3] *(page 210)*—JULES RENARD

Quote 3:

"People who say money can't buy happiness just don't know where to shop."[3] *(page 210)*—TOM SHIVERS

INTERVIEW TOPIC

Interview a relative or close friend over the age of 25 about his or her personal financial bookkeeping. Prepare a questions list that includes literal and interpretive questions: "Do you keep a household budget? How is it organized? How do you keep track of bills to pay and paid bills? What type of system have you developed to keep your personal financial papers organized? Do you include some type of savings account (regular bank savings account, CD, stocks, retirement fund, IRA, etc.) to prepare for your future? Why did you choose this type of savings system?"

PREVIEW WORDS

Neale S. Godfrey	*FICA*	*financial planners*
Margie Mullen	*Karen Altfest*	

WORD-ORIGIN STUDY

finance: The word *finance* originates from a word meaning "to pay a fine or tax." Finances are the money or resources of a person, organization, or government. A financial planner helps you plan the best, most efficient use of your income.

---

[1] Refer to *Quotation Footnotes for Level 8* on page 272.

[3] Refer to *Quotation Footnotes for Level 8* on page 272.

income: *Income* simply means the money that is coming into your
                              possession. It can include your salary, money earned on
                              rental property, interests from loans or savings accounts,
                              or profits from stocks.

List other words beginning with the prefix *in-*. Write the words and their definitions in your vocabulary notebook.

BOOKS TO READ

Angell, Judie. *Leave the Cooking to Me*. New York: Bantam Books, 1990.

Berry, Joy Wilt. *Every Kid's Guide to Making and Managing Money*. Chicago: Children's Press, 1987.

_____. *A Kid's Guide to Managing Money: A Children's Book About Money Management*. Chicago: Children's Press, 1982.

Bodnar, Janet. *Dr. Tightwad's Money-Smart Kids (Expanded and Updated)*. Washington, DC: Kiplinger Books, 1997.

_____. *Kiplinger's Money-Smart Kids (and Parents, Too!)*. Washington, DC: Kiplinger Books, 1993.

Bywater, Sharon. *Using a Checking Account*. New York: New Readers Press, 1980.

Dolan, Ken and Daria Dolan. *Straight Talk on Money: Ken and Daria Dolan's Guide to Family Money Management*. New York: Simon & Schuster, 1993.

Godfrey, Neale S. *A Penny Saved: Teaching Your Children the Values of Life Skills They Need to Live in the Real World*. New York: Simon & Schuster, 1995.

Klass, Sheila Solomon. *Credit-Card Carole*. New York: Scribner, 1987.

Paulsen, Gary. *The Tent: A Parable in One Sitting*. San Diego: Harcourt Brace, 1995.

Schmitt, Lois. *Smart Spending: A Young Consumer's Guide*. New York: Scribner, 1989.

Sprouse, Mary L. *"If Time Is Money, No Wonder I'm Not Rich": The Busy Investor's Guide to Successful Money Management*. New York: Simon & Schuster, 1993.

Strassels, Paul N. *Money Matters: The Hassle-Free, Month-by-Month Guide to Money Management*. Reading, MA: Addison-Wesley Publishing Co., 1986.

Wall, Ginita. *Our Money, Our Selves: Money Management for Each Stage of a Woman's Life*. Yonkers, NY: Consumer Reports Books, 1992.

Weeks, Doug. *Saving and Investing*. New York: New Readers Press, 1980.

ARTICLES

Branch, Shelly. "How to Teach a Teen the Value of a Buck." *Money*, December 1995, vol. 24, no. 12, pp. 132-138.

BOOK CLUB

Read Gary Paulsen's *The Tent: A Parable in One Sitting*, or Judie Angell's *Leave the Cooking to Me*, or *Credit-Card Carole* by Sheila Solomon Klass.

INTRODUCTORY ACTIVITIES

DAY ONE

Objective: The students will survey other students at the school to learn about the teens' predictions for their financial futures.

Hand out copies of the interview form. Enlarge a copy of the form to display in front of the class. Ask the students to fill in the information on the first line of the form with their own predictions. Call on each student to read what he or she wrote, and write this information onto the enlarged copy. Save the enlarged copy for use in the Extension Activities.

The students interview other teens who do not attend this class. They ask about the subjects' predictions concerning their own personal financial future. They are not to take names so that the interview information remains confidential. After completing the interviews, the students attach a short report (2 to 3 paragraphs) stating what conclusions they can draw from the information they obtained from their peers.

DAY TWO

STORY LESSON

Follow the *Presenting the Story Lesson* instructions in the Introduction. Each story lesson follows the same procedure; however, say the following in step 4: "The title of the story we're reading today is *Where Does All the Money Go?* What do you think the story is about? What do you already know about money-management?"

EXTENSION ACTIVITIES

1. Invite a money-management consultant to class. Retired volunteers might be available. Ask them to discuss the real-life financial concerns the students will face in the future. How does a person prepare a budget? How much money should a person put into savings, and why? End the discussion with a question-and-answer session.

   Show the speaker the enlarged interview survey the students made during Day One of the Introductory Activities. Discuss which beliefs expressed on the chart are accurate, and which are unrealistic. In what ways are the beliefs unrealistic?

INTERVIEW FORM

Future Occupation	Expected Salary	Expected Take-Home Pay	Expected Cost of Housing	Expected Luxuries
1. _____				
2. _____				
3. _____				
4. _____				
5. _____				
6. _____				
7. _____				
8. _____				
9. _____				
10. _____				
11. _____				
12. _____				
13. _____				
14. _____				
15. _____				
16. _____				
17. _____				
18. _____				
19. _____				
20. _____				

Name _____   Date _____

2. Neale S. Godfrey's book *A Penny Saved: Teaching Your Children the Values of Life Skills They Need to Live in the Real World* gives many excellent activities to help teens learn about money management. There are several books on the market available at your local library that list effective and meaningful activities for teens.

3. Share the interviews conducted during the Interview Topic. How did the interview subjects care for their personal finances? Were there any ideas or systems that were particularly interesting?

   The students then prepare an imaginary financial management system. They set up a budget form including a section for savings. They prepare a filing system or other organizational system for bills, paid bills, receipts, checking account and savings statements, etc. The students will share their system with their parents.

WHERE DOES ALL THE MONEY GO?

"Money doesn't grow on trees!" How many times have you heard your parents say that? It's difficult for anyone to understand the value of money unless you earn it yourself. Looking at the income-earning, self-supporting world from the outside makes it appear easy. Surely it doesn't cost too much to "get by," and have money left over for the good things in life.

According to Neale S. Godfrey, author of A *Penny Saved*, most teens have an unrealistic view of how much money they can earn, and how far the money will go. She lists three false perceptions teens have about money:

- Teenagers think they'll earn a lot more money than they will.
- Teenagers think they'll take home a lot more money than they will.
- Teenagers think things cost a lot less than they do.

To snap teens out of their money dream world, Godfrey suggests they complete exercises in money reality and personal finance. Some of her activities include estimating future income, and comparing it with actual incomes. Teens should learn the difference between a salary and actual take-home pay, as well as taxes and FICA. This alone is enough to send the typical teen into financial-reality shock.

In her book, *Kiplinger's Money-Smart Kids (and Parents, Too!)*, Janet Bodnar states that teenagers should learn the cost of living with hands-on experience. She suggests parents let teens make out the family checks for one month of bills. She also believes teenagers don't realize exactly how much money they spend. Young adults who keep a list of their monthly expenditures quickly see the reasons behind their parents' concerns over expensive clothes, concert tickets, etc.

To be fair, teens aren't the only people with money fantasies. Most adults, even in the upper-income brackets, have difficulty managing their expenses and saving for the future. One typical example is a family with a total income of $95,104 with a savings of only $230. Financial planners Margie Mullen and Karen Altfest tell parents they set the example of financial responsibility. Their teens are most likely to follow this example for the rest of their lives.

QUESTIONS FOR WHERE DOES ALL THE MONEY GO?

Literal Questions:

THE FACTS:

1. List Neale S. Godfrey's three false perceptions teens have about money.

_____

_____

_____

2. How does Janet Bodnar believe teenagers should learn about the cost of living?

_____

_____

_____

3. Who are Margie Mullen and Karen Altfest?

_____

_____

_____

4. What do Mullen and Altfest tell parents about teaching teens financial responsibility?

_____

_____

_____

SEQUENCE OF EVENTS:

5. What does Neale S. Godfrey feel teens must do before they can snap out of their money dream world?

_____

_____

_____

6. What must parents do before they can teach their children about financial responsibility?

_____

_____

_____

Name _____   Date _____

Interpretive Questions:

DRAWING CONCLUSIONS:

7. How would you describe most teenagers' attitudes towards personal finance?

_____

_____

_____

_____

MAKING INFERENCES:

8. How does the author view most people's ability to manage their money? What did the author say that influenced your answer?

_____

_____

_____

_____

MAKING PREDICTIONS:

9. After reading this article, do you think you will become more aware of your personal finances? Why do you feel this way?

_____

_____

_____

_____

IDENTIFICATION OF CAUSE:

10. What was the author's motive for writing this article?

_____

_____

_____

_____

IDENTIFICATION OF THE MAIN IDEA:

11. Write a title for the story. Use as few words as possible.

_____

_____

Name _____   **Date** _____

COMPARISON:

12. How are your personal finances like those of an adult? How are they different?

_____

_____

_____

_____

SUMMARIZE:

13. In your own words, tell about Janet Bodnar's suggestions to teach teens financial responsibility.

_____

_____

_____

_____

EFFECT:

14. What effect will developing good financial habits early in life have on your future? Why do you feel this way?

_____

_____

_____

_____

FACT AND OPINION:

15. The story said, "It's difficult for anyone to understand the value of money unless you earn it yourself." Is this a fact or the author's opinion? How can you prove your answer?

_____

_____

_____

_____

ON YOUR OWN:

16. Write a question about the story for a teacher or another student to answer.

_____

_____

Name _____ **Date** _____

4. THE HALE HOUSE OF HARLEM
Reading Level = 8.17

ABOUT THE STORY

Clara "Mother" Hale opened her home to babies of drug-addicted mothers and AIDS babies at a time when she planned to retire. She used her savings to begin the Hale House of Harlem which grew into a charity filling the space of two brownstones. President Ronald Reagan appointed both Mother Hale and her daughter to the National Drug-Free America Task Force. After Mother Hale's death, her daughter, Dr. Lorraine Hale, continues to operate the Hale House of Harlem.

QUOTES OF THE WEEK

Quote 1:

"Let us not paralyze our capacity for good by brooding over man's capacity for evil."[3] *(page 93)*—DAVID SARNOFF

Quote 2:

"The worst sin toward our fellow creatures is not to hate them, but to be indifferent to them: that's the essence of inhumanity."[3] *(page 93)* —GEORGE BERNARD SHAW

Quote 3:

"Science may have found a cure for most evils; but it has found no remedy for the worst of them all—the apathy of human beings."[3] *(page 93)* —HELEN KELLER

INTERVIEW TOPIC

Interview a volunteer in your community to learn why that person volunteers his or her time. You might look for a local chapter of Volunteers-in-Action (VIA) or your school's Volunteers in Public Schools (VIP) for subjects for the interview. Prepare a questions list that includes literal and interpretive questions. "What organization do you volunteer for? What service do you perform when you volunteer? Why do you volunteer? What is your definition of charity? What do you hope to achieve through volunteering your time?"

PREVIEW WORDS

drug-addicted   *federal grant*   *chiropractic*

WORD-ORIGIN STUDY

charity: *Charity* comes from a Latin word meaning "dearness, or affection." An act of charity comes from a dearness, or affection, in the heart for another person.

[3] Refer to *Quotation Footnotes for Level 8* on page 272.

163

benevolence: *Bene* means "a prayer or boon." *Benevolence* comes from a Latin word meaning "to wish well, or offer a prayer of good will." A *benevolent* person offers good will through charitable acts.

List other words beginning with *bene-*, and write their definitions in your vocabulary notebook. Also list and define synonyms for the word *benevolence*.

BOOKS TO READ

Brilliant, Eleanor L. *The United Way: Dilemmas of Organized Charity*. New York: Columbia University Press, 1990.

Mackey, Philip English. *The Giver's Guide: Making Your Charity Dollars Count*. Highland Park, NJ: Catbird Press, 1990.

McCarroll, Tolbert. *Morning Glory Babies: Children with AIDS and the Celebration of Life*. New York: Simon & Schuster, 1990.

Morgan, Nina. *Mother Teresa: Saint of the Poor*. Austin, TX: Raintree Steck-Vaughn, 1998.

Oyler, Chris, Laurie Becklund, and Beth Polson. *Go Toward the Light*. New York: Harper & Row, 1988.

Pfeffer, Susan Beth. *The Sebastian Sisters: Thea at Sixteen*. New York: Bantam Books, 1988.

Spink, Kathryn. *Mother Teresa: A Complete Authorized Biography*. San Francisco, CA: HarperCollins, 1997.

Teresa, Mother. *No Greater Love*. Novato, CA: New World Library, 1995.

ARTICLES

"Clara Hale Dies: Cared for 1,000 Drug-Addicted Babies." *Jet*, January 11, 1993, vol. 83, no.11, page 56.

Cunningham, Ann Marie. "Loving the Unloved Children: Following Her Mother's Example, Dr. Lorraine Hale Brings Hope to the Neediest Kids." *Ladies Home Journal*, November 1997, vol. 114, no. 11, page 206.

BOOK CLUB

Read Susan Beth Pfeffer's *The Sebastian Sisters: Thea at Sixteen*.

INTRODUCTORY ACTIVITIES

DAY ONE

Objective: The students will learn about charitable works performed by local individuals, and discuss what drives a person to donate his or her time to a charitable organization.

Invite a local representative from a charitable organization to the class. Ask the representative to bring a person from the community who donates his or her time in an extraordinary way. The students discuss how charitable organizations help the community, not only by aiding those in need, but also the savings in tax dollars generated by volunteers. "What charitable organizations are active in the community? What do these organizations do? Why do people donate their time to these charities? How did the charitable organization begin? Who founded the organization? What can teens do to contribute to these organizations? What are the greatest areas of need in the community?"

DAY TWO

STORY LESSON

Follow the *Presenting the Story Lesson* instructions in the Introduction. Each story lesson follows the same procedure; however, say the following in step 4: "The title of the story we're reading today is *The Hale House of Harlem*. What do you think the story is about?"

EXTENSION ACTIVITIES

1. Call local charitable organizations, such as the United Way, for directories of local charities. The students choose a local charity and write a report about the charity's purpose, goals, services, and needs. The report should include interviews of the head of the charity, volunteers and/or employees involved in the organization, and, with permission, interviews of people affected by the charity.

2. The students read the reports from Extension Activity 1 to the class, and choose one charity that needs their support. For example, the Light House for the Blind might need recordings of books read by the students. A local children's hospital might need donated children's books, or a women's shelter might need help cleaning the property. Be sure to get the proper permission before beginning the project. The students organize and prepare their donations or volunteer time.

3. Look for an outstanding volunteer in the local community. Suggestions might come from the Volunteers in Public Schools or local charitable organizations. The students prepare a brief biography of their favorite volunteer. After presenting their nominees to the class, the students vote for their Volunteer of the Year. The students make a poster to present to the volunteer which represents the impact he or she has had on the community.

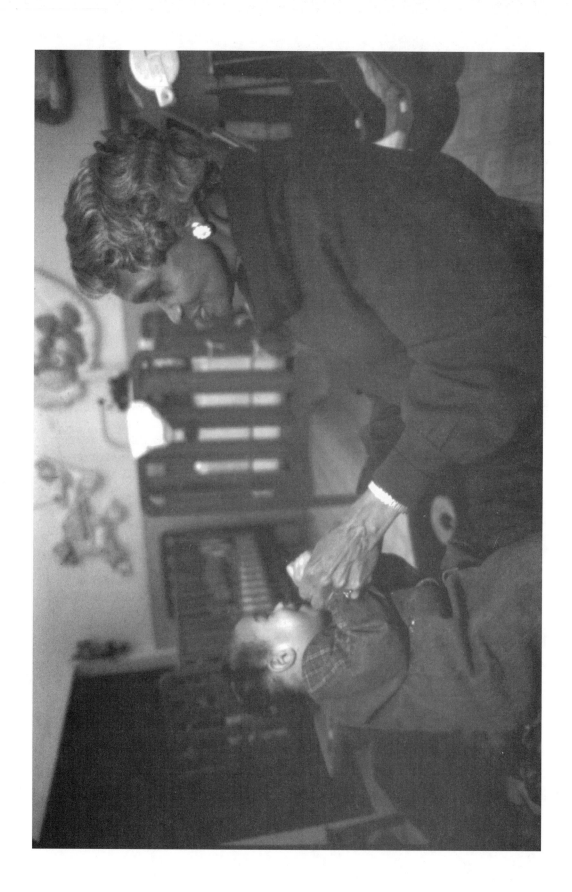

THE HALE HOUSE OF HARLEM

Clara "Mother" Hale lived in Harlem. A widowed housekeeper, she worked to support her three children: Lorraine, Nathan, and Kenneth. In 1941, she began taking in foster children of single working mothers. She planned to retire at the age of 65 having nurtured 40 children.

Her daughter Lorraine, grown and working as a guidance counselor, felt discouraged by the lack of meaningful assistance she could offer children. While visiting her mother, Lorraine saw a young mother, high on drugs, cradling a baby in her arms as she sat on the curb. Unable to simply pass by, Lorraine gave the young woman her mother's address. Soon Mother Hale and Lorraine set out on a quest to help babies of drug-addicted mothers.

Using their savings, the Hales applied for a federal grant at the Office of Economic Opportunity. With this grant they founded the Hale House of Harlem in Mother Hale's small apartment. Twenty-two cribs filled the tiny living space within three months.

Seeing the importance of their dedicated work, the city leased a brownstone to the Hale House for one dollar a year. As the children required more space, a church donated the adjoining brownstone. Funding for the nonprofit organization comes from donations.

In 1986, President Ronald Reagan commended Mother Hale in his State of the Union address. The President then appointed both mother and daughter to the National Drug-Free America Task Force.

Mother Hale died on December 18, 1992. Her daughter, Dr. Lorraine Hale, continues the work she began with her mother. The Hale House trains workers from around the world in the rearing of drug-addicted infants. No matter how many children enter the door, each child receives abundant love and affection, nutritional meals, chiropractic medicine, and massage therapy.

After rearing about 3,000 children, the work continues. The arms of Dr. Hale now reach out to embrace mothers and infants infected by the AIDS virus. Never tiring of her work, Dr. Hale explains, "The children keep me going."

Questions for the Hale House of Harlem

Literal Questions:

THE FACTS:

1. Where did Clara "Mother" Hale live?

_____

_____

_____

2. Where did Lorraine Hale take the young woman with a baby?

_____

_____

_____

3. Who commended Mother Hale in his 1986 State of the Union address?

_____

_____

_____

4. How many children have the Hales helped?

_____

_____

_____

SEQUENCE OF EVENTS:

5. What did Clara Hale do before she opened the Hale House?

_____

_____

_____

6. Who continued the work of the Hale House after Mother Hale died?

_____

_____

_____

Name _____   **Date** _____

Interpretive Questions:

DRAWING CONCLUSIONS:

7. What one word best describes Mother Hale?

_____

_____

MAKING INFERENCES:

8. Did Mother Hale love children? What specific information in the story led you to your answer?

_____

_____

_____

_____

MAKING PREDICTIONS:

9. Will the Hale House continue to help children in the future? Why do you feel this way?

_____

_____

_____

_____

IDENTIFICATION OF CAUSE:

10. Why did Mother and Lorraine Hale take on the responsibility of helping so many drug-addicted infants?

_____

_____

_____

_____

IDENTIFICATION OF THE MAIN IDEA:

11. Write a title for the story. Use as few words as possible.

_____

_____

_____

Name _____   Date _____

COMPARISON:

12. How was Mother Hale's first job as foster mother like the work she did for the Hale House? How was it different?

_____

_____

_____

_____

SUMMARIZE:

13. In your own words, tell about the work done by Mother and Lorraine Hale at the Hale House.

_____

_____

_____

_____

EFFECT:

14. What effect did Mother Hale have on the lives of the infants she cared for? Why do you feel this way?

_____

_____

_____

_____

FACT AND OPINION:

15. The story said, "The President then appointed both mother and daughter (the Hales) to the National Drug-Free America Task Force." Is this a fact or the author's opinion? How can you prove your answer?

_____

_____

_____

_____

ON YOUR OWN:

16. Write a question about the story for a teacher or another student to answer.

_____

_____

Name _____ **Date** _____

5. SIR WALTER RALEIGH'S LOST COLONY
Reading Level = 8.19

ABOUT THE STORY

In the late 1500s, a group of colonists sponsored by Sir Walter Raleigh attempted to settle in the New World. Led by Governor John White, the colonists soon ran low on supplies. White sailed to England for provisions, leaving the families behind. When White returned he could find no sign of Sir Walter Raleigh's Lost Colony.

QUOTES OF THE WEEK

Quote 1:

"(History) hath triumphed over time, which besides it nothing but eternity hath triumphed over."[1] *(page 173)*—SIR WALTER RALEGH*, *HISTORY OF THE WORLD, PREFACE*

Quote 2:

"Legend remains victorious in spite of history."[3] *(page 444)*
—SARAH BERNHARDT

INTERVIEW TOPIC

If possible, interview someone whose ancestors were colonists in early America. Prepare a questions list including literal and interpretive questions: "Where did your ancestors immigrate from? Why did they come to America? What colony were they in? How did you learn that you were a descendent of early American colonists? What was life like for your colonial ancestors?"

PREVIEW WORDS

Sir Walter Raleigh	*Croatoan*
Roanoke Island	*Lumbees*

WORD-ORIGIN STUDY

colony: The word *colony* comes from a Latin word meaning "cultivate." A *colony* is a group of people who cultivate, or promote, the development of a remote region under the political domain of their native country.

folklore: *Folklore* is the teaching and learning through stories told by common people, or folk.

Look up words based on the word *colony*. Write the words and their definitions in your vocabulary notebook.

---

* According to *Webster's Dictionary*, also spelled Releigh.

[1] Refer to *Quotation Footnotes for Level 8* on page 272.

[3] Refer to *Quotation Footnotes for Level 8* on page 272.

BOOKS TO READ

Bosco, Peter I. *Roanoke: The Story of the Lost Colony*. Brookfield, CT: Millbrook Press, 1992.

Cates, Edwin H. *The English in America: Revised Edition*. Minneapolis: Lerner Publications Company, 1978.

Cumming, William Paterson. *British Maps of Colonial America*. Chicago: University of Chicago Press, 1974.

Foulke, Patricia. *Colonial America: A Traveler's Guide*. Old Saybrook, CT: Globe Pequot Press, 1995.

Glubok, Shirley. *The Art of Colonial America*. Riverside, NJ: Macmillan Co., 1970.

Harter, Eugene C. *The Lost Colony of the Confederacy*. Jackson: University Press of Mississippi, 1985.

Lacy, Dan Mabry. *Lost Colony: A First Book*. New York: Franklin Watts, 1972.

Levitin, Sonia. *Roanoke: A Novel of the Lost Colony*. New York: Atheneum, 1973.

Lizon, Karen Helene. *Colonial American Holidays and Entertainment*. New York: Franklin Watts, 1993.

Noël Hume, Ivor. *Guide to Artifacts of Colonial America*. New York: Knopf, 1969.

Reader's Digest Staff. *Strange Stories, Amazing Facts: Stories That Are Bizarre, Unusual, Odd, Astonishing & Often Incredible*. Pleasantville, NY: Reader's Digest Association, Inc., 1976.

Stainer, M.L. *The Lyon's Cub*. Circleville, NY: Chicken Soup Press, 1997.

_____. *The Lyon's Pride*. Circleville, NY: Chicken Soup Press, 1998.

_____. *The Lyon's Roar*. Circleville, NY: Chicken Soup Press, 1997.

BOOK CLUB

Read *The Lyon Saga* by M.L. Stainer, a five-book series beginning with *The Lyon's Roar*, or read Sonia Levitin's *Roanoke: A Novel of the Lost Colony*.

INTRODUCTORY ACTIVITIES

DAY ONE

Objective: The students will discuss the history of the first American colonists.

Discuss the history of the first American colonists. What do the students know about the American colonies? Why did the colonists come to America? Although the students should have a basic understanding of the American colonies, many times they have forgotten or are incorrectly remembering the history. This lesson is to review the facts and to clear up any misconceptions before beginning the story lesson.

Invite a historian, teacher, professor, or an amateur with an interest in colonial America to the class. Ask the speaker to tell the students why he or she finds colonial America an interesting or compelling subject. Why should the students learn about colonial America?

DAY TWO

STORY LESSON

Follow the *Presenting the Story Lesson* instructions in the Introduction. Each story lesson follows the same procedure; however, say the following in step 4: "The title of the story we're reading today is *Sir Walter Raleigh's Lost Colony*. What do you think the story is about? What do you already know about the early American colonies?"

EXTENSION ACTIVITIES

1. Break the students into groups. Each group conducts research on an early American colony. Each group writes a seven-page report about the colony with an outline, cover page, and bibliography.

2. The students make a flag of the country from which their colony originated. The flag can be made of fabric or paper.

3. Using the material of their choosing, the students make a model of their colony. They must include examples of the tools used and clothing worn by the colonists.

4. The students prepare a menu for breakfast, lunch, and dinner based on the authentic meals served in their colony. They make a sample of one of the items to share with the class.

Engraved for Middleton's Complete System of Geography.

SIR WALTER RALEIGH ordering the STANDARD of Queen Elizabeth to be erected on the Coast of VIRGINIA.

SIR WALTER RALEIGH'S LOST COLONY

In 1578, England granted Sir Humphrey Gilbert a charter that allowed him to settle colonies in the New World. The challenge proved fatal, and Gilbert did not return to England after his second attempt in 1583. Gilbert's half brother, Sir Walter Raleigh, took up the task a year later. Little did he know his expedition would lead him and his colonists into American folklore.

Raleigh discharged a scouting party to survey the Atlantic coast of North America. The party explored Roanoke Island on North Carolina's coast. Believing the area was safe, Raleigh sent Governor John White with 100 men, women, and children to establish a settlement.

As time passed, White realized the colony would need supplies to survive. White took a small crew back to England, promising to return. He told the colonists to leave a sign "in a conspicuous place" showing where they went if they were unable to stay in Roanoke.

Delayed by the war between England and Spain, White did not return until 1590. The fortress stood looted and abandoned without any sign of the colonists. White found only the word "Croatoan" carved in a post. No one saw the colonists again.

Where did Raleigh's lost colonists go? Some believe the word Croatoan names the Native American tribe that attacked the settlement and massacred the colonists.

Others point to the island of Croatoan inhabited by the friendly Hatteras tribe. Perhaps the settlers joined the tribe, which later migrated to the Lumber River Valley. Now known as the Lumbees, these Native Americans have gray eyes and skin tones ranging from dark to very fair. It is not unusual to see a member of the Lumbee tribe with blond hair and blue eyes.

The Lumbee language is a derivative of English, and tribesmen report that their ancestors could "talk in a book," or read. The most overwhelming evidence comes from the 41 surnames of Raleigh's colonists found among the Lumbee people, including Sampson, Cooper, and Dare.

QUESTIONS FOR SIR WALTER RALEIGH'S LOST COLONY

Literal Questions:

THE FACTS:

1. In what year did England grant Sir Humphrey Gilbert a charter to settle colonies in the New World?

_____

_____

_____

2. Who was Sir Walter Raleigh?

_____

_____

_____

3. Where did Raleigh's colony settle?

_____

_____

_____

4. Why did Governor John White leave the colonists and return to England?

_____

_____

_____

SEQUENCE OF EVENTS:

5. List the following events in chronological order: White found only the word "Croatoan" carved in a post; the war between England and Spain delayed White's return; England granted Sir Humphrey Gilbert a charter to settle colonies in the New World.

_____

_____

_____

6. What happened after Raleigh's scouting party finished its survey of the Atlantic coast of North America?

_____

_____

_____

Name _____   Date _____

Interpretive Questions:

DRAWING CONCLUSIONS:

7. What do you believe happened to the lost colony? What specific information led you to your conclusion?

_____

_____

_____

_____

MAKING INFERENCES:

8. Was White concerned about leaving the colony when he returned to England for supplies? Why do you feel this way?

_____

_____

_____

_____

MAKING PREDICTIONS:

9. Will historians ever learn what happened to the lost colony? Why do you feel this way?

_____

_____

_____

_____

IDENTIFICATION OF CAUSE:

10. Why did Gilbert and Raleigh want to establish a colony in the New World when it was obviously dangerous?

_____

_____

_____

_____

IDENTIFICATION OF THE MAIN IDEA:

11. Write a title for the story. Use as few words as possible.

_____

_____

Name _____ **Date** _____

COMPARISON:

12. How are the two theories concerning the disappearance of the colony alike? How are they different?

_____

_____

_____

_____

SUMMARIZE:

13. In your own words, tell about the failed attempt to settle a colony on Roanoke Island.

_____

_____

_____

_____

EFFECT:

14. What effect might the loss of the Raleigh colony have had on other people wanting to settle in the New World? Why do you feel this way?

_____

_____

_____

_____

FACT AND OPINION:

15. The story said, "Perhaps the settlers joined the tribe, which later migrated to the Lumber River Valley." Is this a fact or someone's opinion? How can you prove your answer?

_____

_____

_____

_____

ON YOUR OWN:

16. Write a question about the story for a teacher or another student to answer.

_____

_____

Name _____ **Date** _____

6. LEWIS WICKES HINE
Reading Level = 8.21

ABOUT THE STORY

Lewis Wickes Hine, born in 1874, was a photographer who began his career photographing immigrants as they arrived at Ellis Island. The National Child Labor Committee admired Hine's work, and asked him to photograph children in the work place to document the horrors of child labor.

QUOTES OF THE WEEK

Quote 1:

"Whereas, We, Children of America, are declared to have been born free and equal, and

Whereas, We are yet in bondage in this land of the free; are forced to toil the long day or the long night, with no control over the conditions of labor, as to health or safety or hours or wages, and with no right to the rewards of our service, therefore be it

Resolved, I—That childhood is endowed with certain inherent and inalienable rights, among which are freedom from toil for daily bread; the right to play and to dream; the right to the normal sleep of the night season; the right to an education, that we may have equality of opportunity for developing all that there is in us of mind and heart.

Resolved, II—That we declare ourselves to be helpless and dependent; that we are and of right ought to be dependent, and that we hereby present the appeal of our helplessness that we may be protected in the enjoyment of the rights of childhood.

Resolved, III—That we demand the restoration of our rights by the abolition of child labor in America."[8]
—NATIONAL CHILD LABOR COMMITTEE (1913), *Declaration of Dependence*
by the children of America in mines and factories and workshops assembled

Quote 2:

"Never . . . be mean in anything; never be false; never be cruel."[1]
(page 548)—CHARLES DICKENS, *DAVID COPPERFIELD*, Chapter 15

Quote 3:

"Mankind owes to the child the best it has to give . . ."[3] *(page 391)*—Opening words of the United Nations' Declaration of the Rights of the Child

INTERVIEW TOPIC

Interview a person over the age of 50 who has been active in the work place for the majority of his or her life. Discuss changes in the work place that have occurred over his or her working life. Prepare a questions list including literal and interpretive questions: "What was your first job, and when did you begin your first job? What

---

[8] Refer to *Quotation Footnotes for Level 8* on page 272.

[1] Refer to *Quotation Footnotes for Level 8* on page 272.

[3] Refer to *Quotation Footnotes for Level 8* on page 272.

were the working conditions? How has the American work place changed since your first job? What has changed for the better? What has changed for the worse? Do you have any information about child labor at the turn of the century? Do you have a story to tell about child labor?"

PREVIEW WORDS

apprentices   *chronicled*   *overseer*

WORD-ORIGIN STUDY

chronicled: The word *chronicle* comes from the Greek word *chronos*, meaning "time." The noun *chronicle* is a historical account of factual events. The verb *to chronicle* means "to record or recount historical events."

photograph: The prefix *photo-* comes from a Greek word meaning "light" while the suffix *-graph* comes from a Greek word meaning "a writing or drawing." Therefore, a *photograph* is a drawing produced by light.

List other words beginning with the prefix *photo-*. Write the words and their definitions in your vocabulary notebook.

BOOKS TO READ

Cahn, Rhoda. *No Time for School, No Time for Play*. Englewood Cliffs, NJ: Messner, 1972.

Cole, Sheila. *Working Kids On Working*. New York: Lothrop, Lee & Shepard Books, 1980.

Curtis, Verna Posever and Stanley Mallach. *Photography and Reform: Lewis Hine and the National Child Labor Committee*. Milwaukee, WI: Milwaukee Art Museum, 1984.

Dickens, Charles. *Oliver Twist*.

Doherty, Jonathan L. (editor) *Women at Work: 153 Photographs by Lewis W. Hine*. New York: Dover Publications, 1981.

Evans, Martin Marix (editor). *Contemporary Photographers*. Detroit, MI: St. James Press, 1995.

Freedman, Russell. *Kids at Work: Lewis Hine and the Crusade Against Child Labor*. New York: Clarion Books, 1994.

Geddes, Ann. *Down in the Garden*. San Rafael, CA: Cedco, 1996.

Goldberg, Vicki. *The Power of Photography: How Photographs Changed Our Lives*. New York: Abbeville Press, 1991.

Gutman, Judith Mara. *Lewis W. Hine and the American Social Conscience*. New York: Walker and Company, 1967.

_____. *Lewis W. Hine: Two Perspectives*. New York: Grossman Publishers, 1974.

Hine, Lewis W. *Men at Work: Photographic Studies of Modern Men and Machines*. New York: Dover Publications and the International Museum of Photography at George Eastman House, 1977.

Kaplan, Daile (editor). *Photo Story: Selected Letters and Photographs of Lewis W. Hine*. Washington, D.C.: Smithsonian Institution Press, 1992.

Kemp, John R. (editor). *Lewis Hine: Photographs of Child Labor in the New South*. Jackson: University Press of Mississippi, 1986.

Kramer, Stephen P. *Eye of the Storm: Chasing Storms with Warren Faidley*. New York: G.P. Putnam's Sons, 1997.

LeMieux, A.C. *The T.V. Guidance Counselor*. New York: Tambourine Books, 1993.

McLean, Cheryl. *Careers for Shutterbugs and Other Candid Types*. Lincolnwood, IL: VGM Career Horizons, 1995.

Meltzer, Milton. *Cheap Raw Material*. New York: Viking, 1994.

Nickel, Joe. *Camera Clues: A Handbook for Photographic Investigation*. Lexington: University Press of Kentucky, 1994.

Parks, Gordon. *Half Past Autumn: A Retrospective*. Boston, MA: Bulfinch Press, 1997.

Rosenblum, Naomi, Walter Rosenblum, and Alan Trachtenberg. *America and Lewis Hine*. New York: Aperture, 1977.

Schulman, Audrey. *The Cage*. New York: Avon Books, 1995.

Senior, Kathryn. *Photography*. Chicago: World Book, 1996.

Stein, R. Conrad. *The Story of Child Labor Laws*. Chicago: Children's Press, 1984.

Trattner, Walter I. *Crusade for the Children: A History of the National Child Labor Committee and Child Labor Reform in America*. New York: Quadrangle Books, 1970.

VIDEOS

Rosenblum, Nina and Daniel V. Allentuck. *America and Lewis Hine*. New York: The Cinema Guild, 1984.

BOOK CLUB

Read A.C. LeMieux's *The T.V. Guidance Counselor*.

INTRODUCTORY ACTIVITIES

DAY ONE

Objective: The students will talk to a local photographer about the art of photography.

Invite a local photographer to the class. The photographer might be employed by a local newspaper or television station, or be an independent professional or amateur photographer. Ask the speaker to talk about why he or she enjoys photography. What are his or her favorite subjects?

Include information about how photography can chronicle history or the human condition. How can photographs influence public opinion? How can photographs lead to a change in laws or political viewpoints? What important events or circumstances are currently investigated and documented by photographers?

DAY TWO

STORY LESSON

Follow the *Presenting the Story Lesson* instructions in the Introduction. Each story lesson follows the same procedure; however, say the following in step 4: "The title of the story we're reading today is *Lewis Wickes Hine*. What do you think the story is about?"

EXTENSION ACTIVITIES

Note: Be sure to obtain written parent permission for these activities. Explain the activity clearly, preferably in writing, to every parent and guardian.

1. Discuss local issues and concerns that lend themselves to documentation through photography. Examples might be poor housing for the elderly, loneliness in nursing homes, graffiti, or positive issues such as the building of a Habitat for Humanity house, a Boy Scout food drive, marching band competition, etc. Make a list of ideas presented in class.

2. Break the class into groups. Each group chooses an issue or situation to photograph. Recruit local photographers, parents, or teachers to help the children take photographs of their group's subject. Call local photograph developers to ask for discounted developing fees for the students. Some local merchants might donate film, photo albums, or frames for school projects.

    The students go on-site to photograph their subjects. Several students can share one camera. Set a reasonable minimum and limit to the number of photographs taken by each group.

3. After the photographs are developed, each group displays its photographs in a format of its choosing. Perhaps the group would like to arrange framed photographs on the wall, make a collage, or make a book of photographs using a photo album. Encourage creativity. Each group must give its photograph collection a title.

Important: If you choose to display the photographs publicly or share them with the school or local newspaper, be sure you obtain written consent from the subject, the subject's guardian, and any other agency featured in the photograph collection.

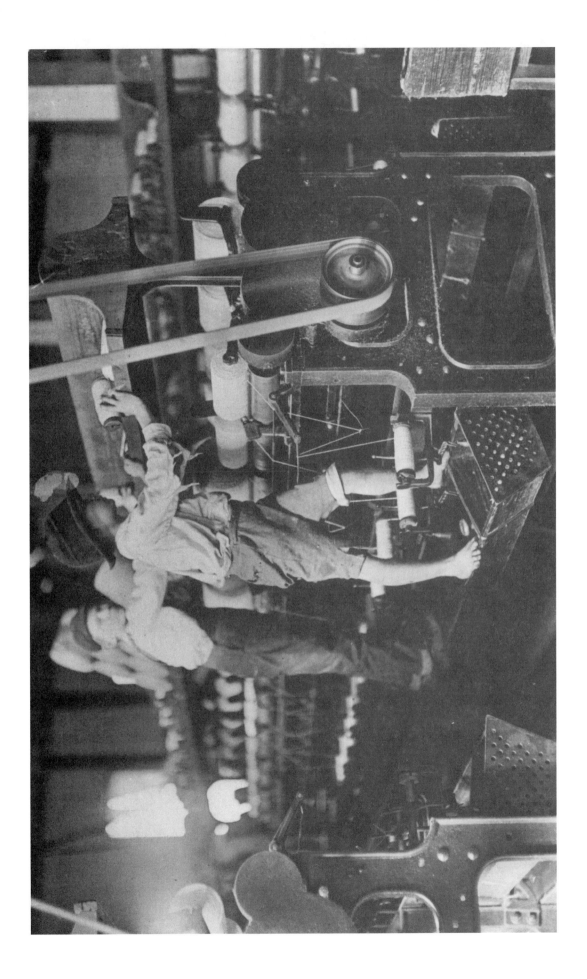

LEWIS WICKES HINE

Born on September 26, 1874 Lewis Wickes Hine grew up in Oshkosh, Wisconsin. Lewis worked in a furniture factory as a teen after his father passed away. Lucky to have a job, Lewis realized that factories replaced adult workers with lower-waged children. "The little work there is to be had should be done at decent wages and the little ones sent to school," declared the newspapers.

Later, as a teacher at New York City's Ethical Culture School, Lewis took up photography. His photographs of students lead him to Ellis Island where he photographed newly arrived immigrants.

His photographs attracted the attention of the National Child Labor Committee (NCLC). The organization asked Lewis to document the horrors of child labor in a series of photographs. Inspired by the task, Lewis took up his heavy box camera and began his journey.

Lewis didn't object to children working odd jobs after school or doing their chores. Since the beginning of the country, young children worked as apprentices. Lewis felt that the children gained a skill from the experience. Only the factory owners benefited from child labor.

As Lewis travelled throughout the country, he found children working long hours in dangerous conditions. Lewis's photographs chronicled the intense poverty of America's working children.

Children below the age of ten worked in textile mills. Lewis noted, "A twelve-year-old doffer boy fell into a spinning machine and the unprotected gearing tore out two of his fingers. 'We don't have any accidents in this mill,' the overseer told me. 'Once in a while a finger is mashed or a foot, but it don't amount to anything.'"

In mines too dangerous for adult men, children worked in the darkness. Many of the boys suffered from chronic cough. Children working in canneries shelled oysters and shrimp. Acid from the shrimp burned the children's swollen, bleeding fingers.

In 1938, President Franklin Roosevelt signed the Fair Labor Standards Act which set limits on child labor. Lewis's photographic style fell out of favor, and he died in poverty on November 4, 1940.

QUESTIONS FOR LEWIS WICKES HINE

Literal Questions:

THE FACTS:

1. When was Lewis Wickes Hine born?

_____

_____

_____

2. Where did Hine work as a teacher?

_____

_____

_____

3. List two industries discussed in the story that used child labor.

_____

_____

_____

4. What did President Franklin Roosevelt sign in 1938?

_____

_____

_____

SEQUENCE OF EVENTS:

5. What did Hine photograph before he began documenting child labor abuses?

_____

_____

_____

6. What did the National Child Labor Committee ask Hine to do after it saw his photographs of immigrants?

_____

_____

_____

Name _____   Date _____

Interpretive Questions:

DRAWING CONCLUSIONS:

7. What one word best describes Hine's feelings about child labor? What specific passages led you to your conclusion?

_____

_____

_____

MAKING INFERENCES:

8. Hine's quoted one overseer as stating, "We don't have any accidents in this mill. Once in a while a finger is mashed or a foot, but it don't amount to anything." How did the overseer feel about his child employees? Why do you feel this way?

_____

_____

_____

MAKING PREDICTIONS:

9. Many companies throughout the world use low-waged child labor. Will this practice continue? If you said yes, why do you feel this way? If you said no, what will bring about an end to the use of child labor?

_____

_____

_____

IDENTIFICATION OF CAUSE:

10. Why did the National Child Labor Committee ask a photographer (Hine) to document the horrors of child labor instead of sending a reporter?

_____

_____

_____

IDENTIFICATION OF THE MAIN IDEA:

11. Write a title for the story. Use as few words as possible.

_____

_____

Name _____   Date _____

COMPARISON:

12. How is your life similar to the children described in the story? How is your life different?

_____

_____

_____

_____

SUMMARIZE:

13. In your own words, tell about the examples of child labor discussed in the story.

_____

_____

_____

_____

EFFECT:

14. What effect did Hine's photographs have on the general public? On what specific information do you base your answer?

_____

_____

_____

_____

FACT AND OPINION:

15. The story quoted a newspaper as declaring, "The little work there is to be had should be done at decent wages and the little ones sent to school." Is this a fact or the reporter's opinion? Why do you feel this way?

_____

_____

_____

_____

ON YOUR OWN:

16. Write a question about the story for a teacher or another student to answer.

_____

_____

Name _____   Date _____

7. MYSTERIOUS CRASH OF AIRSHIP <u>AKRON</u>: 73 FEARED DEAD

Reading Level = 8.45

ABOUT THE STORY

This is a *Moments in Time* story about the crash of the U.S. Airship *Akron* in 1931. One of two military airships, the *Akron* held a crew of 77 men, and had the capacity to hold and launch five airplanes. A lightning strike appeared to be the cause of the crash of this giant airship.

QUOTE OF THE WEEK

> "Passengers are looking out the windows waving; the ship is standing still now. The vast motors are just holding it, just enough to keep it from . . . It's broken into flames. . . . This is terrible, this is one of the worst catastrophes in the world. Oh, the humanity and all the passengers . . . This is the worst thing I've ever witnessed. . . ."[5] *(pages 191-192)*—HERB MORRISON, radio correspondent for Station WLS Chicago on the burning of the airship *Hindenburg* in May of 1937

INTERVIEW TOPIC

Interview a person who lived in the 1930s. Ask the person about his or her memories of the giant dirigibles of the time. Such a person might be found in a nursing home. Prepare a questions list including literal and interpretive questions: "Did you ever see or ride in a dirigible? What do you remember about the giant airships? Is there a story, such as the burning of the airship *Hindenburg*, that you could share?"

PREVIEW WORDS

Karl Arnstein	*dirigibles*	*Zeppelins*
behemoth	*Barnegat Inlet*	

WORD-ORIGIN STUDY

blimp: The term *blimp* began to be associated with airships in 1917 as a nickname coined for one of the original dirigible's U.S. Navy classification: "Dirigible, Type B, Limp." (Jackson, Robert. *Airships*. Garden City, NY: Doubleday & Company, Inc., 1973, page 197)

behemoth: *Behemoth* originated from the word *b'hemoth* meaning "a huge beast." Reference to the giant creature appears in Job 40.15–24 of the Old Testament.

---

[5] Refer to *Quotation Footnotes for Level 8* on page 272.

Look up the words *colossus, goliath, titan, Titanic,* and *leviathan*. Write their definitions and origins in your vocabulary notebook.

BOOKS TO READ

Block, Thomas H. *Airship Nine*. New York: G.P. Putnam's Sons, 1984.

Botting, Douglas. *The Giant Airships*. Chicago: Time-Life Books, 1980.

Cohen, Daniel. *The Great Airship Mystery: A UFO of the 1890s*. New York: Dodd, Mead & Company, 1981.

Collier, Basil. *Airship: A History*. New York: Putnam, 1974.

Florence, Ronald. *Zeppelin: A Novel*. New York: Arbor House, 1982.

Jackson, Robert. *Airships: A Popular History of Dirigibles, Zeppelins, Blimps, and Other Lighter-than-Air Craft*. New York: Doubleday, 1973.

Mondey, David. *The Illustrated History of Aircraft*. New York: Galahad Books, 1980.

Percefull, Aaron W. *Balloons, Zeppelins, and Dirigibles*. New York: Franklin Watts, 1983.

Shalit, Nathan. *Cup and Saucer Chemistry*. New York: Grosset & Dunlap, 1972.

Thayer, James Stewart. *The Stettin Secret: A Novel*. New York: Putnam, 1979.

Verne, Jules. *Around the World in Eighty Days*. New York: Dell Publishing, 1975.

Whitehouse, Arch. *Zeppelin Fighters*. New York: Doubleday, 1966.

Wood, Robert W. *Science for Kids*. Blue Ridge Summit, PA: Tab Books, 1991.

BOOK CLUB

Read Jules Verne's *Around the World in Eighty Days* or Thomas H. Block's *Airship Nine*.

INTRODUCTORY ACTIVITIES

DAY ONE

Objective: The students will learn about the helium and hydrogen used to give dirigibles lift, and why early airships tended to burn.

Invite a scientist, teacher, professor, a college science student, or retired scientist to class. Ask the speaker to discuss the gases used to make a dirigible float. "Why did the blimps of the 1930s tend to explode? What could ignite these explosions? Are the blimps we see today as dangerous? Why is this true?"

If a teacher is not available, conduct experiments on hydrogen that illustrate the lighter-than-air quality of hydrogen. Check out "Hydrogen" in Nathan Shalit's *Cup and Saucer Chemistry*, pages 88-89.

DAY TWO

STORY LESSON

Follow the *Presenting the Story Lesson* instructions in the Introduction. Each story lesson follows the same procedure; however, say the following in step 4: "The title of the story we're reading today is *Mysterious Crash of the Airship* Akron: *73 Feared Dead*. What do you think the story is about? What do you already know about airships?"

EXTENSION ACTIVITIES

1. Break the students into groups. Assign one of the following topics to each group:

   The First Dirigibles and Their Designs

   Wartime Uses for Airships

   Early Peacetime Uses for Airships

   Modern Airships

   The groups research their topic and write 2- to 4-page essays. They must include an outline, bibliography, cover page, and illustrations.

2. The students make models of past and present airships. The students will need:

long balloons	papier-mâché
egg cartons cut into sections	toothpicks
tape	string
white labels	

PROCEDURE:

a. Choose a dirigible from the past or present. Use a picture of the balloon as a guide. An excellent source for pictures is Douglas Botting's *The Giant Airships* from Time–Life Books.

b. Blow up an oblong-shaped balloon. Tape part of an egg carton in the correct position of the cabin of the airship.

c. Cover the balloon and egg carton with papier mâché. Let dry.

d. Paint the model to match the original dirigible.

e. Label the dirigible with a white sticker label stating the name of the dirigible, the date produced, the date it crashed or retired, and a brief description of what the airship was used for.

f. Drive a toothpick into the tail and nose ends of the model. Tie a string from one toothpick to the other giving enough length to allow the model to hang freely from the ceiling.

g. Hang the dirigible models from the ceiling.

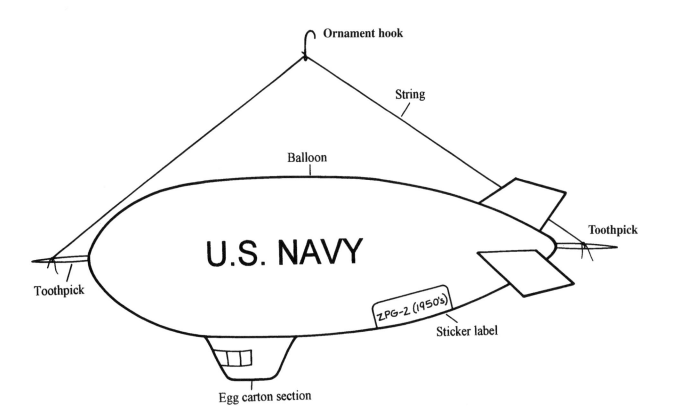

MYSTERIOUS CRASH OF AIRSHIP <u>AKRON</u>: 73 FEARED DEAD

Almost two years ago, on August 8, 1931, over 150,000 people converged on Akron, Ohio. There they witnessed the president's wife, Mrs. Herbert Hoover, christen the first of two huge navy dirigibles, the <u>U.S.S. Akron.</u> Americans cheered and looked forward to the completion of *Akron's* sister ship, the *Macon.*

Karl Arnstein designed the eight-million-dollar *Akron* based on his designs of several German wartime Zeppelins. The *Akron* held 6,500,000 cubic feet of helium. With a diameter of 133 feet and a length of 785 feet, the *Akron* was six times larger in cubic capacity than its German predecessors. Spectators marvelled at the sight of the behemoth-like ship as it rose in the air. The massive shadow silently slipping over the crowd created an eerie and awesome sight.

The size of the *Akron* allowed room for large living quarters. Suspended from the huge belly of the airship was an airplane hangar with sliding bottom doors. This hangar stored up to five uniquely designed airplanes. Movement of the planes in the immense hangar relied on overhead monorails. On completion of refueling and maintenance, a trapeze swung the airplanes out from below for take-off. The process repeated itself when the planes re-entered the hangar upon the conclusion of the flight.

According to reports, the *Akron* crashed near the Barnegat Inlet off the coast of New Jersey. Rescuers could reach only 4 of the 77 men. Navy spokesmen gave no cause for the tragedy. Many speculate that lightning ignited the volatile helium, sparking an explosion. Officials have not pinpointed the exact cause of this catastrophic loss. However, the Navy will not delay the launching of the *Macon* later this month.

QUESTIONS FOR MYSTERIOUS CRASH OF AIRSHIP AKRON: 73 FEARED DEAD

Literal Questions:

THE FACTS:

1. When was the *U.S.S. Akron* christened?

_____

_____

_____

2. Who designed the *Akron*?

_____

_____

_____

3. How many airplanes could the *Akron's* hangar store?

_____

_____

_____

4. Where did the *Akron* crash?

_____

_____

_____

SEQUENCE OF EVENTS:

5. What did Karl Arnstein design before he designed the *Akron*?

_____

_____

_____

6. Which happened first: the crash of the *Akron* or the launch of the *Macon*?

_____

_____

_____

Name _____   Date _____

Interpretive Questions:

DRAWING CONCLUSIONS:

7. Why was the president's wife chosen to christen the *U.S.S. Akron*?

_____

_____

_____

_____

MAKING INFERENCES:

8. What was the Navy's attitude toward the crash of the *Akron*? What specific information led you to your answer?

_____

_____

_____

_____

MAKING PREDICTIONS:

9. Based on the information from the story, what do you think happened to the *Macon*? Look for information about the *Macon* to learn if your prediction was correct.

_____

_____

_____

_____

IDENTIFICATION OF CAUSE:

10. Why didn't the Navy delay the launch of the *Macon*?

_____

_____

_____

_____

IDENTIFICATION OF THE MAIN IDEA:

11. Write a title for the story. Use as few words as possible.

_____

_____

Name _____ **Date** _____

COMPARISON:

12. How was the *Akron* like modern aircraft carriers? How was it different?

_____

_____

_____

_____

SUMMARIZE:

13. In your own words, describe the *Akron*.

_____

_____

_____

_____

EFFECT:

14. What effect might the crash of the *Akron* have had on the men assigned to the *Macon*? Why do you feel this way?

_____

_____

_____

_____

FACT AND OPINION:

15. The story said, "Many speculate that lightning ignited the volatile helium, sparking an explosion." Is this a fact or someone's opinion? Why do you feel this way?

_____

_____

_____

_____

ON YOUR OWN:

16. Write a question about the story for a teacher or another student to answer.

_____

_____

Name _____ **Date** _____

8. THE TRUE POOH

Reading Level = 8.45

ABOUT THE STORY

A.A. Milne wrote the stories of Winnie-the-Pooh based on toys owned by his son, Christopher Robin. Ernest Howard Shepard illustrated the books, modeling Pooh after his child's favorite toy bear, Growler.

QUOTES OF THE WEEK

Quote 1:

"I am a Bear of Very Little Brain, and long words Bother me."[1] *(page 778)*—A.A. MILNE, *WINNIE-THE-POOH*

Quote 2:

"I never did, I never did, I never *did* think much of 'Not up there, dear!' It's no good saying it. They don't understand."[6] *(page 17)*—A.A. MILNE

INTERVIEW TOPIC

Read a Winnie-the-Pooh story to a young child. Interview the child on his or her feelings about the story. Prepare a very short list of literal and interpretive questions: "Did you like the story? Why do you feel this way? Who is your favorite person or animal in the story? Why do you feel this way? What was your favorite part of the story? Why do you feel this way?"

PREVIEW WORDS

A.A. Milne	*Ernest Howard Shepard*	*Steiff*
Harry Colebourn	*Winnipeg*	

WORD-ORIGIN STUDY

author: *Author* comes from a Latin word meaning "to make grow or increase." An author can be anyone who creates, or "makes grow" something. As an author of books, the writer creates a world of his or her own in words that grow from the imagination.

illustrator: The prefix *il-* can mean "in." An illustrator lets in the light or enlightens a written composition.

List other words using the prefix *il-* and look up their meanings. Write the words and their definitions in your vocabulary notebook.

---

[1] Refer to *Quotation Footnotes for Level 8* on page 272.

[6] Refer to *Quotation Footnotes for Level 8* on page 272.

BOOKS TO READ

Hoff, Benjamin. *The Tao of Pooh*. New York: E.P. Dutton, 1982.

_____. *The Te of Piglet*. New York: Dutton, 1992.

Melrose, A.R. *The Pooh Dictionary: The Complete Guide to the Words of Pooh and All the Animals in the Forest*. New York: Dutton Children's Books, 1995.

Milne, A.A. *The Complete Tales of Winnie-the-Pooh*. New York: Dutton Children's Books, 1994.

_____. *A Gallery of Children*. New York: David McKay Company, 1925.

_____. *House on Pooh Corner*. New York: Dutton, 1956.

_____. *Now We Are Six*. New York: E.P. Dutton & Co., Inc., 1927.

_____. *Pooh Story Book*. New York: E.P. Dutton & Co., Inc., 1965.

_____. *When We Were Very Young*. New York: Dutton, 1961.

_____. *Winnie-the-Pooh*. New York: Dutton, 1974.

Milne, Christopher. *Enchanted Places*. New York: Dutton, 1975.

Toby, Marlene. *A.A. Milne: Author of Winnie-the-Pooh*. Chicago: Children's Press, 1995.

BOOK CLUB

Read A.A. Milne's *House at Pooh Corner, Winnie-the-Pooh*, or *The Complete Tales of Winnie-the-Pooh*. Try to locate other books illustrated by Ernest Howard Shepard.

INTRODUCTORY ACTIVITIES

DAY ONE

Objective: The students will listen to a story written by A.A. Milne and discuss the style of writing.

Read "In Which We Are Introduced to Winnie-the-Pooh and Some Bees, and the Story Begins" from A.A. Milne's *Winnie-the-Pooh* to the class. Discuss the introduction. How does Milne grab the interest of his readers? Does Milne use unique phrasing that makes his writing distinctive? Give examples. Many adults enjoy reading *Winnie-the-Pooh*. Why would adults as well as children enjoy the Pooh stories?

DAY TWO

STORY LESSON

Follow the *Presenting the Story Lesson* instructions in the Introduction. Each story lesson follows the same procedure; however, say the following in step 4: "The title of the story we're reading today is *The True Pooh*. What do you think the story is about? What do you already know about Winnie-the-Pooh?"

EXTENSION ACTIVITIES

1. Collect new stuffed toys, one for each student. You might obtain toys from local merchants as donations. The students write a story using their toy as a main character. Because the stories will be donated to young children, the stories should not contain high-level vocabulary or sentence structure. Encourage the students to use creative-writing techniques that would hold the attention of young children.

2. The students illustrate their stories. If possible, they should type the stories onto the computer where the text can be produced in the larger, primary-size, print.

3. Students draw coloring-book-size pictures of the main events of the story. Trace over the lines with wide markers so that young children can successfully color the pictures.

4. Students bind the stories into books including the illustrated story, blank lined notebook paper, and the coloring-book pictures.

5. Collect the books with the companion toys, and deliver them to local children's hospitals, homeless shelters, or other charities for children. The children can read the story, write their own stories about the toy on the blank notebook pages, and color the pictures. If possible, include a small set of crayons with each book.

THE TRUE POOH

Most people associate author A.A. Milne with Winnie-the-Pooh. Yet the creation of the charming bear may never have taken place without his illustrator, Ernest Howard Shepard. A.A. Milne was born in London in 1882 to a headmaster of a private school. Although they never met until adulthood, Shepard was born only two years earlier around the corner from Milne's school.

The two met working on a famous weekly comic magazine called *Punch*. As editor, Milne appreciated the talents of his illustrator. The first rendering of the future Winnie-the-Pooh appeared in *Punch* on November 26, 1913 as an unassuming stuffed bear in a toy shop display. According to Shepard, he based Pooh on his son's Steiff bear, Growler. Shepard later noted, ". . . Growler was a real character and played an important part in the career of Winnie-the-Pooh."

World War I disrupted the careers of Milne and Shepard for several years. Miraculously, both men survived, and A.A. Milne went on to a career as a writer of children's books. The *New York Times* described Milne's first book, *Once on a Time*—although billed as a book for children-as "an entertaining mockery of war."

In the meantime, the third figure in the Pooh story moved to the London Zoo in 1914. An army veterinarian, Harry Colebourn, bought an orphaned bear. He named the cub after the Canadian town of Winnipeg, and nicknamed the little bear Winnie. Winnie became a popular attraction until his death in 1934.

The final character in the Pooh saga was born in 1920 with the name Christopher Robin Milne. Not long after Christopher Robin's birth, a stuffed bear named after Winnie moved into the Milnes' home. It was not until much later that Winnie adopted the name Pooh, which originally belonged to a swan.

After acquiring a toy donkey named Eeyore in 1921 and a pig-like figure called Piglet, the cast was complete. Pooh's debut came in the book *When We Were Young* under the unassuming title of "Teddy Bear." Finally, Pooh entered the literary world on Christmas Eve, 1925 in the pages of London's *Evening News*. "So they went off together. . . . a little boy and his Bear. . . ."

QUESTIONS FOR THE TRUE POOH

Literal Questions:

THE FACTS:

1. Who was A.A. Milne?

_____

_____

_____

2. Who was Ernest Howard Shepard?

_____

_____

_____

3. Who was Harry Colebourn?

_____

_____

_____

4. In what book did Winnie-the-Pooh make his debut?

_____

_____

_____

SEQUENCE OF EVENTS:

5. What were Milne's and Shepard's occupations before World War I?

_____

_____

_____

6. Who moved into the Milnes' home after the birth of Christopher Robin?

_____

_____

_____

Name _____   Date _____

Interpretive Questions:

DRAWING CONCLUSIONS:

7. Did A.A. Milne find the inspiration for his fictional stories in his real life? What specific information in the story led you to your conclusion?

_____

_____

_____

_____

MAKING INFERENCES:

8. How did A.A. Milne feel about his son, Christopher Robin? What specific information led you to your answer?

_____

_____

_____

_____

MAKING PREDICTIONS:

9. As we move into the twenty-first century and the age of technology, will the appeal of Winnie-the-Pooh continue? Why do you feel this way?

_____

_____

_____

_____

IDENTIFICATION OF CAUSE:

10. Why did A.A. Milne and Ernest Howard Shepard write and illustrate stories about a little boy and his toy bear? What information in the story led you to your answer?

_____

_____

_____

_____

IDENTIFICATION OF THE MAIN IDEA:

11. Write a title for the story. Use as few words as possible.

_____

_____

Name _____   **Date** _____

COMPARISON:

12. How was Milne's work on *Winnie-the-Pooh* similar to Shepard's? How was it different?

_____

_____

_____

_____

SUMMARIZE:

13. In your own words, tell how the characters of *Winnie-the-Pooh* came from real-life events.

_____

_____

_____

_____

EFFECT:

14. What effect, if any, do you believe the stories of Winnie-the-Pooh had on the real Christopher Robin? Why do you feel this way? (To learn more about the real Christopher Robin, read his autobiography, *Enchanted Places*, included in Books to Read.)

_____

_____

_____

_____

FACT AND OPINION:

15. The story said, "The *New York Times* described Milne's first book, *Once on a Time* . . . as 'an entertaining mockery of war.'" Is this a fact or the critic's opinion? Why do you feel this way?

_____

_____

_____

_____

ON YOUR OWN:

16. Write a question about the story for a teacher or another student to answer.

_____

_____

Name _____   **Date** _____

9. SCOTT JOPLIN: RAGTIME KING
Reading Level = 8.53

ABOUT THE STORY

Scott Joplin developed his ragtime musical style in the late 1880s. Ragtime stands apart from other genres of music with its complicated and continuous syncopation. Today Joplin's music continues to be popular among musicians and audiences alike.

QUOTES OF THE WEEK

Quote 1:

"Music is the universal language of mankind. . . ."[1] *(page 509)*
—HENRY WADSWORTH LONGFELLOW, *OUTRE-MER*

Quote 2:

"It is from the blues that all that may be called American music derives its most distinctive characteristic."[1] *(page 733)*—JAMES WELDON JOHNSON, *BLACK MANHATTAN*

Quote 3:

"Lady, if you got to ask you ain't got it."[1] *(page 847)*—THOMAS (FATS) WALLER in response to the question "What is rhythm?"

Quote 4:

"Man, if you gotta ask you'll never know."[1] *(page 847)*—LOUIS ARMSTRONG in response to the question "What is jazz?"

INTERVIEW TOPIC

Choose a person of any age. Play a recording of a piece of Scott Joplin music. Ask the person if he or she liked the music. Prepare a question list including literal and interpretive questions: "Did you like the music? How did it make you feel? Have you heard Scott Joplin's music before? Where and when did you hear it?"

PREVIEW WORDS

Texarkana, Texas   *syncopation*   *Treemonisha*

WORD-ORIGIN STUDY

ragtime: The name *ragtime* came from the words "ragged time" which described the fast, syncopated, ragged, rhythm of music played on Mississippi riverboats in the 1890s. It was at its height of popularity between 1890 and 1915. It is believed that *ragtime* led to the development of jazz.

---

[1] Refer to *Quotation Footnotes for Level 8* on page 272.

syncopation: *Syncopate* comes from a word meaning "swooning or cutting short." *Syncopated* music sets the rhythm to the unaccented beat which produces an impression that the notes are cut short. The music takes on a swooning rhythm.

List other words beginning with the prefix *syn-*. Write the words and their definitions in your vocabulary notebook.

BOOKS TO READ

Berendt, Joachim Ernst. *The Jazz Book: From Ragtime to Fusion and Beyond.* Brooklyn, NY: Lawrence Hill Books, 1992.

Doctorow, E.L. *Ragtime.* New York: Random House, 1975.

Gamond, Peter. *Scott Joplin and the Ragtime Era.* New York: St. Martin's Press, 1975.

Haskins, James. *Scott Joplin.* Garden City, NY: Doubleday & Co., 1978.

Mitchell, Barbara. *Raggin': A Story About Scott Joplin.* Minneapolis: Carolrhoda Books, 1987.

Preston, Katherine K. *Scott Joplin.* New York: Chelsea House Publishers, 1988.

Schafer, William John. *The Art of Ragtime: Form and Meaning of an Original Black American Art.* Baton Rouge: Louisiana State University Press, 1973.

Shaw, Arnold. *Black Popular Music in America: From the Spirituals, Minstrels, and Ragtime to Soul, Disco, and Hip-Hop.* New York: Schirmer Books, 1986.

Waldo, Terry. *This Is Ragtime.* New York: Hawthorn Books, 1976.

Whitcomb, Ian. *Irving Berlin and Ragtime America.* New York: Limelight Editions, 1988.

CDs, RECORDS, AND CASSETTES

Joplin, Scott. *Entertainer Ballet* (Cassette). New York: Columbia Records, 1974.

_____. *Gladrags* (CD). London, England: EMI Records, 1983.

BOOK CLUB

Read *Scott Joplin* by Katherine K. Preston or another biography of Scott Joplin matched to the student's reading ability.

INTRODUCTORY ACTIVITIES

DAY ONE

Objective: The students will listen to two piano solos, *Moonlight Sonata* by Beethoven and Scott Joplin's *The Entertainer*, and write a compare/contrast essay about the two pieces.

Tell the students that they will listen to two solos played on the same instrument, the piano. The pieces are Beethoven's *Moonlight Sonata* and Joplin's *The Entertainer*. The students are to listen to the sounds produced by the instrument, the differences or similarities in the rhythms, and the feelings evoked by each piece.

After listening to the songs, discuss how the pieces are alike and how they are different. The students then write a short compare/contrast essay about what they heard.

DAY TWO

STORY LESSON

Follow the *Presenting the Story Lesson* instructions in the Introduction. Each story lesson follows the same procedure; however, say the following in step 4: "The title of the story we're reading today is *Scott Joplin: Ragtime King*. What do you think the story is about? What do you already know about Scott Joplin? What do you know about ragtime music?"

EXTENSION ACTIVITIES

1. Invite a pianist to come to the school to discuss and play ragtime music. Ask the pianist to play a composition by Scott Joplin. Instruct the students to watch the movement of the hands. Request a short classical piece, also instructing the students to watch the hands. How were the movements of the hands alike or different when the pianist played the different styles of music? Hold a question-and-answer session with the pianist.

2. The students research American jazz and ragtime musicians. They choose one musician and make a poster that includes a drawing of the musician, a collage depicting how the musician's music makes the student feel, and a brief biography of the musician. Encourage the students to be creative using a variety of materials for the collage. Students share the posters with the class and play music performed or composed by their subject.

3. Play recordings of ragtime and jazz music as the students work on their posters. The music might include Louis Armstrong, Scott Joplin, and Thomas "Fats" Waller.

SCOTT JOPLIN: RAGTIME KING

Riverboat scenes appear in many movies set in the American South of the early 1900s. If you close your eyes and listen, you'll hear the piano player completing the picture with his bouncing bass lines and irregular rhythms. That's ragtime!

The father of ragtime was a black man named Scott Joplin. Joplin was born in Texarkana, Texas, in 1868. His mother encouraged the study of music, much to his father's disapproval, and Joplin began playing the piano at age seven.

Joplin's father soon left, and his mother became caretaker of a black church. It was in the music of the church where Joplin learned the rhythm of music as he studied classically at home.

At the age of twenty, Scott Joplin wandered with a group of travelling musicians until he reached St. Louis in 1885. Joplin perfected "ragtime" music while playing in night clubs throughout the city.

Joplin's ragtime music carried a complicated syncopation. Irregular accents and rocking bass lines gave ragtime a musical flavor unlike any other.

Scott Joplin realized that "Maple Leaf Rag" was the jewel of his compositions; yet leery publishers wouldn't buy such complicated music. Publishers believed most piano players would find ragtime too difficult. Finally, Joplin sold his first song, "Original Rags," which led to the purchase of "Maple Leaf Rag" for $50.00 and royalties. As Joplin predicted, "Maple Leaf" was popular and sold hundreds of copies.

Looking to stretch his talents, Joplin wrote a ragtime opera, *Treemonisha*, in 1908. Unable to find backers, Joplin financed the production with his own funds. Perhaps too early for its time, *Treemonisha* closed after one performance.

Joplin died with a broken spirit in 1917. His family buried him on Long Island in an unmarked grave. In 1972, the Atlanta Arts Center performed *Treemonisha* to rave reviews, and his ragtime "The Entertainer" became the theme song to the award-winning movie *The Sting*. Today, Americans attend and compete in ragtime festivals. To demonstrate their musical skill, every contestant must play "Maple Leaf Rag," Joplin's most loved tune, and the standard of ragtime skill.

QUESTIONS FOR SCOTT JOPLIN: RAGTIME KING

Literal Questions:

THE FACTS:

1. When and where was Scott Joplin born?

_____

_____

_____

2. Where did Joplin perfect "ragtime" music?

_____

_____

_____

3. Name two of Joplin's piano pieces.

_____

_____

_____

4. What was the name of Joplin's ragtime opera?

_____

_____

_____

SEQUENCE OF EVENTS:

5. What did Joplin's mother do after his father left home?

_____

_____

_____

6. Which event happened first: Joplin sold "Maple Leaf Rag" for $50.00 or Joplin financed *Treemonisha* with his own funds?

_____

_____

_____

Name _____   Date _____

Interpretive Questions:

DRAWING CONCLUSIONS:

7. Why did Joplin's musical compositions, such as "The Entertainer" and *Treemonisha*, become popular nearly sixty years after his death?

_____

_____

_____

_____

MAKING INFERENCES:

8. Why did Joplin die with a broken spirit? What specific information led you to your answer?

_____

_____

_____

_____

MAKING PREDICTIONS:

9. With the popularity of rock music and the use of electronically produced music, will Scott Joplin's ragtime continue to be popular in the future? Why do you feel this way?

_____

_____

_____

_____

IDENTIFICATION OF CAUSE:

10. As you watch the movie *The Sting*, listen to the music carefully. Why did the producers choose Scott Joplin's ragtime, "The Entertainer," as the theme song?

_____

_____

_____

_____

IDENTIFICATION OF THE MAIN IDEA:

11. Write a title for the story. Use as few words as possible.

_____

_____

Name _____   Date _____

COMPARISON:

12. Listen to recordings of Joplin's "Maple Leaf Rag" and "The Entertainer." How are the songs alike? How are they different?

_____

_____

_____

_____

SUMMARIZE:

13. In your own words, tell about the life of Scott Joplin.

_____

_____

_____

_____

EFFECT:

14. What effect did the early failure of _Treemonisha_ have on Joplin's life? How might his life have been different if it had met with favorable reviews when it opened in 1908?

_____

_____

_____

_____

FACT AND OPINION:

15. The story said, "Publishers believed most piano players would find ragtime too difficult." Was this a fact or the publishers' opinion? How can you prove your answer?

_____

_____

_____

_____

ON YOUR OWN:

16. Write a question about the story for a teacher or another student to answer.

_____

_____

Name _____   **Date** _____

10. BETTY FORD: A TRUE FIRST LADY

Reading Level = 8.54

ABOUT THE STORY

Betty Ford, born in 1918, was a first among first ladies. She was the first wife of a president to come from a divorce, and the first to openly discuss her breast cancer. Before marriage she was a dancer who performed at Carnegie Hall. After her husband's term in the White House, she opened the world-famous Betty Ford Center for those addicted to drugs or alcohol.

QUOTES OF THE WEEK

Quote 1:

"Like the invisible worm that eats at the heart of the rose, drugs and alcohol are dark secret lovers that destroy. I have heard those patients who say, 'Cocaine loves me.' It wasn't until 1955 that the American Medical Association finally said—out loud, and in print—'Alcoholism is a disease.'"[9] *(page 163)*—BETTY FORD, *BETTY: A GLAD AWAKENING*, Chapter 13

Quote 2:

"No one can make you feel inferior without your consent."[3] *(page 126)* —ELEANOR ROOSEVELT

INTERVIEW TOPIC

Interview a person over the age of 30 about his or her favorite First Lady. Prepare a questions list that includes literal and interpretive questions: "Who was your favorite First Lady? Why did you like her? Did she accomplish something that touched your life? What is your favorite story about the First Lady?"

PREVIEW WORDS

Carnegie Hall   *Spiro T. Agnew*   *candid*

WORD-ORIGIN STUDY

alcohol: *Alcohol* comes from the Arabic *al-*, "the" and *kohl*, which is the powder of antimony. The powder of antimony was a stain or paint used to color the eyebrows and as a compound in medicines. *Alcohol* began its history as the powder of antimony, but now refers to impalpable powder (a powder too fine to be felt). Today *alcohol* also refers to alcohol compounds used in industry as fuel, in medicine as an antiseptic, or in intoxicating liquor.

---

[9] Refer to *Quotation Footnotes for Level 8* on page 272.

[3] Refer to *Quotation Footnotes for Level 8* on page 272.

| *addict:* | The prefix *ad-* means "to, or unto." *Addict* comes from a Latin word meaning "to devote, or to deliver over." An *addict* "gives (oneself) up habitually." When people become addicted, they deliver themselves, or gives themselves up to, the substance or act to which they are addicted. |

List other words beginning with the prefix *ad-*. Write the words and their meanings in your vocabulary notebook.

Books to Read

Anthony, Carl Sferrazza. *America's Most Influential First Ladies*. Minneapolis: Oliver Press, 1992.

Behrens, June. *Barbara Bush: First Lady of Literacy*. Chicago: Children's Press, 1990.

Feinman, Jeffrey. *Betty Ford*. New York: Award, 1976.

Ford, Betty and Chris Chase. *Betty: A Glad Awakening*. Garden City, NY: Doubleday, 1987.

Giblin, James Cross. *Edith Wilson: The Woman Who Ran the United States*. New York: Viking, 1992.

Gorman, Edward. *The First Lady*. New York: Forge, 1995.

Gould, Lewis L. (ed.) *American First Ladies: Their Lives and Their Legacy*. New York: Garland Publishing, Inc., 1996.

Grimes, Ann. *Running Mates: The Making of a First Lady*. New York: William Morrow, 1990.

Radcliffe, Donnie. *Hillary Rodham Clinton: A First Lady of Our Time*. New York: Warner Books, 1993.

_____. *Simply Barbara Bush: A Portrait of America's Candid First Lady*. New York: Warner Books, 1989.

Roosevelt, Elliott. *The Hyde Park Murder*. New York: St. Martin's Press, 1985. (One of a series of Elliott Roosevelt mysteries using his mother, Eleanor Roosevelt, as a main character.)

_____. *Murder and the First Lady*. New York: St. Martin's Press, 1984.

_____. *Murder at the Palace*. New York: St. Martin's Press, 1988.

_____. *The White House Pantry Murder*. New York: St. Martin's Press, 1987.

Truman, Margaret. *First Ladies*. New York: Random House, 1995.

Weidenfeld, Sheila Rabb. *First Lady's Lady*. New York: Berkley, 1979.

Weidt, Maryann N. *Stateswoman to the World: A Story About Eleanor Roosevelt*. Minneapolis: Carolrhoda Books, 1991.

Videos

Blaugrund, Andrea and Bettina Gregory. *Hillary Rodham Clinton: Changing the Rules*. New York: A&E Home Video, 1994.

Furneaux, Charles (director). *Jackie*. Bethesda, MD: Discovery Channel Video, 1995.

Lerman, Rhoda. *Eleanor: First Lady of the World*. Burbank, CA: Columbia Tristar Home Video, 1992.

BOOK CLUB

Read *Murder and the First Lady* by Elliott Roosevelt.

INTRODUCTORY ACTIVITIES

DAY ONE

Objective: The students will watch three videos about three different first ladies. They will discuss how the women are alike and how they are different.

Show the three videos listed in the Videos section, or three other biographical videos about a first lady. "How were Eleanor Roosevelt, Hillary Rodham Clinton, and Jackie Kennedy Onassis alike? How were they different? How did their duties as First Lady reflect the times they lived in? How will the duties of the First Lady (or first gentleman) change in the future? Why do you feel this way?

DAY TWO

STORY LESSON

Follow the *Presenting the Story Lesson* instructions in the Introduction. Each story lesson follows the same procedure; however, say the following in step 4: "The title of the story we're reading today is *Betty Ford: A True First Lady*. What do you think the story is about? What do you already know about Betty Ford? What do you already know about first ladies?"

EXTENSION ACTIVITIES

1. Usually the First Lady is the President's wife. However, a daughter, daughter-in-law, sister, and niece have served as First Ladies. Current First Ladies have their own executive staff and control a large household staff. In the past, wives of presidents performed their own household duties, such as laundry.

   Assign each student a First Lady. The students write a brief essay using three references about the life and times of their First Lady. A list of First Ladies is provided.

TERM	PRESIDENT	FIRST LADY
1789–1797	George Washington	Martha Dandridge Custis
1797–1801	John Adams	Abigail Smith
1801–1809	Thomas Jefferson	Martha Jefferson Randolph*
1809–1817	James Madison	Doll[e]y Payne Todd
1817–1825	James Monroe	Elizabeth Kort[w]right
1825–1829	John Quincy Adams	Louisa Catherine Johnson
1829–1837	Andrew Jackson	Rachel Donelson Robards*
1837–1841	Martin Van Buren	Angelica Singleton Van Buren*
1841–1841	William Henry Harrison	Ann Tuthill Symmes
1841–1845	John Tyler	Letitia Christian Julia Gardiner
1845–1849	James Knox Polk	Sarah Childress
1849–1850	Zachery Taylor	Margaret Mackall Smith
1850–1853	Millard Fillmore	Abigail Powers
1853–1857	Franklin Pierce	Jane Means Appleton
1857–1861	James Buchanan	Harriet Lane Johnston*
1861–1865	Abraham Lincoln	Mary Ann Todd
1865–1869	Andrew Jackson	Eliza McCardle
1869–1877	Ulysses Simpson Grant	Julia Dent
1877–1881	Rutherford Birchard Hayes	Lucy Ware Webb
1881–1881	James Abram Garfield	Lucretia Rudolph
1881–1885	Chester Alan Arthur	Mrs. John McElroy*
1885–1889	Stephen (Grover) Cleveland	Frances Clara Folsom
1889–1893	Benjamin Harrison	Caroline Lavinia Scott
1893–1897	Stephen (Grover) Cleveland	Frances Clara Folsom
1897–1901	William McKinley	Ida Saxton
1901–1909	Theodore Roosevelt	Edith Kermit Carow
1909–1913	William Howard Taft	(Nellie) Helen Herron
1913–1921	Thomas (Woodrow) Wilson	Ellen Louise Axson Edith Bolling Galt
1921–1923	Warren Gamaliel Harding	Florence Kling DeWolfe
1923–1929	Calvin Coolidge	Grace Anna Goodhue
1929–1933	Herbert Clark Hoover	Lou Henry
1933–1945	Franklin Delano Roosevelt	Anna (Eleanor) Roosevelt
1945–1953	Harry S Truman	(Bess) Elizabeth Virginia Wallace
1953–1961	Dwight David Eisenhower	Mamie Geneva Doud
1961–1963	John Fitzgerald Kennedy	Jacqueline Lee Bouvier

TERM	PRESIDENT	FIRST LADY *(Cont'd)*
1963–1969	Lyndon Baines Johnson	(Lady Bird) Claudia Alta Taylor
1969–1974	Richard Milhous Nixon	(Patricia or Pat) Thelma Catherine Ryan
1974–1977	Gerald Rudolph Ford	(Betty) Elizabeth Ann Bloomer
1977–1981	(Jimmy) James Earl Carter	Eleanor (Rosalynn) Smith
1981–1989	Ronald Wilson Reagan	(Nancy) Anne Frances Robbins Davis
1989–1993	George Herbert Walker Bush	Barbara Pierce
1993–2000	(Bill) William Jefferson Clinton	Hillary Rodham

* Denotes first ladies who were not the presidents' wives; ( ) denotes a preferred name; [ ] denotes an alternate spelling.

2. Using a long piece of bulletin board paper, students make a timeline starting with George Washington in 1789. Mark off the dates of each presidential term. Display a picture of the First Lady on the timeline along with her name, the president she served with, and their years in office. Hang the essay corresponding with each First Lady under her picture. In a contrasting color write in important events in American history along the timeline such as the Civil War, the beginning of the Industrial Revolution, the first astronaut in space, etc.

3. Have the students take the timeline to a local elementary school classroom and share interesting information about the First Ladies with the younger children. It is best if the visit coincides with Presidents' Day.

BETTY FORD: A TRUE FIRST LADY

Born April 8, 1918, Betty Ford set on a road that would touch the hearts of every American. From the age of eight, Betty demonstrated a talent for dancing which she described as her "happiness." She eventually became a student under the legendary Martha Graham, and danced at Carnegie Hall.

In the 1930s society forced women to choose between a family and a career. Torn between the two worlds, Betty married Bill Warren. Unfortunately, her marriage, which she later described as "the five-year misunderstanding," ended quickly. Shortly after her divorce she met a handsome young lawyer who became the love of her life, Gerald R. Ford, whom she married in 1948.

Betty became active in her husband's political career. Public service took Mr. Ford away from home 280 days of the year, leaving Betty to raise their four young children.

In 1968, Richard M. Nixon became president with Vice President Spiro T. Agnew by his side. By 1973 Agnew resigned his vice presidency, pleading guilty to accepting kickbacks from contractors. Mr. Ford's popularity made him the obvious replacement. Then, in 1974, Nixon resigned his presidency, and Gerald Ford became the first man to serve as vice president and president without winning an election.

In the White House Mrs. Ford became known as a candid, outspoken First Lady. She had a divorce in her past and her views on abortion drew criticism from many Americans, yet the hearts of the country rallied behind her when she became a victim of breast cancer. Instead of keeping silent about her illness, she encouraged all women to get a check-up. The advice touched close to home when Happy Rockefeller, the vice president's wife, learned that she too suffered from breast cancer.

Mrs. Ford never spoke of her pain from arthritis and a pinched nerve, and found herself addicted to painkillers and alcohol. After seeking help, she dedicated her life to those afflicted with addiction. In 1982 the Betty Ford Center opened its doors. Gerald Ford summed up the feelings of America when he said, "We're proud of you, Mom. . . . We want you to know that we love you."

QUESTIONS FOR BETTY FORD: A TRUE FIRST LADY

Literal Questions:

THE FACTS:

1. When was Betty Ford born?

_____

_____

_____

2. Who did Betty Ford marry in 1948?

_____

_____

_____

3. When did Gerald R. Ford become America's president?

_____

_____

_____

4. Who does the Betty Ford Center serve?

_____

_____

_____

SEQUENCE OF EVENTS:

5. What happened before Gerald Ford took the office of president?

_____

_____

_____

6. What did Betty Ford do after she learned she had breast cancer?

_____

_____

_____

Name _____ **Date** _____

Interpretive Questions:

DRAWING CONCLUSIONS:

7. After reading the biography, what one word would you use to describe Betty Ford? Why do you feel this way?

_____

_____

_____

_____

MAKING INFERENCES:

8. Why did Mrs. Ford keep silent about her pain from arthritis and a pinched nerve?

_____

_____

_____

_____

MAKING PREDICTIONS:

9. Will America always remember Betty Ford's commitment to those addicted to drugs? Why do you feel this way?

_____

_____

_____

_____

IDENTIFICATION OF CAUSE:

10. Why did Betty Ford talk about her breast cancer at a time when most people kept such a disease private?

_____

_____

_____

_____

IDENTIFICATION OF THE MAIN IDEA:

11. Write a title for the story. Use as few words as possible.

_____

_____

Name _____   Date _____

COMPARISON:

12. How was Betty Ford's response to her breast cancer similar to her response to her addiction to painkillers and alcohol? How was it different?

_____

_____

_____

_____

SUMMARIZE:

13. In your own words, describe the events that led to the opening of the Betty Ford Center.

_____

_____

_____

_____

EFFECT:

14. What effect did marriage have on Betty Ford's life? How might her life be different if she chose dancing over marriage?

_____

_____

_____

_____

FACT AND OPINION:

15. The story said, "In the White House Mrs. Ford became known as a candid, outspoken first lady." Is this a fact or the author's opinion? How can you prove your answer?

_____

_____

_____

_____

ON YOUR OWN:

16. Write a question about the story for a teacher or another student to answer.

_____

_____

Name _____   **Date** _____

11. RACHEL CARSON:
THE COMING OF A SILENT SPRING
Reading Level = 8.58

ABOUT THE STORY

Rachel Carson grew up with an appreciation of the countryside in Springdale, Pennsylvania. While attending college, Rachel Carson studied English and biology which gave her the skills she needed to eloquently express her concerns about the environment in her best-selling book *Silent Spring*.

QUOTES OF THE WEEK

Quote 1:

"As crude a weapon as the cave man's club, the chemical barrage has been hurled against the fabric of life."[1] *(page 870)*—RACHEL CARSON, *SILENT SPRING*

Quote 2:

"The most alarming of all man's assaults upon the environment is the contamination of air, earth, rivers, and sea . . . . This pollution is for the most part irrecoverable."[2] *(page 171)*—RACHEL CARSON

Quote 3:

"We won't have a society if we destroy the environment."[2] *(page 171)* —MARGARET MEAD

INTERVIEW TOPIC

Interview a person who has lived in the community for 30 years or longer. Prepare a question list that includes literal and interpretive questions based on the topic, "How has our community's environment changed over the time you have lived here?" "What was the environment of our community like when you first lived here? What changes made the greatest impact on the environment? Have the changes been for the better? Why do you feel this way? In retrospect, compare the benefits and detriments of the impact of people on the land."

PREVIEW WORDS

pristine	*ecology*
pesticide	*magna cum laude*

WORD-ORIGIN STUDY

environment: *Environment* comes from a French word meaning "to surround." The *environment* is all the circumstances and elements that make up the surroundings in which an organism or group of organisms grow.

---

[1] Refer to *Quotation Footnotes for Level 8* on page 272.

[2] Refer to *Quotation Footnotes for Level 8* on page 272.

ecology: Eco- comes from a Greek word meaning "house," while the suffix *-logy,* when used in science, means "the doctrine or theory of." *Ecology* is a branch of biology dealing with the interaction between an organism and its environment, or the study of the environment which is our home and our affect upon it.

List other words beginning with the prefix *eco-*. Write the words and their definitions in your vocabulary notebook.

BOOKS TO READ

Anticaglia, Elizabeth. *Twelve American Women.* Chicago: Nelson-Hall, 1975.

Archer, Jules. *To Save the Earth: The American Environmental Movement.* New York: Viking, 1998.

Bernards, Neal (ed.). *The Environmental Crisis: Opposing Viewpoints.* San Diego: Greenhaven Press, 1991.

Carson, Rachel. *The Sea Around Us.* New York: Penguin Books, 1979.

_____. *The Sense of Wonder.* New York: Harper, 1965.

_____. *Silent Spring.* New York: Houghton Mifflin, 1962.

Cohn, Susan. *Green at Work: Finding a Business Career That Works for the Environment.* Washington, D.C.: Island Press, 1992.

Gore, Albert (U.S. Vice-President). *Earth in the Balance: Ecology and the Human Spirit.* New York: Plume, 1993.

Hawley, T.M. *Against the Fires of Hell: The Environmental Disaster of the Gulf War.* New York: Harcourt Brace Jovanovich, Publishers, 1992.

Heloise. *Heloise's Hints for a Healthy Planet.* New York: Perigee Books, 1990.

Henricksson, John. *Rachel Carson: The Environmental Movement.* Brookfield, CT: Millbrook Press, 1991.

Kallen, Stuart A. *Earth Keepers.* Edina, MN: Abdo & Daughters, 1993.

Killingsworth, Monte. *Circle Within a Circle.* New York: M.K. McElderry Books, 1994.

Klass, David. *California Blue.* New York: Scholastic, 1994.

Kudlinski, Kathleen V. *Rachel Carson: Pioneer of Ecology.* New York: Puffin Books, 1989.

Makower, Joel. *The Green Consumer.* New York: Penguin Books, 1993.

Miller, Louise. *Careers for Nature Lovers and Other Outdoor Types.* Lincolnwood, IL: VGM Career Horizons, 1996.

Naar, Jon. *Design for a Livable Planet: How You Can Help Clean Up the Environment.* New York: Harper & Row, Publishers, 1990.

Paehlke, Robert (ed.). *Conservation and the Environmentalism: An Encyclopedia.* New York: Garland Publishers, 1995.

Presnall, Judith Janda. *Rachel Carson.* San Diego: Lucent Books, 1995.

Sabin, Francene. *Rachel Carson: Friend of the Earth* (book/cassette set). Mahwah, NJ: Troll Associates, 1993.

Sharpe, Susan. *Waterman's Boy*. New York: Bradbury Press, 1990.

Teitel, Martin. *Rain Forest in Your Kitchen: The Hidden Connection Between Extinction and Your Supermarket*. Washington, D.C.: Island Press, 1992.

United States: Environmental Protection Agency, Information Access Branch. *Access EPA*. Washington, D.C.: Environmental Protection Agency, Information Access Branch, 1995.

Veglahn, Nancy. *Women Scientists*. New York: Facts on File, 1991.

VIDEOS

Feinerman, Lynn. *Eco Rap: Voices From the Hood*. Oakland, CA: The Video Project, 1993.

BOOK CLUB

Read *Waterman's Boy* by Susan Sharpe (a Junior Library Guild selection), *Circle Within a Circle* by Monte Killingsworth (also a Junior Library Guild selection), or David Klass's *California Blue*.

INTRODUCTORY ACTIVITIES

DAY ONE

Objective: The students will learn how environmental concerns affect their lives and community.

Invite a member of the local branch of the Environmental Protection Agency, or a member of the local city council, to discuss local environmental concerns including the effects of development on the environment versus the growing needs of the population. "What are the greatest environmental concerns facing the city/town? How are local authorities addressing these concerns? How can the community grow with the least amount of impact on the environment? What are the future concerns of the area in respect to the environment? What can individuals do to make a difference?" End the lesson with a question-and-answer session.

DAY TWO

STORY LESSON

Follow the *Presenting the Story Lesson* instructions in the Introduction. Each story lesson follows the same procedure; however, say the following in step 4: "The title of the story we're reading today is *Rachel Carson: The Coming of a Silent Spring*. What do you think the story is about?"

EXTENSION ACTIVITIES

1. Identify areas of environmental concern in your area. Perhaps car emissions and increased freeway (and highway) traffic need to be addressed. Check the Internet or with your local state representatives for issues debated on the local, state, or national levels that affect the environment in your area. Discuss these concerns in the classroom. Encourage a variety of viewpoints on each issue.

   Each student chooses an issue that interests him or her. Students research the matter in current newspapers, articles, and books to learn as much as possible about all angles and viewpoints. After they are educated on the issue, they form an opinion and write a letter to the appropriate agency or representative expressing their feelings, basing their opinions on stated facts found in their research. Your local library can help you locate any addresses or e-mail addresses needed to complete the assignment.

2. As a class, make a list of actions the school itself can take to improve the environment. Learn about programs already used by the school system, such as recycling, and look for other ways to not only help the environment, but also save the school money. Reference books such as Jon Naar's *Design for a Livable Planet: How You Can Help Clean Up the Environment* can offer suggestions. The class then writes a letter to the principal outlining what they learned.

3. Make a booklet on ways to live that can reduce an individual's impact on the environment. Break the class into groups. Assign each group an area of daily living, and locate environmentally friendly alternatives to common pollution produced around the home. Examples of subjects are:

   > Saving Water
   > The Environmentally Friendly Kitchen
   > Cleaning and Maintenance Around the House
   > Gardening
   > The Environmentally Aware Consumer
   > Air Pollution: Indoors and Out
   > Your Car
   > Renewable Energy

   Each group researches its topic listing alternative ways to function that have less of an impact on the environment. Reference books such as *Heloise's Hints for a Healthy Planet*, Jon Naar's *Design for a Livable Planet: How You Can Help Clean Up the Environment*, and Joel Makower's *The Green Consumer* offer good advice. For example, Heloise suggests using vinegar mixed with cinnamon and cloves warmed in the microwave to absorb odors rather than using a commercially produced air deodorizer that simply masks odors (page 78).

   Compile a booklet using each group section as a chapter. Make an index and cover page. Give the booklet a title, and make copies for each student to take home.

RACHEL CARSON:
THE COMING OF A SILENT SPRING

"Only within the moment of time represented
by the present century has one species—man—acquired
significant power to alter the nature of his world."

—Rachel Carson,
Silent Spring

Born on May 27, 1907, Rachel Carson grew up on 65 acres of pristine countryside in Springdale, Pennsylvania. Her mother, a former school teacher, encouraged Rachel's interest in all that lived in the grass, trees, and streams. One day Rachel would popularize the term *ecology*, and forever change the way the world viewed the environment.

Rachel's life-long aspiration was to become a writer. She majored in English at the Pennsylvania College for Women where her teachers instantly recognized her talents. As a course requirement, Rachel took a class in biology. Suddenly, her life changed, and science became her passion. Her professors and fellow students warned her that the world would not embrace a woman scientist. Not persuaded, Rachel changed her major to zoology. She graduated from college with a B.A. in Science, magna cum laude. Later she attended Johns Hopkins University earning an M.A. in Zoology. The real test was yet to come. Could a woman find employment as a scientist?

In the 1950s, Rachel began to see ominous signs of poisons in the environment. Pesticide manufacturers produced deadly products, such as DDT. Pesticides poisoned livestock which made its way to America's dinner tables. Silently, Rachel began her quest to warn the world of a coming disaster. During this time her beloved mother died, and Rachel suffered from arthritis, flu, and a stomach ulcer. Not even a diagnosis of terminal cancer kept her from her work.

Rachel Carson's crowning achievement came in 1962 with the publication of *Silent Spring*. She alerted the world to a future where spring would come in silence, and pesticides would devastate the earth's ecology. *Silent Spring* became an immediate bestseller. Scientists argued that Rachel was an alarmist, but no one could disprove her facts. *Silent Spring* prompted a congressional investigation, and Rachel spent her last days defending her work. Rachel died on April 14, 1964, at the age of 56.

QUESTIONS FOR RACHEL CARSON:
THE COMING OF A SILENT SPRING

Literal Questions:

THE FACTS:

1. When was Rachel Carson born?

_____

_____

_____

2. What was Rachel Carson's first major at the Pennsylvania College of Women?

_____

_____

_____

3. When did Rachel Carson begin to see ominous signs of poisons in the environment?

_____

_____

_____

4. What did Rachel Carson's book, *Silent Spring*, alert the world to?

_____

_____

_____

SEQUENCE OF EVENTS:

5. What did Rachel Carson do after she saw ominous signs of poisons in the environment?

_____

_____

_____

6. What did Congress do after *Silent Spring* alerted the world to the environmental problems caused by pesticides?

_____

_____

_____

Name _____   Date _____

Interpretive Questions:

DRAWING CONCLUSIONS:

7. After reading the biography, what one word best describes Rachel Carson? What specific information led you to your conclusion?

_____

_____

_____

_____

MAKING INFERENCES:

8. What was the common perception of women scientists in the 1940s and 1950s? What information in the story led you to your answer?

_____

_____

_____

_____

MAKING PREDICTIONS:

9. Are we continuing to poison our environment with pesticides? Will this practice continue in the future? Why do you feel this way? (For more information, read *Something's Wrong With the Frogs* in Reading Level Twelve of this series.)

_____

_____

_____

_____

IDENTIFICATION OF CAUSE:

10. Why did Rachel Carson continue her crusade against pesticides even after she became ill with terminal cancer?

_____

_____

_____

_____

IDENTIFICATION OF THE MAIN IDEA:

11. Write a title for the story. Use as few words as possible.

_____

_____

Name _____   Date _____

COMPARISON:

12. How was Rachel Carson's decision to major in science similar to her decision to write *Silent Spring*? How was it different?

_____

_____

_____

_____

SUMMARIZE:

13. In your own words, tell about Rachel Carson's life and achievements.

_____

_____

_____

_____

EFFECT:

14. What effect did *Silent Spring* have on the way we view ecology? What specific information led you to your answer?

_____

_____

_____

_____

FACT AND OPINION:

15. In *Silent Spring,* Rachel Carson wrote, "Only within the moment of time represented by the present century has one species—man— acquired significant power to alter the nature of his world." Is this a fact or Rachel Carson's opinion? How can you prove your answer?

_____

_____

_____

_____

ON YOUR OWN:

16. Write a question about the story for a teacher or another student to answer.

_____

_____

Name _____ **Date** _____

12. THE RETURN OF SUPERSONIC FLIGHT

Reading Level = 8.61

ABOUT THE STORY

After the development of the *Concorde,* supersonic planes lost their popularity. Operating costs, low passenger capacity, and noise regulation made the supersonic plane too costly. Today NASA and independent airplane manufacturers are taking a new look at supersonic flight.

QUOTES OF THE WEEK

Quote 1:

"In the space age, man will be able to go around the world in two hours—one hour for flying and the other to get to the airport."[3] *(page 343)*
—NEIL H. MCELROY

Quote 2:

"I owned the world that hour as I rode over it . . . free of the earth, free of the mountains, free of the clouds, but how inseparably I was bound to them."[3] *(page 343)*—CHARLES A. LINDBERGH

INTERVIEW TOPIC

Interview a person 25 years old or older about supersonic air travel. Prepare a question list including literal and interpretive questions: "Do you fly often? Would you like it if all airplanes traveled at supersonic speed? Why do you feel this way? Would you like to fly in a plane that traveled about 1,500 miles per hour, and could travel 7,000 miles without stopping to refuel? Why do you feel this way?"

PREVIEW WORDS

Concorde	*supersonic*
Boeing	*stealth*

WORD-ORIGIN STUDY

sonic:	*Sonic* comes from a Latin word meaning "sound." Although *sonic* can refer to anything related to sound, it is also used to describe a speed equal to the speed of sound (approximately 1,087 feet per second or 738 miles per hour).
supersonic:	The prefix *super-* means "above, over, or higher." *Supersonic* is a speed above or faster than the speed of sound.

---

[3] Refer to *Quotation Footnotes for Level 8* on page 272.

List other words beginning with the prefix *super-*. Write the words with their definitions in your vocabulary notebook.

BOOKS TO READ

Allen, Richard Sanders. *Revolution in the Sky: The Lockheeds of Aviation's Golden Age*. New York: Orion Books, 1993.

Angelucci, Enzo. *Airplanes From the Dawn of Flight to the Present Day*. New York: McGraw Hill Book Company, 1973.

Hallion, Richard. *Designers and Test Pilots*. Alexandria, VA: Time–Life Books, 1983.

Hamlen, Joseph R. *Flight Fever*. New York: Doubleday, 1971.

Hammer, Charles. *Wrong-Way Ragsdale*. New York: Farrar, Straus, Giroux, 1987.

Mondey, David. *Illustrated History of Aircraft*. New York: Galahad Books, 1980.

Sutton, Larry. *Taildraggers High*. New York: Farrar, Straus, Giroux, 1985.

Wragg, David W. *Flight With Power: The First Ten Years*. New York: St. Martin's Press, 1978.

ARTICLES

Weingarten, Tara. "Beyond the Concorde, and Other Fantasy Flights." *Newsweek*, February 23, 1998, vol. 131, no. 8, p. 12.

BOOK CLUB

Read *Taildraggers High* by Larry Sutton or *Wrong-Way Ragsdale* by Charles Hammer.

INTRODUCTORY ACTIVITIES

DAY ONE

Objective: The students will learn about the history of airplanes from the Wright Brothers to supersonic flight.

If possible, the students should visit an aeronautics museum and take notes on the various airplanes. Allow the students to share a camera to take pictures (if permissible) of the planes for a classroom scrapbook.

If you cannot visit a museum, invite a speaker with knowledge of airplanes to your class. This might be a pilot (civilian or military), a collector of model planes, or a historian. Discuss the history of flight and how civilization changed when people could travel easily throughout the world. Describe, show models, or look at pictures of early cross-country flight in which passengers slept in beds aboard the plane. End with a discussion of the future of flight.

DAY TWO

STORY LESSON

Follow the *Presenting the Story Lesson* instructions in the Introduction. Each story lesson follows the same procedure; however, say the following in step 4: "The title of the story we're reading today is *The Return of Supersonic Flight*. What do you think the story is about? What do you already know about supersonic airplanes?"

EXTENSION ACTIVITIES

1. Hold a model airplane exhibition. Contact local model clubs for a list of possible members who would be interested in displaying their airplanes. Stores specializing in models might also be interested in participating.

   The students choose a model plane and write a brief essay on the original plane on which the model was patterned. Include information such as the year the plane first flew, what was the purpose of the plane, who designed the plane, and interesting facts surrounding the aircraft.

2. If your class went to an airplane museum, make a scrapbook of the photographs, making note of any information about the plane provided by the museum. Include any flyers or brochures from the museum.

3. Students make a shadow box, 3-D collage of an airplane. They will need:

   > magazines with photographs of airplanes and of scenic countryside
   > scissors
   > thin cardboard (such as that found in dress shirt packages)
   > Styrofoam plates
   > all-purpose, nontoxic glue
   > glue stick
   > posterboard
   > shallow boxes with rigid sides (such as shirt boxes)
   > construction paper, glitter, or other miscellaneous items to decorate the picture

PROCEDURE:

Students should use their imagination and creativity. There are no set patterns.

a. Cut out pictures of airplanes from magazines.

b. Choose scenic photographs that would complement the airplane. These could be layered to give the picture depth.

c. Cut a piece of posterboard to fit inside the bottom of the shallow box. Do not put it in yet.

d. Cut a scenic picture to cover the posterboard, or use construction paper or drawing paper and create your own background. Glue it to the posterboard with a glue stick.

e. Cut out pictures of trees or buildings to layer over the background. You can mix color photos with black-and-white photos, or use your own art work. Glue the picture onto the thin cardboard with a glue stick. Cut around the picture so that the cardboard does not show around the edges.

f. Cut the Styrofoam into small pieces, and glue them to the back of the pictures from step e using all-purpose glue. Glue this picture onto the background. The trees or building will stand off the background.

g. Cut out a picture of an airplane. Glue the picture onto thin cardboard with a glue stick. Cut around the picture so that the cardboard does not show around the edges.

h. Cut a second piece of cardboard the exact shape of the airplane. Glue Styrofoam pieces on the back of the blank airplane cardboard with all-purpose glue. Glue the blank board in place on your picture.

i. Using all-purpose glue, attach Styrofoam pieces to the back of the airplane picture. Glue this cut-out over the blank airplane cardboard at the bottoms of the Styrofoam pieces. The airplane will stand out over the trees or buildings to give the picture depth.

j. Glue the entire piece to the inside bottom of the cardboard box. Hang the shadow boxes around the room.

k. The students might want to mount their pictures into actual shadow box frames found in local craft stores or frame shops.

The students can put the plane farther in the background, use glitter to decorate a night sky, etc.

THE RETURN OF SUPERSONIC FLIGHT

Concorde, the supersonic plane of the early 1970s, entered the transportation industry with eager anticipation. Streaking through the sky at 1,320 mph, the *Concorde* dramatically reduced flight time to destinations around the world.

In September of 1973, *Concorde* made its first flight in the United States. The supersonic plane participated in the opening ceremonies of the new Dallas-Fort Worth Airport. While DFW Airport went on to become one of the busiest international airports in the world, *Concorde* floundered. The cost of flying *Concorde* and the low passenger capacity caused ticket prices to soar. Complaints of loud "sonic booms" rattling windows and disturbing livestock restricted the *Concorde* to oversea flights. Yet with all the pitfalls encountered by the *Concorde*, the dream of supersonic flight continues.

The High-Speed Civil Transport hit the NASA and Boeing drawing boards in the late 1990s. It will fly 25 percent faster than the *Concorde*, and will accommodate three times as many passengers. With 300 people on board, the High-Speed Civil Transport could fly at about 1,500 mph. You could fly from Los Angeles to Tokyo in four hours. Friction from such high speeds would heat the fuselage to 350 degrees Fahrenheit causing the plane to glow.

NASA's *Hyper*-X travels at speeds of up to 7,000 mph with an altitude of 100,000 feet. Like the High-Speed Civil Transport, friction heat would raise the body temperature of the plane to 3,000 degrees, melting the engine. If successful, *Hyper*-X would fly from Los Angeles to Sydney in less than two hours.

Maybe speed doesn't impress you, but cutting down on delayed flights would. NASA and Boeing's Blended Wing Body (BWB) plane might be what you're looking for. Plans for the double-decker jetliner includes space for 800 passengers compared with the 400 of the popular 747. Ecology conscious, the BWB will cut fuel use by one third, and decrease air-polluting emissions. Similar in design to the "flying wing" stealth bomber, the BMB could travel nonstop for up to 7,000 miles.

QUESTIONS FOR THE RETURN OF SUPERSONIC FLIGHT

Literal Questions:

THE FACTS:

1. What type of plane is the *Concorde?*

_____

_____

_____

2. When did *Concorde* enter the transportation industry?

_____

_____

_____

3. Name two supersonic airplane designs.

_____

_____

_____

4. How fast will NASA's *Hyper-X* travel?

_____

_____

_____

SEQUENCE OF EVENTS:

5. Which supersonic airplane did the story discuss first: the *Hyper-X* or the *Concorde?*

_____

_____

_____

6. What happened to the *Concorde* after its introduction at the new Dallas–Fort Worth Airport in 1973?

_____

_____

_____

Name _____ **Date** _____

Interpretive Questions:

DRAWING CONCLUSIONS:

7. Did the lack of popularity of *Concorde* discourage the development of supersonic airplanes? What led you to your conclusion?

_____

_____

_____

_____

MAKING INFERENCES:

8. Who has made the greater investment in supersonic flight: the U.S. government or private corporations? What information led you to your answer?

_____

_____

_____

_____

MAKING PREDICTIONS:

9. If NASA and Boeing's Blended Wing Body appears in the marketplace, will it become a popular mode of transportation? Why do you feel this way?

_____

_____

_____

_____

IDENTIFICATION OF CAUSE:

10. Why are airplane manufacturers continuing to develop supersonic flight even after the *Concorde* met with little success?

_____

_____

_____

_____

IDENTIFICATION OF THE MAIN IDEA:

11. Write a title for the story. Use as few words as possible.

_____

_____

Name _____   **Date** _____

COMPARISON:

12. How are the High-Speed Civil Transport and the *Hyper-X* alike? How are they different?

_____

_____

_____

_____

SUMMARIZE:

13. In your own words, describe two of the supersonic airplanes discussed in the story.

_____

_____

_____

_____

EFFECT:

14. What effect, if any, might the use of NASA and Boeing's Blended Wing Body plane have on the transportation industry? Why do you feel this way?

_____

_____

_____

_____

FACT AND OPINION:

15. The story said, "While DFW Airport went on to become one of the busiest international airports in the world, *Concorde* floundered." Is this a fact or the author's opinion? How can you prove your answer?

_____

_____

_____

_____

ON YOUR OWN:

16. Write a question about the story for a teacher or another student to answer.

_____

_____

Name _____   **Date** _____

13. THE GUEST STAR
Reading Level = 8.70

ABOUT THE STORY

In 1054, people around the world reported seeing a bright new star in the sky. The light lingered for three months, and was visible even in daylight. Astronomers believe this "guest star" was the explosion of what we now call the Crab Nebula.

QUOTES OF THE WEEK

Quote 1:

"Ice is the silent language of the peak;
and fire the silent language of the star."[1] *(page 812)*—CONRAD AIKEN,
AND IN THE HUMAN HEART

Quote 2:

"We had the sky, up there, all speckled with stars, and we used to lay on our backs and look up at them, and discuss about whether they was made, or only just happened."[7] *(page 217)*—MARK TWAIN, *HUCKLEBERRY FINN*

INTERVIEW TOPIC

Interview a person of any age about an astronomical sight (a solar or lunar eclipse, a comet, a meteor shower, etc.) he or she personally witnessed. Prepare a question list that includes literal and interpretive questions: "What was the event you witnessed? When did you see it? How did it make you feel? Do you know the scientific facts that caused the event? If so, what are they? Do you know any folktales or legends about the type of event you saw? What are they?"

PREVIEW WORDS

terrestrial	*Crab Nebula*	*supernova (supernovae)*
Tycho Brahe	*Johannes Kepler*	*catastrophic*

WORD-ORIGIN STUDY

nova: In astronomy, a *nova* is a star that suddenly becomes much brighter then slowly fades. A *supernova* is a nova that is much brighter and larger than usual, and can be as luminous as the galaxy in which it resides. The plural form of *nova* is *novas,* or *novae.*

terrestrial: The word *terra* means "the earth." *Terrestrial* is anything pertaining to the Earth, and is the opposite of *celestial,* pertaining to heaven. *Extraterrestrial* means outside, or beyond the limits, of Earth.

---

[1] Refer to *Quotation Footnotes for Level 8* on page 272.

[7] Refer to *Quotation Footnotes for Level 8* on page 272.

List other words beginning with the prefix *terra-*. Write the words and their definitions in your vocabulary notebook.

BOOKS TO READ

Asimov, Isaac. *Ancient Astronomy*. Milwaukee, WI: Gareth Stevens Publishers, 1988.

Asimov, Isaac, Martin H. Greenberg, and Charles G. Waugh (eds.). *Young Star Travelers*. New York: Harper & Row, Publishers, 1986.

Berman, Bob. *Secrets of the Night Sky: The Most Amazing Things in the Universe You Can See With the Naked Eye*. New York: William Morrow, 1995.

Clark, Stuart. *Stars and Atoms: From the Big Bang to the Solar System*. New York: Oxford University Press, 1995.

Hadingham, Evan. *Early Man and the Comos*. New York: Walker and Co., 1984.

Hawkins, Gerald S. *Stonehenge Decoded*. New York: Doubleday, 1965.

Hotaling, Billie. *Count the Stars Through the Cracks*. Unionville, NY: KAV Books, 1992.

Krupp, E.C. *In Search of Ancient Astronomers*. New York: Doubleday and Co., 1978.

Lampton, Christopher. *Supernova!* New York: Franklin Watts, 1988.

Sagan, Carl. *Cosmos*. New York: Random House, 1980.

Thorne, Kip S. *Black Holes and Time Warps: Einstein's Outrageous Legacy*. New York: W.W. Norton, 1993.

VanCleave, Janice Pratt. *Janice VanCleave's 202 Oozing, Bubbling, Dripping, and Bouncing Experiments*. New York: John Wiley, 1996.

VIDEOS

Bates, Robin. *Death of a Star*. Boston: WGBH Educational Foundation, 1987.

COMPUTER PROGRAMS

Nutt, Jan. *Using the Internet to Explore Astronomy*. Austin, TX: Steck-Vaughn, 1997.

BOOK CLUB

Read *Young Star Travelers* edited by Isaac Asimov, Martin H. Greenberg, and Charles G. Waugh.

INTRODUCTORY ACTIVITIES

DAY ONE

Objective: The students will visit a planetarium, or listen to a speaker focusing on unique astronomical events such as supernovae.

Take the students on a field trip to a planetarium, or have a speaker come to class, and discuss unique astronomical events such as supernovae, black holes, meteors hitting planets, etc. The speaker might be a university professor of astronomy, a professional astronomer, or a student of astronomy recommended by a professor. Prior to the visit, prepare a list of questions with the students that includes literal and interpretive questions: "What is a nova? What is a supernova? Has a supernova exploded close to Earth? Can Earth ever feel the effects of a supernova, and in what way would the effects be felt?" End the presentation with a question-and-answer session.

DAY TWO

STORY LESSON

Follow the *Presenting the Story Lesson* instructions in the Introduction. Each story lesson follows the same procedure; however, say the following in step 4. "The title of the story we're reading today is *Guest Star*. What do you think the story is about?"

EXTENSION ACTIVITIES

1. Hold a *Night Among the Stars* event in the evening to allow the students an opportunity to see the Crab Nebula and/or other interesting features of the night sky. Seek advice from an astronomer for the best night to star gaze. (Be sure to obtain the proper parental and school permission.) Which objects the students are able to see depends on the season. Perhaps you can time the event with a lunar eclipse or a meteor shower.

   a. Invite professional or amateur astronomers to bring their telescopes, and join the students for an evening of star gazing. (Students and teachers as well as the school system might have telescopes they are willing to share.) Ask each astronomer to set up his or her telescope to look at a specific object in the sky. Make a poster to display at the telescope which names the object it is focusing on.

   b. Invite local astronomy clubs to set up a booth to inform students about the club, and what it offers members.

   c. Hold a "Find the Constellation" contest. Hand out a set of index cards, each showing the names and layout of constellations visible on the night of the *Night Among the Stars*. Give the students who can locate the most constellations astronomy-related prizes.

   d. Bob Berman's *Secrets of the Night Sky: The Most Amazing Things in the Universe You Can See With the Naked Eye* is a good reference for students without telescopes.

2. Do the activities listed in Jan Nutts's *Using the Internet to Explore Astronomy*.

3. The students make *Starry Night* posters.

Display a print of Vincent van Gogh's *Starry Night* (1889). (Your local library might offer prints for check out.) Write the following quote on the board:

> **"I have . . . a terrible need . . . shall I say the word? . . . of religion. Then I go out at night and paint the stars."[7]** *(page 217)*
>
> —**Vincent van Gogh**

Prepare an example poster before the lesson. You need:

posterboards (half sheet for each student)

fluoresecent crayons or markers

many dark blue or black crayons (this is a good way to use up broken crayons)

dark earth-tone (brown, green, etc.) crayons

various sized objects used to scratch off layers of crayon, such as empty disposable pens, coins, paper clips (use what is available, but avoid sharp objects)

PROCEDURE:

a. Using only the fluorescent colors, cover the entire poster with random colors.

b. Following the flowing style of the dark colors in Van Gogh's *Starry Night*, color the entire poster with thick dark blue and black crayons covering all the fluorescent colors.

c. Using various objects, scratch off the layers of dark crayon to reveal the fluorescent colors underneath, and create a design similar to van Gogh's. (The fluorescent colors will make up the circular stars.)

d. To give the picture depth, use the dark, earth-tone crayons to make mountains in the foreground similar to the peak in the foreground of *Starry Night*.

e. Mount the pictures in a well-lighted room for several hours. Turn off the lights to see how the glow-in-the-dark colors shine through the dark crayon.

BOOKS ABOUT VINCENT VAN GOGH:

Harrison, Peter. *Art for Young People: Vincent van Gogh*. New York: Sterling Publishing Co., Inc., 1996

Honour, Alan. *Tormented Genius: The Struggles of Vincent van Gogh*. New York: William Morrow and Company, 1967.

Lucas, Eileen. *Vincent van Gogh*. New York: Franklin Watts, 1991.

Venezia, Mike. *Getting to Know the World's Greatest Artists: Van Gogh*. Chicago: Children's Press, 1988.

Welsh-Ovcharov, Bogomila. *Van Gogh in Perspective*. Englewood Cliffs, NJ: Prentice-Hall, Inc., 1974.

THE GUEST STAR

On July 4, 1054 Chinese astronomers recorded the sighting of an unusually bright light in the sky. The "guest star," located in the constellation of Taurus, was more dazzling than any other star in the sky. Moslem astronomers also noted the same celestial event. In the American southwest desert, a Native American tribe known as the Anasazi painted a pictorial version of this unique event. Strangely, scholars never mentioned such a sighting in Europe.

According to astronomers, the bright light lingered in the sky for three months. After two years observers saw the light with the naked eye. It was visible even in the glare of the sun. At night its glow allowed people to read by its light. What was this strange light in the sky? Was this a visit from extraterrestrial life recorded by our ancestors?

Astronomers believe the world witnessed the explosion of a star we now call the Crab Nebula. Gases from the exploded star continue to expand into the universe at the speed of 1,300 kilometers per second.

Supernovae occur in any given galaxy about once every 100 years. Tycho Brahe and Johannes Kepler each recorded a supernova in our galaxy in 1572 and 1604, respectively. Unfortunately, since the invention of the telescope, astronomers have not witnessed a supernova in this galaxy.

Will our star, the sun, ever go supernova, and spread its molecules across the universe? Astronomers tell us that the sun is not immense enough to explode. A star must be at least ten times more massive than our Sun in order to die by explosion. The good news is that smaller stars use energy at a slower rate. Stars that become supernova burn through their energy source of hydrogen at such rapid rates that any life forms within the star's solar system cannot evolve into higher forms.

Perhaps by the time you read this article, a star in the Milky Way galaxy will explode into a brilliant supernova. You will have witnessed a catastrophic event astronomers dream of. If not, keep your eyes open. You never know when a supernova will light up the sky.

QUESTIONS FOR THE GUEST STAR

Literal Questions:

THE FACTS:

1. When did Chinese astronomers record the sighting of an unusually bright light in the sky?

_____

_____

_____

2. What do astronomers believe the world witnessed?

_____

_____

_____

3. How often do supernovae occur in any given galaxy?

_____

_____

_____

4. What happens to a star that becomes a supernova?

_____

_____

_____

SEQUENCE OF EVENTS:

5. What did the Anasazi of the American southwest do after they saw the light in the sky?

_____

_____

_____

6. What does a star do before it explodes into a supernova?

_____

_____

_____

Name _____   **Date** _____

Interpretive Questions:

DRAWING CONCLUSIONS:

7. Why do you think scholars never mentioned a sighting of the supernova in Europe?

_____

_____

_____

_____

MAKING INFERENCES:

8. How did the Anasazi artist feel about the strange light in the sky? What specific information from the story led you to your answer?

_____

_____

_____

_____

MAKING PREDICTIONS:

9. How will people around the world react when the next supernova appears in the sky? How will you feel when you see the bright light in the sky?

_____

_____

_____

_____

IDENTIFICATION OF CAUSE:

10. Why did the Chinese, Moslems, and the Anasazi artist record the event of the supernova?

_____

_____

_____

_____

IDENTIFICATION OF THE MAIN IDEA:

11. Write a title for the story. Use as few words as possible.

_____

_____

Name _____   **Date** _____

COMPARISON:

12. If a supernova occurred today, how would the reactions of witnesses be different from that of people who saw the 1054 supernova? How would their reactions be similar?

_____

_____

_____

_____

SUMMARIZE:

13. In your own words, describe a supernova.

_____

_____

_____

_____

EFFECT:

14. What effect, if any, would the occurrence of a modern supernova have on the science of astronomy?

_____

_____

_____

_____

FACT AND OPINION:

15. The story said, "Astronomers believe the world witnessed the explosion of a star we now call the Crab Nebula." Is this statement a fact, or is it the astronomers' opinion? How can you prove your answer?

_____

_____

_____

_____

ON YOUR OWN:

16. Write a question about the story for a teacher or another student to answer.

_____

_____

Name _____   **Date** _____

14. THERE LIVES A MONSTER IN THE LOCH
Reading Level = 8.76

ABOUT THE STORY

Theories on the existence of a monster in Scotland's Loch Ness are explored from the myths of kelpies to the popular speculation of a prehistoric dinosaur surviving in the lake's bottom. Although many people consider the monster of Loch Ness as nothing more than a folktale, researchers continue to comb the loch for the monster.

QUOTES OF THE WEEK

Quote 1:

"Ingratitude, thou marble-hearted fiend,
More hideous, when thou show'st thee in a child,
Than the sea-monster."[1] *(page 233)*—SHAKESPEARE, *KING LEAR*, I, iv, 283

Quote 2:

"Whoever fights monsters should see to it that in the process he does not become a monster. And when you look long into an abyss, the abyss also looks into you."[1] *(page 657)*—FRIEDRICH WILHELM NIETZSCHE, *BEYOND GOOD AND EVIL*, IV, 146

Quote 3:

There Leviathan
Hugest of living creatures, on the deep
Stretched like a promontory sleeps or swims,
And seems a moving land, and at his gills
Draws in, and at his trunk spouts out a sea."[1] *(page 286)*—JOHN MILTON, *PARADISE LOST*

INTERVIEW TOPIC

Interview a person of any age about monsters. Prepare a question list of literal and interpretive questions: "Do you believe in monsters? Why do you feel this way? When you hear the word *monster* what creature do you think of? Do you know about a monster in local folklore? What is it, and what is the legend? Why do you think people still talk about monsters even in modern times?"

PREVIEW WORDS

Mealfourvonie Mountain	*kelpies*
conglomerate	*plesiosaurs*

---

[1] Refer to *Quotation Footnotes for Level 8* on page 272.

250

WORD-ORIGIN STUDY

kelpie: *Kelpie,* also spelled *kelpy,* is a water monster from Gaelic folklore. The *kelpie* appears in the form of a horse and comes to drown people, or warn them of their drowning.

monster: The word *monster* originated from a Latin word that meant any unusual event or unnatural development that is sent as a message from the gods. The event is to admonish or warn people. Today, *monster* refers to any hideously malformed plant or creature.

List other words based on the word *monster.* Write the words with their definitions in your vocabulary notebook.

BOOKS TO READ

Ables, Harriette Sheffer. *Loch Ness Monster*. Mankato, MN: Crestwood House, 1987.

Baurer, Henry H. *The Enigma of Loch Ness: Making Sense of a Mystery*. Urbana: University of Illinois Press, 1986.

Berke, Sally Senzell. *Monster at Loch Ness*. Chicago: Raintree Editions, 1977.

Costello, Peter. *In Search of Lake Monsters*. New York: Coward McCann, 1974.

Epstein, Perle S. *Monsters*. Garden City, NY: Doubleday, 1973.

Farson, Daniel. *Mysterious Monsters*. London, England: Bloomsbury Books, 1979.

Gilleo, Alma. *Learning About Monsters*. Chicago: Children's Press, 1982.

Grant, John. *Monster Mysteries*. Secaucus, NJ: Chartwell Books, 1992.

Hall, Angus. *Monsters and Mythic Beasts*. Danbury, CT: Danbury Press, 1975.

Herbst, Judith. *Animal Amazing*. New York: Atheneum, 1991.

Holiday, F.W. *The Great Orm of Loch Ness: A Practical Inquiry Into the Nature and Habits of Water-Monsters*. New York: W.W. Norton & Company, Inc., 1969.

King-Smith. Dick, *The Water Horse*. New York: Crown Publishers, Inc., 1990.

MacGill-Callahan, Sheila. *The Last Snake in Ireland: A Story About St. Patrick*. New York: Holiday House, 1999.

Mackal, Roy P. *Monsters of Loch Ness*. Chicago: Swallow Press, 1980.

_____. *Searching for Hidden Animals*. Garden City: Doubleday, 1980.

Noonan, R.A. *Enter at Your Own Risk*. New York: Aladdin Paperbacks, 1995.

Reed, Don C. *The Kraken*. Honesdale, PA: Boyds Mills Press, 1995.

Sanchez, Isidro. *Monsters and Extraterrestrials*. Milwaukee, WI: Gareth Stevens Pub., 1996.

Steffens, Bradley. *The Loch Ness Monster*. San Diego: Lucent Books, 1995.

Time-Life Books. *Mysterious Creatures*. Alexandria, VA: Time–Life Books, 1988.

_____. *The Mysterious World*. Alexandria, VA: Time–Life Books, 1992.

Wilson, Colin. *Mysteries of the Universe*. New York: DK Publishing, 1997.

Zindel, Paul. *The Doom Stone*. New York: HarperCollins, 1995.

VIDEOS

Forsberg, Rolf. *Touring Scotland*. Chicago: Questar Home Video, 1990.

BOOK CLUB

Read Dick King-Smith's *The Water Horse* or Don C. Reed's *The Kraken*.

INTRODUCTORY ACTIVITIES

DAY ONE

Objective: The students will list monsters they have heard about, then discuss whether they believe the monsters are real or imaginary.

Make a poster-size chart with two horizontal lines dividing the chart into three sections. Label the first column MONSTER; the second, REAL; and the third, IMAGINARY. Ask the students to list monsters. As the students call out names such as Bigfoot, Loch Ness, Frankenstein's monster, etc., list the monsters in column one. Next, call out the names of each monster asking students to raise their hands if they think the monster is real. Note in column two the number of students raising their hands. Then ask the students to raise their hands if they think the monster is imaginary. Enter the number of raised hands in column three. Continue until the chart is complete.

Discuss which animals received the most votes for being real or being imaginary. Why do people feel this way? What do the monsters most people felt were real have in common? What do the monsters most people felt were imaginary have in common? Why do the students feel that people believe in monsters even in modern times?

Note: This chart can be used for Math assignments. For example, what percent of the class believes the Loch Ness monster is real? What percent of the class believes Bigfoot is imaginary? Based on the information found on the chart, what is a good estimate of the number of people in a group of 200 who would believe that the Loch Ness monster is real?

DAY TWO

STORY LESSON

Follow the *Presenting the Story Lesson* instructions in the Introduction. Each story lesson follows the same procedure; however, say the following in step 4: "The title of the story we're reading today is *There Lives a Monster in the Loch*. What do you think the story is about? What do you already know about the Loch Ness monster?"

EXTENSION ACTIVITIES

1. List the following monsters on the board:

Bigfoot	Leviathan
Water Kelpie	cockatrice
dragon	gargoyle
ogre	satyr
bogeyman	vampire
werewolf	zombie
Abominable Snowman	Dracula
Frankenstein's monster	Godzilla
King Kong	Gorgon
Harpy	Hydra
Minotaur	Ogopogo (of Okanagan Lake)
Manipogo (of Lake Manitoba)	mermaids (sirens)

    Students choose a monster and write a brief report (3 to 5 pages) about their monster. "Where does it live? What culture and country does it originate from? What are its unique features and personality traits? Can you show any proof of the monster's existence? Give examples of stories, legends, or sightings surrounding the monster. How does the monster reflect the belief system and culture of the people who began telling the legend of the monster?"

2. Read the story *The Last Snake in Ireland: A Story About St. Patrick* by Sheila MacGill-Callahan to the class. The story tells about the legend of St. Patrick driving the snakes out of Ireland, but the last remaining snake he tosses into Loch Ness.

    The students write a legend of their own about their monster from Extension Activity 1. They explain where the monster came from, why it lives the way it does, and where it goes when no one can see it. Encourage the students to use their imaginations.

3. The students make a model of their monster from Extension Activity 1. Use whatever materials the students would like—from boxes to clay to papier-mâché. Be as creative as possible. A good reference book is Isidro Sanchez's *Monsters and Extraterrestrials* which provides ideas and instructions on making model monsters.

4. Students look for legends of local monsters. "Are there any stories of monsters in your area? Look into Native American folklore. Talk to long-time residents. For example, Texas folklore tells of a monster living on Greer Island in Lake Worth just outside Fort Worth. Write the legend in your own words."

THERE LIVES A MONSTER IN THE LOCH

The eerie dark depths of Loch Ness, Scotland invites the imagination to conger visions of slithering, flesh-eating monsters. The mile-wide ribbon of water runs 23 miles with a maximum depth of 754 feet. Situated in the center of the valley of Glenmore, steep wooded mountains rim the lake. Rising 2,284 feet, Mealfourvonie Mountain stands guard. The water itself is murky, stained with peat, and maintains a chilling temperature of 42 degrees F.

For centuries, legend reports a monster living in the lake. These creatures are not unusual in Scottish and Irish folklore. Many Celtic myths dating as far back as the tenth century tell of kelpies living in waters throughout the region. The heads resemble that of a horse, hence the common name "horse-eels." Some observers compare the two raised ears to that of the horns, or tentacula, of a snail.

Popular theories compare the monster to plesiosaurs (marine reptiles of the dinosaur age). A sighting in 1933 by Mr. and Mrs. Spicer describes such a creature lumbering onto the shore of the lake. Horrified, the couple watched the monster snatch a lamb in its sharp-toothed mouth, then return to the waters with its meal.

Due to the large number of visitors to Loch Ness, more than 100,000 each year, observations of such a beast should be common. With sightings a rarity, some speculators believe the monster lurks in the depths feeding on plankton, perhaps in the form of a giant squid. However, large quantities of plankton needed to sustain such a large creature only live near the surface of the lake.

Perhaps, according to one hypothesis, the monster is a rare form of giant eel. Several members of the eel family live at the bottom of water feeding at the surface only at night.

More likely, the water kelpie is only a shadowy conglomerate of stories told for hundreds of years around the glow of a campfire. Perhaps the monster of Loch Ness is nothing more than a primeval memory of dark, liquid demons and imaginary phantoms dancing in the mist of decaying peat.

QUESTIONS FOR THERE LIVES A MONSTER IN THE LOCH

Literal Questions:

THE FACTS:

1. How long and wide is Loch Ness?

_____

_____

_____

2. What did Mr. and Mrs. Spicer report seeing in 1933?

_____

_____

_____

3. How many people visit Loch Ness each year?

_____

_____

_____

4. What is a giant eel?

_____

_____

_____

SEQUENCE OF EVENTS:

5. According to the sightings of Mr. and Mrs. Spicer, what did the monster do after it snatched a lamb in its sharp-toothed mouth?

_____

_____

_____

6. What is the last theory of the Loch Ness monster presented in the story?

_____

_____

_____

Name _____   Date _____

Interpretive Questions:

DRAWING CONCLUSIONS:

7. Drawing only from the information given in the story, what is a water kelpie?

_____

_____

_____

_____

MAKING INFERENCES:

8. Which theory of the Loch Ness monster does the author find most plausible? Why do you feel this way?

_____

_____

_____

_____

MAKING PREDICTIONS:

9. Will people continue to tell stories about the Loch Ness monster in the future? Why do you feel this way?

_____

_____

_____

_____

IDENTIFICATION OF CAUSE:

10. Why do thousands of people visit Loch Ness every year?

_____

_____

_____

_____

IDENTIFICATION OF THE MAIN IDEA:

11. Write a title for the story. Use as few words as possible.

_____

_____

Name _____   **Date** _____

COMPARISON:

12. Some people believe the Loch Ness monster is a giant squid while others believe it is a giant eel. How are these two theories alike? How are they different?

_____

_____

_____

_____

SUMMARIZE:

13. In your own words, tell which theory you believe is most likely true. Give supporting information to back up your hypothesis.

_____

_____

_____

_____

EFFECT:

14. What effect would the capture of the Loch Ness monster have on the folktale? Why do you feel this way?

_____

_____

_____

_____

FACT AND OPINION:

15. The story said, "With sightings a rarity, some speculators believe the monster lurks in the depths feeding on plankton, perhaps in the form of a giant squid." Is this statement a fact or an opinion? Why do you feel this way?

_____

_____

_____

_____

ON YOUR OWN:

16. Write a question about the story for a teacher or another student to answer.

_____

_____

Name _____ **Date** _____

15. "D. B. COOPER—WHERE ARE YOU?"
Reading Level = 8.76

ABOUT THE STORY

On November 24, 1971, a man calling himself D.B. Cooper hijacked an airplane in Portland, Oregon. After demanding and receiving $200,000 and a parachute, D.B. Cooper leapt from the plane just outside of Seattle, Washington. After an intense manhunt and thorough searches from hopeful treasure hunters, no trace of Cooper or the ransom were found.

QUOTES OF THE WEEK

Quote 1:

"If you give to a thief he cannot steal from you, and he is then no longer a thief."[1] *(page 875)*—WILLIAM SAROYAN, *THE HUMAN COMEDY*

Quote 2:

"Show me a liar, and I'll show thee a thief."[1] *(page 270)*—GEORGE HERBERT, *JACULA PRUDENTUM*, no. 652

INTERVIEW TOPIC

Conduct the interview after reading the Story Lesson. Interview a person who remembers the hijacking by D.B. Cooper in 1971. Give scant details only to jog the person's memory. Take careful notes of the person's recollections without correcting any errors he or she might make. After all the interviews are complete, compare the stories told by all the interview subjects. "How are their recollections alike? How are they different? Why are the stories of the same event told differently by each person? What does this tell you about the development of folktales?"

PREVIEW WORDS

hijacker   *tenacity*   *enterprising*

WORD-ORIGIN STUDY

hijack: *Hijack,* also spelled highjack, has evolved from its original meaning which finds its roots in the highwayman, a thief who would lay wait for victims travelling along a highway. Bootleggers, makers and sellers of illegal liquor, were often targets of highwaymen. Rumrunners referred to theft by highwaymen as a highjack, or hijack. Highwaymen specializing in stealing moonshine were called highjackers. Today *hijack* means to commandeer a vehicle of transportation—such as a train, car, airplane, or ship—and hold the innocent passengers as a means of obtaining money, safe passage, or other demands.

---

[1] Refer to *Quotation Footnotes for Level 8* on page 272.

tenacity: *Tenacity* comes from a word meaning "to hold." A tena-
                         cious person is persistent, and firmly holds his or her
                         ground.

List other words beginning with *ten-*, which have their roots in the word meaning "to hold." Write the words and their definitions in your vocabulary notebook.
Examples: tenacious, tenable, tenaculum, tenaille, tenancy, tenant, etc.

BOOKS TO READ

Adams, Barbara Johnston. *Crime Mysteries*. New York: Franklin Watts, 1988.

Arey, James A. *Sky Pirates*. New York: Charles Scribner's Sons, 1972.

Avi. *Windcatcher*. New York: Avon Books, 1992.

Blair, Ed. *Odyssey of Terror*. Nashville, TN: Broadman Press, 1977.

Burgess, Robert Forrest. *They Found Treasure*. New York: Dodd, Mead, 1977.

Conatser, Estee. *The Sterling Legend: The Facts Behind the Lost Dutchman Mine*. Dallas, TX:
    Ram Publishing Company, 1972.

Cussler, Clive. *Treasure: A Novel*. New York: Simon & Schuster, 1988.

Floyd, E. Randall. *Great American Mysteries: Raining Snakes, Fabled Cities of Gold, Strange
    Disappearances, and Other Baffling Tales*. Little Rock, AR: August House Publishers,
    1991.

Groushko, Michael. *Lost Treasures of the World*. London, England: Multimedia Books, 1993.

Hirschman, Dave. *Hijacked: The True Story of the Heroes of Flight 705*. New York: William
    Morrow, 1997.

Hubbard, David G. *Skyjackers: His Flights of Fantasy*. New York: The Macmillan
    Company, 1971.

_____. *Winning Back the Sky: A Tactical Analysis of Terrorism*. San Francisco: Saybrook
    Publishers, 1986.

Lehman, Ernest. *The French Atlantic Affair*. New York: Atheneum, 1977.

Marks, James M. *Hijacked!* Nashville, TN: Thomas Nelson Inc., Publishers, 1973.

Marx, Robert F. *Always Another Adventure*. Cleveland, OH: World Publishing Co., 1967.

Nance, John J. *The Last Hostage*. New York: Doubleday, 1998.

Noyes, Alfred. *The Highwayman*. San Diego: Harcourt Brace Jovanovich, Publishers, 1990.

Peretti, Frank E. *Trapped at the Bottom of the Sea*. Wheaton, IL: Crossway Books, 1988.

Reid, Struan. *The Children's Atlas of Lost Treasures*. Brookfield, CT: Millbrook Press, 1997.

Schwartz, Alvin. *Gold and Silver, Silver and Gold: Tales of Hidden Treasure*. New York:
    Farrar, Straus, Giroux, 1988.

Strasser, Todd. *Beyond the Reef*. New York: Dell Publishers, 1991.

Svidine, Nicholas. *Cossack Gold: The Secret of the White Army Treasure*. Boston: Little,
    Brown & Company, 1975.

Testrake, John. *Triumph Over Terror on Flight 847*. Old Tappan, NJ: F.H. Revell Co., 1987.

Titler, Dale Milton. *Haunted Treasures*. Englewood Cliffs, NJ: Prentice-Hall, 1976.

Wallace, Bill. *Danger in Quicksand Swamp*. New York: Pocket Books, 1991.

Westlake, Donald E. *Kahawa*. New York: Viking Press, 1982.

Williams, Brad and Choral Pepper. *Lost Treasures of the West*. New York: Holt, Rinehart and Winston, 1975.

Wilson, Kirk. *Unsolved: Great Mysteries of the Twentieth Century*. New York: Carroll & Graf, 1990.

Wulffson, Don L. *Amazing True Stories*. New York: Cobblehill Books, 1991.

Yenne, Bill. *Hidden Treasure: Where to Find It, How to Get It*. New York: Avon Books, 1997.

BOOK CLUB

Read John J. Nance's *The Last Hostage*, Frank E. Peretti's *Trapped at the Bottom of the Sea*, or *Hijacked!* by James M. Marks.

INTRODUCTORY ACTIVITIES

DAY ONE

Objective: The students will read a handout detailing the history of airplane hijacking in the late 1960s to early 1970s.

Make a copy of the story *Sky Piracy: Hijacking of the Sky* for each student. (See reproducible story on following page.) Prior to reading the article, discuss security measures at airports. "What security measures are obvious to the traveller? What security measures take place behind the scenes? Why are these measures taken? Do you feel secure from crime in the airport or in a plane? Why do you feel this way?"

After reading the story, complete the assignment at the bottom of the page.

DAY TWO

STORY LESSON

Follow the *Presenting the Story Lesson* instructions in the Introduction. Each story lesson follows the same procedure; however, say the following in step 4: "The title of the story we're reading today is 'D.B. Cooper—Where are You?' What do you think the story is about?"

SKY PIRACY: HIJACKING OF THE SKY

Sky piracy, airline hijacking, was a major concern to the flying public in the late 1960s to the early 1970s. Airlines became susceptible to hijacking because airplanes in flight securely held captive passengers and crew to the will of the hijackers.

Although we often think of hijacking as a fairly recent criminal ploy, sky piracy began just after World War II. Eleven hijackings took place between 1947 and 1950 by people looking to escape the Communist tyranny behind the Iron Curtain. Yet between 1930 and 1968 there were only sixteen successful U.S. skyjackings.

The majority of hijackings in the 1960s were also politically motivated. The first United States hijacker seized a plane as transport to Cuba. In 1968, thirteen commercial and five private planes were hijacked to Cuba. Suddenly, in 1969, hijacking of U.S. airplanes skyrocketed to forty attempted skyjackings. In most of these cases the hijackings ended without injury to passengers and crew.

Sky piracy took a violent turn in 1970. Members of the Popular Front for the Liberation of Palestine hijacked four airliners within days of each other demanding the release of fellow comrades from Israeli prisons. In the end, with one Arab hijacker killed and 300 innocent people held captive, Israel released seven prisoners. In response, the guerrillas blew up three jetliners.

On the national front, security measures such as metal detectors, an airline guard force of 2,000 special agents, and international efforts to prosecute and punish hijackers, helped to lower the incidence of airline piracy by more than fifty percent by 1970. Yet with all the extra security measures, hijackers continued to plague the airlines. These episodes included a demand for a one-million-dollar ransom which ended peacefully, and the shooting death of a pilot after a struggle broke out in the cockpit of a hijacked plane. Concerned pilots began to ask to carry guns for protection. As the battle over safety in the sky continued, hijackers wounded two Soviet pilots and killed a stewardess on October 15, 1970.

ASSIGNMENT:

Continue the story. Research the history of airline piracy. Did the world come together with an international agreement on the prosecution of hijackers? Did the occurrence and level of violence of hijacking decrease, and why?

EXTENSION ACTIVITIES

1. Read the poem *The Highwayman* by Alfred Noyes (1880-1958) to the class. "What information in the story tells you that the Highwayman is a robber? Who alerted the red-coat troop to the Highwayman's visits to Bess? Why do you think he reported the Highwayman's activities? How was the Highwayman like modern-day hijackers? How are they different?"

2. Is there a lost treasure in your area? Students look in reference books such as *Hidden Treasure: Where to Find It, How to Get It* by Bill Yenne, or talk to long-time residents to learn about legends of lost treasure in or around their community. Students write a report telling about how the treasure was hidden or lost, the folklore that grew out of the lost treasure, and attempts to find the treasure.

3. Students write a fictional mystery story based on the case of D.B. Cooper. "Place yourself in the story as a detective, treasure hunter, or simply a curious mystery buff. Continue the story where it left off. Did you find D.B. Cooper? Who was he? Where is he and the money? Create an exciting fictional mystery based on the factual events."

"D.B. COOPER—WHERE ARE YOU?"

On November 24, 1971, a man calling himself D.B. Cooper boarded a Northwest Airlines Boeing 727 in Portland, Oregon. Nothing in the quiet man's appearance raised anyone's suspicion. In his mid-forties, he wore an ordinary coat, slacks, tie, and overcoat. Clean shaven, the only distinguishing item was a pair of brown-tinted glasses firmly set on his nose.

After the flight began, Cooper signaled for the hostess. He asked her to take a note to the pilot. To encourage her to comply, he displayed what looked like several sticks of dynamite inside his briefcase. The demands in the note were short and precise: $200,000 in $20 bills placed in a knapsack, two backpacks, and two chest parachutes.

The pilot landed the plane full of confused passengers at the Seattle airport for refueling. Finally, Cooper received a white cloth sack filled with 10,000 $20 bills weighing 24 pounds which he placed in a carton measuring 8″ × 6″ × 27″.

After leaving Seattle, Cooper ordered the pilot to fly to Mexico City by way of Reno, Nevada. The pilot was to maintain an altitude of 7,000 feet, use 15% flaps, keep the landing gear down, and fly at a speed of about 200 miles per hour.

Twenty minutes after leaving Seattle, with the parachute and money bag strapped to his body, Cooper jumped from the plane. A search party immediately embarked using a computer to estimate his landing site. Searchers found no trace of Mr. Cooper after scouring the heavily wooded area about 30 to 40 miles north of Portland at the base of the Cascade Mountains. Tantalized by the tenacity of Cooper's escapade, enterprising merchants began selling T-shirts imprinted with the words "D.B. Cooper—Where Are You?"

A discovery of $3,000 of Cooper's marked bills near a river bank seven years later set off an explosion of treasure hunters, yet no one found the remaining $197,000. The brazen highjacker evaporated into the fabric of American folklore.

QUESTIONS FOR "D. B. COOPER—WHERE ARE YOU?"

Literal Questions:

THE FACTS:

1. When did D.B. Cooper board an airplane in Portland, Oregon?

_____

_____

_____

2. What did D.B. Cooper ask the hostess to do?

_____

_____

_____

3. What did D.B. Cooper demand in his note?

_____

_____

_____

4. When and where did someone discover $3,000 of Cooper's marked bills?

_____

_____

_____

SEQUENCE OF EVENTS:

5. What did D.B. Cooper do after the plane left Seattle, Washington?

_____

_____

_____

6. Write these events in chronological order: Cooper jumped from the plane with the parachute and money bag strapped to his body; Searchers found no trace of Mr. Cooper after scouring the heavily wooded area north of Portland; Cooper received a white cloth sack filled with 10,000 $20 bills.

_____

_____

_____

Name _____   **Date** _____

Interpretive Questions:

DRAWING CONCLUSIONS:

7. Based on the information in the story, what one word best describes D.B. Cooper?

_____

_____

_____

_____

MAKING INFERENCES:

8. How did the public feel about D.B. Cooper's adventure? On what information do you base your answer?

_____

_____

_____

_____

MAKING PREDICTIONS:

9. Will D.B. Cooper ever step forward and solve the mystery he began over 25 years ago? Why do you feel this way?

_____

_____

_____

_____

IDENTIFICATION OF CAUSE:

10. Why did merchants sell T-shirts imprinted with the words "D.B. Cooper—Where Are You?"

_____

_____

_____

_____

IDENTIFICATION OF THE MAIN IDEA:

11. Write a title for the story. Use as few words as possible.

_____

_____

Name _____ **Date** _____

COMPARISON:

12. How was D.B. Cooper like the treasure hunters who searched for the money along a river bank? How was he different?

_____

_____

_____

_____

SUMMARIZE:

13. In your own words, tell how D.B. Cooper stole $200,000.

_____

_____

_____

_____

EFFECT:

14. What effect might D.B. Cooper's hi-jacking have had on America's airport security? Why do you feel this way?

_____

_____

_____

_____

FACT AND OPINION:

15. The story said, "In his mid-forties, he (D.B. Cooper) wore an ordinary coat, slacks, tie, and overcoat." Is this a fact or someone's opinion? How can you prove your answer?

_____

_____

_____

_____

ON YOUR OWN:

16. Write a question about the story for a teacher or another student to answer.

_____

_____

Name _____   **Date** _____

REFERENCES FOR LEVEL 8

IS ANYONE AWAKE OUT THERE?

Cohn, Deborah L. "Walk or Run: Benefits of Exercise." *Current Health*, 20, no. 8 (April 1994), 25(3).

"Latest Teen Excuse: Report in Magazine *Sleep* Indicates Hormones Cause Teenagers to Stay Up Later at Night and Sleep-in Later on the Weekends." *Time*, 141, no. 18 (May 3, 1993), 25.

Martin, Cate. "Dozing At Your Desk?: Doctors Say Teens Need More Sleep and School Should Start Later!" *Science World*, 52, no. 11, 9(3).

Poikolainen, Kari. "Life Events and Other Risk Factors for Somatic Symptoms in Adolescence." *Pediatrics*, 96, no. 1 (July 1995), 59(5).

"Teenagers in High School Need Proper Amount of Sleep to Excel in School, Study Reveals." *Jet*, 91, no. 12 (February 10, 1997), 62.

FERRIS AND HIS WHEEL

Karwatka, Dennis. *Technology's Past: America's Industrial Revolution and the People Who Delivered the Goods.* Ann Arbor, MI: Prakken Publications, Inc., 1996, pp. 142-144.

Pictorial Encyclopedia: People Who Made America. Skokie, IL: United States History Society, Inc., 1973, p. 372.

WHERE DOES ALL THE MONEY GO?

Bodnar, Janet. *Kiplinger's Money-Smart Kids (and Parents, Too!).* Washington, D.C.: Kiplinger Books, 1993, pp. 171-188.

Branch, Shelly. "How to Teach a Teen the Value of a Buck." *Money*, 24, no. 12 (December 1995), 132-138.

Godfrey, Neale S. *A Penny Saved: Teaching Your Children the Values and Life Skills They Need to Live in the Real World.* New York: Simon & Schuster, 1995, pp. 177-189.

THE HALE HOUSE OF HARLEM

"Clara Hale Dies: Cared for 1,000 Drug-Addicted Babies." *Jet*, 83, no. 11 (January 11, 1993), 56(2).

Cunningham, Ann Marie. "Loving the Unloved Children: Following Her Mother's Example, Dr. Lorraine Hale Brings Hope to the Neediest Kids." *Ladies Home Journal*, 114, no. 11 (November 1997), 206(3).

"God Bless the Children: Quotes From Eighteen Wisdom Speakers." *Essence*, 88, no. 7 (May 1995), 6(5).

"Hale, Clara: Obituary." *Current Biography*, 54, no. 2 (February 1993), 58.

"Obituaries: Hale, Clara M." *The Americana Annual: 1993.* Canada: Grolier Incoporated, 1993, p. 406.

SIR WALTER RALEIGH'S LOST COLONY

Gruver, Rebecca Brooks, *An American History* (4th ed.). New York: Alfred A. Knopf, 1985, p. 30.

Reader's Digest Staff. *Strange Stories, Amazing Facts: Stories That Are Bizarre, Unusual, Odd, Astonishing & Often Incredible.* Pleasantville, NY: Reader's Digest Association, Inc., 1976, p. 340.

LEWIS WICKES HINE

Berlau, John. "The Paradox of Child-Labor Reform." *Insight on the News*, 13, no. 43 (November 24, 1997), 20(2).

Cahan, Rhoda and William Cahan. *No Time for School, No Time for Play: The Story of Child Labor in America.* New York: Julian Messner, 1972, pp. 14-15.

Freedman, Russell. *Kids at Work: Lewis Hine and the Crusade Against Child Labor.* New York: Clarion Books, 1994.

MYSTERIOUS CRASH OF AIRSHIP <u>AKRON</u>: 73 FEARED DEAD

"Aviation, History of." *Collier's Encyclopedia* (1953), 2, 579.

Daniel, Clifton (ed.). *Chronicle of the Twentieth Century.* Mount Kisco, NY: Chronicle Publications, 1987, pp. 396, 419.

"Lighter-than-Air Craft." *Collier's Encyclopedia* (1953), 12, 282.

THE TRUE POOH

Milne, Christopher. *The Enchanted Places.* New York: E.P. Dutton & Co., 1975.

Thwaite, Ann. *The Brilliant Career of Winnie-the-Pooh: The Definitive History of the Best Bear in All the World.* New York: Dutton Children's Book, 1992.

SCOTT JOPLIN: RAGTIME KING

Mitchel, Barbara. *Raggin': A Story About Scott Joplin.* Minneapolis: Carolrhoda Books, 1987.

Pictorial Encyclopedia: People Who Made America. Skokie, IL: United States History Society, Inc., 1973, p. 661.

"Ragtime." *Encyclopedia Americana* (1963), 23, 134.

BETTY FORD: A TRUE FIRST LADY

Feinman, Jeffrey. *Betty Ford.* New York: Universal-Award House, Inc., 1976.

"First Ladies of the United States," *Our Wonderful World Encyclopedia* (1962), 18, 129.

Gould, Lewis L. (ed.). *American First Ladies: Their Lives and Their Legacy.* New York: Garland Publishing, Inc., 1996, pp. 536-555.

Rachel Carson: The Coming of a Silent Spring

Carson, Rachel. *Silent Spring*. Boston: Houghton Mifflin Company, 1962, p. 5.

Kudlinski, Kathleen V. *Rachel Carson: Pioneer of Ecology*. New York: Puffin Books, 1988.

Paradise, Jean (ed.). *Collier's Encyclopedia Yearbook* (1965). New York, NY: The Crowell-Collier Publishing Company, 1965, p. 404.

Shores, Louis, ed. *Collier's Encyclopedia Yearbook* (1963). New York: The Crowell–Collier Publishing Company, 1963, pp. 71, 120, 145, 267, 306.

The Return of Supersonic Flight

Lindsey, Robert H. "Air Transportation." *The Americana Annual: 1970*. Canada: Grolier, Inc., 1970, p. 67.

_____. "Air Transportation." *The Americana Annual: 1974*. Canada: Grolier, Inc., 1974, p. 598.

Weingarten, Tara. "Beyond the Concorde, and Other Fantasy Flights." *Newsweek*, 131, no. 8 (February 23, 1998), p. 12.

The Guest Star

Hadingham, Evan. *Early Man and the Cosmos*. New York: Walker and Company, 1984, pp. 142-144.

Sagan, Carl. *Cosmos*. New York: Random House, 1980, pp. 217, 232, 237-238.

There Lives a Monster in the Loch

Grant, John. *Monster Mysteries*. Secaucus, NJ: Cartwell Books, Inc., 1992, pp. 104-110.

Hall, Angus. *Monsters and Mystic Beast*. London, England: The Danbury Press, 1975, pp. 65-67.

"Ness, Loch." *Encyclopedia Americana* (1963) 20, 112.

Stuttaford, Andrew. "Loch Roswell?," *National Review*, 49, no. 17 (September 15, 1997), 24 (2).

"D.B. Cooper—Where Are You?"

Groushko, Michael. *Lost Treasures of the World*. London, England: Multimedia Books Limited, 1993, pp. 152-153.

Hubbard, David G. *Winning Back the Sky: A Tactical Analysis of Terrorism*. San Francisco: Saybrook Publishers, 1986.

Lindsey, Robert H. "Hijacking." *The Americana Annual: 1971*. New York: Americana Corporation, 1971, pp. 86-87.

Webster's Collegiate Dictionary (5th ed.). Springfield, MA: G. & C. Merriam Co., Publishers, 1947, p. 471.

QUOTATION FOOTNOTES
FOR LEVEL 8

[1] Bartlett, John. *Bartlett's Familiar Quotations*. Boston: Little, Brown and Company, 1980.

[2] Peter, Laurance J. *Peter's Quotations: Ideas of Our Times*. New York: William Morrow and Company, Inc., 1977.

[3] Applewhite, Ashton, William R. Evans III, and Andrew Frothingham. *And I Quote: The Definitive Collection of Quotes, Sayings, and Jokes for the Contemporary Speechmaker.* New York: St. Martin's Press, 1992.

[4] Rowes, Barbara. *The Book of Quotes*. New York: E.P. Dutton, 1979.

[5] Jackson, Robert. *Airships: A Popular History of Dirigibles, Zeppelins, Blimps and Other Lighter-than-Air Craft*. Garden City, NY: Doubleday & Company, Inc., 1973.

[6] Milne, A.A. *When We Were Very Young*. New York: E.P. Dutton & Co., Inc., 1924.

[7] Sagan, Carl. *Cosmos*. New York: Random House, 1980.

[8] Freedman, Russell. *Kids at Work: Lewis Hine and the Crusade Against Child Labor*. New York: Clarion Books, 1994.

[9] Ford, Betty and Chris Chase. *A Glad Awakening,* Graden City, NY: Doubleday & Company, Inc., 1987.

WORD-ORIGIN STUDY REFERENCE
FOR LEVEL 8

Unless otherwise noted:

Webster, Noah. *Webster's New Twentieth Century Dictionary of the English Language*. New York: The World Publishing Company, 1964.

READING LEVEL 9

STORY TITLE	READING LEVEL	PAGE
1. Omen in the Sky	9.00	274
2. "Cosmic Rocket:" Soviets Winning the Space Race	9.01	282
3. Witches and Lies: The Salem Witch Hunt	9.10	290
4. The Glorious Tombs of China	9.16	299
5. Automaton	9.18	308
6. America Mourns	9.18	317
7. Dreaming to Remember	9.28	326
8. Summer Camp Isn't What It Used to Be	9.28	336
9. "Ma" Barker Gunned Down by F.B.I.	9.34	344
10. Joseph Cardinal Bernardin	9.44	353
11. What Does "QWERTY" Mean?	9.45	361
12. Adopt-a-Senior	9.46	370
13. 1,200 Dead in Cameroon	9.55	378
14. Predicting the Next Earthquake	9.59	386
15. Charles Kuralt: Journalist of the People	9.64	395
References for Level 9		404
Quotation Footnotes for Level 9		406
Word-Origin Study Reference for Level 9		406

1. OMEN IN THE SKY
Reading Level = 9.00

ABOUT THE STORY

This story tells about the history of superstitions surrounding comets. It includes stories from ancient Rome to modern time.

QUOTES OF THE WEEK

Quote 1:

"When beggars die, there are no comets seen;
The heavens themselves blaze forth the death of princes."[1] *(page 215)*
—WILLIAM SHAKESPEARE, *JULIUS CAESAR*, II, ii, 30

Quote 2:

"A professor can never better distinguish himself in his work than by encouraging a clever pupil, for the true discoverers are among them, as comets amongst the stars."[1] *(page 350)*—LINNAEUS (1707-1778)

Quote 3:

"A fearful star is the comet, and not easily appeased, as appeared in the late civil troubles when Octavius was Consul; a second time by the . . . war of Pompey and Caesar; and, in our own time, when, Claudius Caesar having been poisoned, the empire was left to Domitian, in whose reign there appeared a blazing comet."[5] *(page 25)*—PLINY THE ELDER (c.23-79 A.D.)

INTERVIEW TOPIC

Interview a person who has seen a comet. Prepare a question list that includes literal and interpretive questions: "What was the name of the comet you saw? What was the year and month you saw the comet? In your own words, explain what a comet is. Describe the comet. How did seeing the comet make you feel? Why did you feel this way? Do you believe that comets are omens of disaster or death? Why do you feel this way?"

PREVIEW WORDS

apocalypse	*dirk*	*forewarning*
Emperor Ludwig of Pious	*Pliny*	*prophesized*

WORD-ORIGIN STUDY

astronomy: *Astronomy* is derived from the Greek work *astron*, meaning "star." The suffix, *nomos*, means "to arrange or dis-

---

[1] Refer to *Quotation Footnotes for Level 9* on page 406.

[5] Refer to *Quotation Footnotes for Level 9* on page 406.

tribute." *Astronomy* is the study of the distribution and nature of heavenly bodies including stars, planets, comets, and satellites.

apocalypse: *Apocalypse* comes from Greek words meaning "to remove the cover or concealment." *Apocalypse* means revelation, or disclosure. The apocalypse in Christian writing appears in the last book of the New Testament: The Book of Revelation. The Book of Revelation describes in cryptic form how God will disclose or reveal Himself to His creatures. Many people believed that a comet was a sign from God heralding the apocalypse.

List other words beginning with the prefix *apo-* that mean "off, from, away from, or separation." Write the words and their definitions in your vocabulary notebook.

BOOKS TO READ

Asimov, Isaac. *Asimov's Guide to Halley's Comet*. New York: Walker, 1985.

Benford, Gregory. *Heart of the Comet*. New York: Bantam Books, 1986. (Science Fiction)

Calder, Nigel. *The Comet Is Coming!: The Feverish Legacy of Mr. Halley*. New York: Viking Press, 1981.

Flaste, Richard, Holcomb Noble, Walter Sullivan, and John Noble Wilford. *The New York Times Guide to the Return of Halley's Comet*. New York: Random House, 1985.

Fradin, Dennis B. *Halley's Comet*. Chicago: Children's Press, 1985.

Heckart, Barbara Hooper. *Edmond Halley: The Man and His Comet*. Chicago: Children's Press, 1984.

Krupp, E.C. *The Comet and You*. New York: Macmillan Publishing Co., 1985.

Lancaster-Brown, Peter. *Halley and His Comet*. New York: Sterling Publishing Co., 1985.

Olson, Roberta J.M. *Fire and Ice: A History of Comets in Art*. New York: Walker, 1985.

Pellowski, Anne. *Have You Seen a Comet?* New York: The John Day Company, 1971.

Sagan, Carl and Ann Druyan. *Comet*. New York: Random House, 1985.

United States Government. *Comet Halley Returns: A Teachers' Guide—1985-1986*. Washington, D.C.: Government Printing Office, 1986.

Wiegand, Roberta. *The Year of the Comet*. Scarsdale, NY: Bradbury Press, 1984.

VIDEOS

Comet Halley Returns. Eugene, OR: New Dimension Films, 1985.

Night of the Comet. CBS/Fox, 1984. (rated PG-13)

BOOK CLUB

Read Roberta Wiegand *The Year of the Comet* or Gregory Benford's *Heart of the Comet*.

INTRODUCTORY ACTIVITIES

DAY ONE

Objective: The students will learn about what a comet is and how a comet orbits the sun.

Invite a spokesperson to class who has a background in astronomy, particularly comets. Sources for speakers might be a local astronomy club, university or college professors, college students recommended by their professors, etc.

Ask the speaker to talk about what comets are, and how they orbit the sun. "What are the more famous comets? When is the next known comet due to visit our skies? Are comets astronomical objects that people should fear? Why do you feel this way, and on what do you base your opinion? Why do you find the study of comets and astronomy interesting? Why is astronomy an important field of science?" End the class period with a question-and-answer session.

DAY TWO

STORY LESSON

Follow the *Presenting the Story Lesson* instructions in the Introduction. Each story lesson follows the same procedure; however, say the following in step 4: "The title of the story we're reading today is *Omen in the Sky*. What do you think the story is about? What do you already know about comets?"

EXTENSION ACTIVITIES

1. Each student researches, and designs a comet chart. The charts can be made of any material with any creative design. The charts must consist of information on at least ten comets that are due to visit Earth's skies over the next several years including the comets' names, the orbit periods in years, and the months/years the comets are due to pass Earth. Sources for such information include the Internet, local planetariums, and astronomy clubs.

2. Students recreate artwork featuring comets on ceramic tiles or plates. If your school has a kiln, ask the art teacher for help. Otherwise, invite to the class a representative from a local craft shop specializing in ceramics. Using artwork found in books, such as *Fire and Ice: A History of Comets in Art* by Roberta J.M. Olson or *Comet* by Carl Sagan and Ann Druyan, recreate a comet design on a plate or tile. These books contain several beautiful pieces of art from which to choose. The students can make their own designs after reviewing the illustrations, or recreate a particular design on their ceramic piece.

3. When a comet is within view, have a comet countdown. Ask the school newspaper or local newspaper if your students can write a daily countdown article leading up to the day of the comet. Include in the article student illustrations and interesting facts about the comet or comets in general.

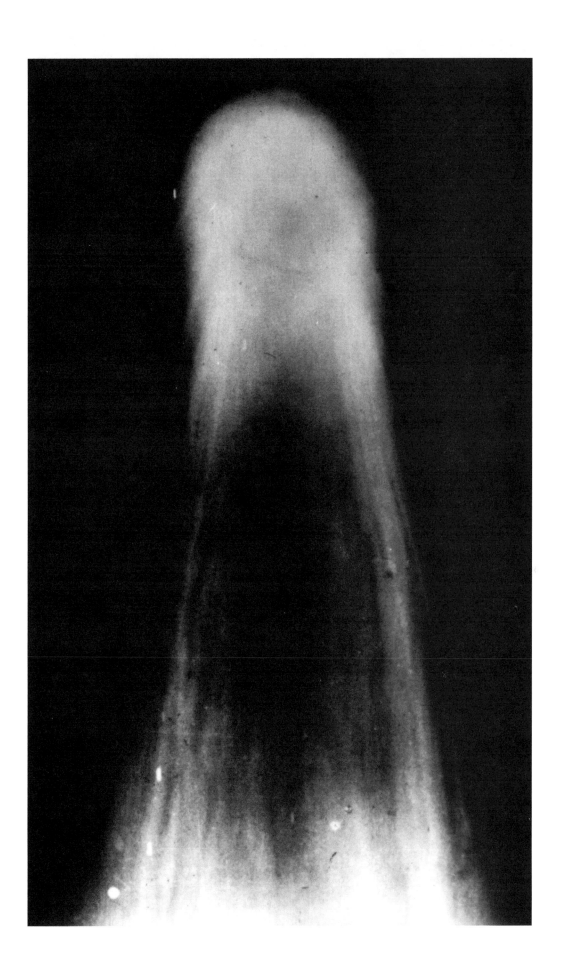

OMEN IN THE SKY

Imagine living in ancient times when there are no telescopes to look deep into space, or electrical lights to obscure the stars. One night you look out over the horizon, and see a giant smear of light attached to a fiery orb hanging in the sky. Where did the object come from? Is it an omen sent from God? Could this be a sign telling of a terrible apocalypse?

With a firm belief in astrology, many early civilizations regarded comets as omens of doom, and superstitions surrounding the comet linger in its name. According to ancient tradition, women in mourning let their hair hang down because they could not find the strength to tend to their hair. Like a beautiful grieving lady, a comet lets its shimmering "hair" trail behind as it passes overhead; therefore we derive our modern word, *comet*, from the Greek **kometes**, meaning "hairy."

Comets inspired other dreadful fantasies of the imagination. Pliny (*c.* 23–79 A.D.), a Roman writer and naturalist, referred to comets as mystical weapons in the form of blazing boulders, swords, and dirks.

Many horrific events seemed to coincide with the appearance of comets, thus reinforcing the comet's image of a forewarning of disaster. The assassination of Julius Caesar in 44 B.C. occurred in the year of a comet, and many astrologers credited the 837 A.D. comet as a precursor to the death three years later of Emperor Ludwig of Pious. Even Mark Twain accurately prophesied his death at the return of Halley's comet.

Not only were comets associated with death, but also with war. The comet of 66 A.D. preceded the fall of Jerusalem to Rome by four years. Astrologers attributed a comet as a predictor of the conquest of England by Normandy.

In 1910, the return of Halley's comet created panic throughout the world. This close encounter prompted rumors of the extinction of all life on Earth as our planet passed through the comet's gaseous tail. Not even the revelations of science can erase the centuries of frightening folklore that flies on the tail of a comet.

QUESTIONS FOR OMEN IN THE SKY

Literal Questions:

THE FACTS:

1. From what language is the word *comet* derived?

_____

_____

_____

2. Who was Pliny?

_____

_____

_____

3. Who prophetized his death at the return of Halley's comet?

_____

_____

_____

4. Why were people afraid of Halley's comet in 1910?

_____

_____

_____

SEQUENCE OF EVENTS:

5. When did the assassination of Julius Caesar occur: before, during, or after the comet of 44 B.C.?

_____

_____

_____

6. What historical event occurred four years after the comet of 66 A.D.?

_____

_____

_____

Name _____   Date _____

Interpretive Questions:

DRAWING CONCLUSIONS:

7. What one word best describes the superstitions surrounding comets?

_____

_____

_____

_____

MAKING INFERENCES:

8. What emotion are people inclined to experience when they are faced with the unknown? What specific information in the story led you to your answer?

_____

_____

_____

_____

MAKING PREDICTIONS:

9. Will people continue to believe comets are omens of doom? Why do you feel this way?

_____

_____

_____

_____

IDENTIFICATION OF CAUSE:

10. Why did people associate comets with tragic events rather than joyous occurrences?

_____

_____

_____

_____

IDENTIFICATION OF THE MAIN IDEA:

11. Write a title for the story. Use as few words as possible.

_____

_____

Name _____   **Date** _____

COMPARISON:

12. How were people's reactions to the comet of 1910 like the reactions of people toward the year 2000, such as the Y2K computer problem? How were they different?

_____

_____

_____

_____

SUMMARIZE:

13. In your own words, summarize the story using as few words as possible.

_____

_____

_____

_____

EFFECT:

14. How would comet superstitions have changed if ancient people saw comets as visions of angels bringing blessings rather than mystical swords and dirks?

_____

_____

_____

_____

FACT AND OPINION:

15. Is it a fact that the comet of 44 B.C. foretold the assassination of Julius Caesar? Why do you feel this way?

_____

_____

_____

_____

ON YOUR OWN:

16. Write a question about the story for a teacher or another student to answer.

_____

_____

Name _____   **Date** _____

2. "COSMIC ROCKET": SOVIETS WINNING THE SPACE RACE

Reading Level = 9.01

ABOUT THE STORY

This story is part of the *Moments in Time* series. In 1959, the Soviet Union launched a probe toward the sun. Its purpose included measuring the moon's "magnetic field, cosmic radiation, and interplanetary space." Due to the success of satellites such as Sputnik, many people predicted that the Soviet Union would win the race to the moon.

QUOTES OF THE WEEK

Quote 1:

"*Sputnik* doesn't worry me one iota. Apparently from what they say, they have put one small ball in the air."[4] *(page 54)*—DWIGHT D. EISENHOWER (1957)

Quote 2:

"There is just one thing I can promise you about the outer-space program: Your tax dollar will go farther."[4] *(page 54)*—WERNHER VON BRAUN

Quote 3:

"This nation has tossed its cap over the wall of space, and we have no choice but to follow it."[4] *(page 54)*—JOHN F. KENNEDY

INTERVIEW TOPIC

Interview a person who remembers the space race of the 1950s and 1960s. Prepare a question list that includes literal and interpretive questions: "What was the affect of *Sputnik* on the United State's public? Why did they react this way? What was the goal of the space race? Did you support the space race? Why did you feel this way? In retrospect, do you think the space race was worth the investment? Why do you feel this way? What was the most memorable moment of the space race? Why do you feel this way?"

PREVIEW WORDS

Lunik	*interplanetary*	*Sputnik*
Lainka	*ramifications*	*iota*

WORD-ORIGIN STUDY

satellite: The origin of the word *satellite* comes from a word meaning "guard or attendant." A satellite accompanies or encircles a person of importance, such as royalty. In astronomy, a satellite, like Earth's moon, circles a planet.

---

[4] Refer to *Quotation Footnotes for Level 9* on page 406.

> *ramifications:*   *Ramification* has its roots in the Latin word *ramus*, meaning "a branch." Ramifying is the arrangement of branches (offshoots) of a plant. *Ramification* in this week's story refers to an offshoot, or consequence of an action.

List other words based on the Latin word *ramus,* such as ramiforn, ramified, ramify, ramose, etc. Write the words and their definitions in your vocabulary notebook.

BOOKS TO READ

Appleton, Victor II. *Tom Swift on the Phantom Satellite.* New York: Grosset & Dunlap, 1956.

Baker, David. *The History of Manned Space Flight.* New York: Crown Publishers, 1982.

Buckley, William F. *Who's on First.* Garden City, NY: Doubleday & Company, 1980.

Clark, Phillip. *The Soviet Manned Space Program: An Illustrated History of the Men, the Missions, and the Spacecraft.* New York: Orion Books, 1988.

Curtis, Anthony R. *Space Almanac: Facts, Figures, Names, Dates, Places, Lists, Charts, Tables, Maps Covering Space From Earth to the Edge of the Universe.* Woodsboro, MD: Arcsoft, 1989.

Dethloff, Henry C. *Suddenly, Tomorrow Came: A History of the Johnson Space Center.* Washington, D.C.: National Aeronautics and Space Administration, 1993.

Kerrod, Robin. *NASA: Visions of Space: Capturing the History of NASA.* Philadelphia: Courage Books, 1990.

Shepard, Alan B. *Moon Shot: The Inside Story of America's Race to the Moon.* Atlanta: Turner Publishing, 1994.

Sobel, Lester A. *Space: From Sputnik to Gemini.* New York: Facts on File, 1965.

Spangenburg, Ray. *Opening the Space Frontier.* New York: Facts on File, 1989.

_____. *Space People from A-Z.* New York: Facts on File, 1990.

Vogt, Gregory. *Space Satellites.* New York: Franklin Watts, 1987.

Von Braun, Wernher. *History of Rocketry and Space Travel.* New York: Thomas Y. Crowell, 1975.

Walter, William J. *Space Age.* New York: Random House, 1992.

BOOK CLUB

Read William F. Buckley, Jr.'s *Who's on First.*

INTRODUCTORY ACTIVITIES

DAY ONE

> *Objective:*   The students will discuss the Cold War and how it affected the space race.

Invite speakers to class with knowledge of the Cold War. They might be retired military personnel, historians, college professors, or history students recommended by college professors. Discuss how the fears surrounding the Cold War affected the development of space technology during the late 1950s and early 1960s. "What was *Sputnik?* Why were the American people and government officials concerned about *Sputnik?* What was the official American response, and why? President Eisenhower seemed to down play the relevance of *Sputnik* (see Quote 2). Why did he feel this way? Why did President Kennedy, the following president, emphasize the space race and the importance of the American space program (see Quote 3)?" End the class with a question-and-answer session.

DAY TWO

STORY LESSON

Follow the *Presenting the Story Lesson* instructions in the Introduction. Each story lesson follows the same procedure; however, say the following in step 4: "The title of the story we're reading today is *'Cosmic Rocket': Soviets Winning the Space Race.* What do you think the story is about? What do you already know about the space race?"

EXTENSION ACTIVITIES

1. The students make a timeline of the important events of the Cold War. They make a second timeline of the Soviet space program's historic accomplishments. Finally, the students make a third timeline tracing the American space program. Each timeline may be constructed by separate groups of students. Be sure the timelines are measured the same. For example, begin with the same year, and keep the same spacing between the years and months along each timeline. In this way the students can easily compare the timelines. "What conclusions, if any, can you draw from studying the timelines? Why do you feel this way? What conclusions can you draw from the development of technology, and the political/historical events that surrounded them?"

2. The students read *Tom Swift on the Phantom Satellite* by Victor Appleton II, written in 1956, one year prior to the launching of the Soviet satellite *Sputnik.* "What does the style and tone of his writing hint about American interest in space? What space technology did the author create that had not been invented when he wrote the story? Did you enjoy the story? Why or why not?"

3. Ask the students to write a science fiction story about a satellite set in the late 1950s or 1960s. They must create a main character, such as Tom Swift, and write a story between seven and ten pages long. Encourage the use of reference books or the Internet to find factual information to bring an air of authenticity to the story.

January 5, 1959

"COSMIC ROCKET:"
SOVIETS WINNING THE SPACE RACE

Moscow claimed yet another victory in the space race as the *Lunik* satellite sped past the moon. The "cosmic rocket," which bears the Soviet hammer-and-sickle, represents not only an important milestone in space exploration, but also Soviet dominance in space.

The Soviets launched *Lunik* on Friday. *Lunik* passed over Hawaii as it began its historic trip into space. Shooting toward its final destination, a solar orbit, *Lunik* travels at the velocity of 5,500 miles per hour. Weighing 3,238 pounds, *Lunik* has now moved 343,750 miles from Earth. *Lunik's* 795 pounds of cargo include instruments to measure the moon's "magnetic field, cosmic radiation, and interplanetary space."

Lunik flies on the successes of several previous Soviet space missions. On October 4, 1957, the Soviet Union proudly announced the acclaimed deployment of *Sputnik*. Weighing 184 pounds, *Sputnik* became the first man-made satellite to orbit our planet.

By November 1957, the Soviets shocked the world again with the announcement of a second satellite. This historic flight included living cargo, a dog named *Lainka*. Soviet spokesmen stated, "It is completely realistic to speak about the launching of a satellite which will exist for tens and hundreds of years."

In these tense years filled with concern for nuclear warfare, President Eisenhower ignored the possible military ramifications. He stated he does not worry "one iota."

In the near future, Soviet space scientists hope to photograph the dark side of the moon. The moon does not revolve on its axis. Therefore, no one has seen the dark side of the moon which constantly faces away from Earth. The Soviet Academy of Sciences hopes to release its finding by October of this year.

QUESTIONS FOR "COSMIC ROCKET": SOVIETS WINNING THE SPACE RACE

Literal Questions:

THE FACTS:

1. When did the story take place?

_____

_____

_____

2. Who launched *Lunik?*

_____

_____

_____

3. How much did *Lunik* weigh?

_____

_____

_____

4. What was *Lainka?*

_____

_____

_____

SEQUENCE OF EVENTS:

5. Write the following events in chronological order: The Soviet Union announced the deployment of *Sputnik;* The Soviets launched *Lunik;* The Soviets launched a second satellite containing living cargo.

_____

_____

_____

6. Where was *Lunik* shooting toward after it passed over Hawaii?

_____

_____

_____

Name _____ **Date** _____

Interpretive Questions:

DRAWING CONCLUSIONS:

7. Why did the author believe the Soviets were winning the space race?

_____

_____

_____

_____

MAKING INFERENCES:

8. Was the author concerned about the military ramifications of the Soviet Union's advances in space? What specific information led you to your answer?

_____

_____

_____

_____

MAKING PREDICTIONS:

9. Will the world ever see another international scientific competition like that of the U.S. and Soviet space race? Why do you feel this way?

_____

_____

_____

_____

IDENTIFICATION OF CAUSE:

10. Why was the Soviet Union working toward dominance in space?

_____

_____

_____

_____

IDENTIFICATION OF THE MAIN IDEA:

11. Write a title for the story. Use as few words as possible.

_____

_____

Name _____ **Date** _____

COMPARISON:

12. At the time of the story, what was the level of the Soviet Union's space technology compared with that of the United States? What specific information led you to your answer?

_____

_____

_____

_____

SUMMARIZE:

13. In your own words, tell about the Soviet Union's advances in space during the 1950s.

_____

_____

_____

_____

EFFECT:

14. What effect, if any, did the launching of Soviet satellites have on America's national pride?

_____

_____

_____

_____

FACT AND OPINION:

15. The story said, ". . . President Eisenhower ignored the possible military ramifications." Is this statement a fact or the author's opinion? How can you prove your answer?

_____

_____

_____

_____

ON YOUR OWN:

16. Write a question about the story for a teacher or another student to answer.

_____

_____

Name _____   Date _____

3. WITCHES AND LIES: THE SALEM WITCH HUNT

Reading Level = 9.10

ABOUT THE STORY

In 1692, several young girls in the Puritan village of Salem, Massachusetts, began to behave in unusual ways. The girls told their families witches tormented them. This set off a witch hunt that ended in the deaths of nineteen accused witches. In the end, the girls admitted the hunt was based on a lie.

QUOTES OF THE WEEK

Quote 1:

"Fear of serious injury cannot alone justify suppression of free speech and assembly. Men feared witches and burned women. It is the function of speech to free men from the bondage of irrational fears."[1] *(page 677)*
—LOUIS DEMBITZ BRANDEIS, *WHITNEY V. CALIFORNIA, 274 U.S. 376* (1927)

Quote 2:

". . . well over a hundred (alleged witches) languished for months in cramped, dark, stinking prisons, hungry and thirsty, never moving from the walls they were chained to, unsure if they would ever go free."[6] *(page 95)*
—FRANCES HILL, author and journalist during the Salem witch trials

Quote 3:

"We walked in clouds and could not see our way. And we have most cause to be humbled for error . . . which cannot be retrieved."[6] *(page 102)*
—REVEREND JOHN HALE OF BEVERLY, in reference to the witch trials (1697)

INTERVIEW TOPIC

Interview a person of any age and background about lying. Prepare a list of literal and interpretive questions: "What are the consequences of lying? How does lying affect friendships and other relationships? Can you tell of a personal experience in which you or someone else lied, and the consequences of that lie? Once you find out a person has lied to you, can that person ever regain your full trust? Why do you feel this way?"

PREVIEW WORDS

Puritan	*Anglican Church*	*charade*
Tituba	*magistrates*	*grudges*

---

[1] Refer to *Quotation Footnotes for Level 9* on page 406.

[6] Refer to *Quotation Footnotes for Level 9* on page 406.

WORD-ORIGIN STUDY

witch: The word *witch* probably originated from the word *wiccian*, meaning "to use sorcery." The Anglo-Saxon word *wicce*, or *wicca* for a female (an early form of witch), referred to a magician or wizard.

crucible: A *crucible* was originally a lamp or pot used for melting metals. Today a *crucible* is a pot made of material such as graphite, porcelain, or platinum that is tempered to withstand extreme heat. Because they are heat resistant, crucibles are used in the melting of ores and metals. *Crucible* later refered to a severe test, or difficult trial.

Puritan: Based on the word *purity*, the *Puritan* movement of England and America in the 16th and 17th centuries aimed to reform the Church of England, and abolish elaborate ceremonies and celebrations. The Puritans were looked upon as extreme in their strict adherence to moral and religious codes.

List other words based on the word *purity*. Write the words and their definitions in your vocabulary notebook.

BOOKS TO READ

Clapp, Patricia. *Witches' Children: A Story of Salem*. New York: Lothrop, Lee & Shepard Books, 1982.

Jackson, Shirley. *The Witchcraft of Salem Village*. New York: Random House, 1984.

Kent, Zachary. *The Story of the Salem Witch Trials*. Chicago: Children's Press, 1986.

Krensky, Stephen. *Witch Hunt: It Happened in Salem Village*. New York: Random House, 1989.

Lasky, Kathryn. *Beyond the Burning Time*. New York: Blue Sky Press, 1994.

Rice, Earle. *The Salem Witch Trials*. San Diego: Lucent Books, 1997.

Rinaldi, Ann. *A Break With Charity: A Story About the Salem Witch Trials*. San Diego: Harcourt Brace Jovanovich, 1992.

Sebald, Hans. *Witch-Children: From Salem Witch-Hunts to Modern Courtrooms*. Amherst, NY: Prometheus Books, 1995.

Starkey, Marion Lena. *The Visionary Girls: Witchcraft in Salem Village*. Boston: Little, Brown & Co., 1973.

Van der Linde, Laurel. *The Devil in Salem Village: The Story of the Salem Witchcraft Trials*. Brookfield, CT: Millbrook Press, 1992.

VIDEOS

Miller, Arthur (screenplay by). *The Crucible*. Beverly Hills, CA: Fox Video, 1997. (rated PG-13)

BOOK CLUB

Read *Beyond the Burning Time* by Kathryn Lasky, Ann Rinaldi's *A Break With Charity: A Story About the Salem Witch Trials*, or *Witches Children: A Story of Salem* by Patricia Clapp.

INTRODUCTORY ACTIVITIES

DAY ONE

Objective: The students will discuss lies and the consequences of lies.

Display a large chart in front of the class. Begin a discussion about lying. "What reasons do people give for lying? What were the consequences of lying?" Ask the students to tell their experiences with lies, and the repercussions of the lies. "Did the lie change the way people related to or trusted the person who lied? Why do you feel this way? In the end, did the lie cause more problems than telling the truth from the start? Why do you feel this way? If you learned a friend lied to you, could the friend ever completely regain your trust? Why do you feel this way?"

Write the following columns on the chart. Ask the students to list reasons for lies and the consequences of the lies. Display the chart throughout the week.

Reasons for Lies	Consequences
1.	1.
2.	2.
3.	3.
4.	4.
5.	5.
etc.	etc.

DAY TWO

STORY LESSON

Follow the *Presenting the Story Lesson* instructions in the Introduction. Each story lesson follows the same procedure; however, say the following in step 4: "The title of the story we're reading today is *Witches and Lies: The Salem Witch Hunt*. What do you think the story is about? What do you already know about lies? What do you already know about the Salem witch hunt?"

EXTENSION ACTIVITIES

1. Watch the video *The Crucible* adapted from Arthur Miller's play. After the movie, discuss the story, its basis in fact, and the effect of lies on innocent people.

2. Role-play an incident where someone tells a lie about a friend. You can dictate the lie, or allow the students to discuss what the lie will be. Randomly choose a student to play the role of the person telling the lie, and another to play the victim of the lie. Address the effects of the lie on both people. "How does the lie affect the people who spread the rumor or lie? In the end, what could be the result of the lie not only on the victim, but the person who started the lie and the friends who believed the lie?" End with a discussion session and the question, "Could a lie in modern times lead to tragic results similar to those of the Salem witch hunt? Give an example."

3. Review Quote 1 of the Quotes of the Week.

   Discuss the connection made by Louis Dembitz Brandeis between "the suppression of free speech and assembly" and the burning of women accused of witchcraft. The students write a short essay expressing their interpretation of this quote.

WITCHES AND LIES:
THE SALEM WITCH HUNT

It all began in the winter of 1692 in the Puritan village of Salem, Massachusetts. Puritanism was a branch of the Anglican Church that set out to reform, or purify, the adopted teaching of the church. Establishing their theology in England, Puritans migrated to America in 1630. They followed stringent rules of conduct based upon the Scriptures.

These strict doctrines forbade most forms of entertainment, and isolated the adolescents of Salem. In search of relief from their tedious lives, several girls met with a Caribbean slave-woman, Tituba. Tituba's skill as a palm reader and fortuneteller fascinated the girls; however, Puritan law forbade these activities. The girls swore to keep their clandestine meetings a secret.

The secret, although initially thrilling, began to prey on the conscious of nine-year-old Betty. For no apparent reason, she fell into a loud fit. To conceal the true cause of Betty's anguish, the girls imitated her seizures, leading village elders to conclude that witches tormented the children.

Witch hunts were common in England where courts condemned hundreds of women and men to death. The practice migrated to America, and eventually to Salem.

Under extreme pressure to name the witches causing their affliction, and in fear of punishment if the truth came out, the girls continued their charade. They accused several local women, including Tituba, of corrupting their souls with witchcraft.

Unlike the others who swore their innocence, Tituba confessed to the practice of witchcraft. The magistrates promised her clemency if she cooperated in the investigation. The witch trials were merciless, and the fever of lies quickly spread. Friends betrayed one another while others settled long-held grudges with false accusations.

Finally, the ministers could no longer let the madness continue, and the witch hunts came to a close. In the end, nineteen people died on the gallows while many others perished in jail.

QUESTIONS FOR WITCHES AND LIES: THE SALEM WITCH HUNT

Literal Questions:

THE FACTS:

1. Where and when does the story take place?

_____

_____

_____

2. Who was Tituba?

_____

_____

_____

3. What was the secret Betty found difficult to keep?

_____

_____

_____

4. Who stopped the madness of the witch hunts?

_____

_____

_____

SEQUENCE OF EVENTS:

5. Write the following events in chronological order: Tituba confessed to the practice of witchcraft; The girls swore to keep their clandestine meetings a secret; The girls accused several local women of corrupting their souls with witchcraft.

_____

_____

_____

6. What did the other girls do after Betty fell into a loud fit?

_____

_____

_____

Name _____ **Date** _____

Interpretive Questions:

DRAWING CONCLUSIONS:

7. What one word best describes the deaths that resulted from the Salem witch hunt? Why do you feel this way?

_____

_____

_____

_____

MAKING INFERENCES:

8. How did the Puritans feel about witches? What specific information led you to your answer?

_____

_____

_____

_____

MAKING PREDICTIONS:

9. Several people died and many lives ruined by the girls' lies. Could a similar event happen again? Why do you feel this way?

_____

_____

_____

_____

IDENTIFICATION OF CAUSE:

10. Why did Tituba confess to practicing witchcraft?

_____

_____

_____

_____

IDENTIFICATION OF THE MAIN IDEA:

11. Write a title for the story. Use as few words as possible.

_____

_____

Name _____   Date _____

COMPARISON:

12. How were the girls' lies similar to those of the neighbors who falsely accused each other of witchcraft? How were they different?

_____

_____

_____

_____

SUMMARIZE:

13. In your own words, tell about the events that led to the Salem witch hunt.

_____

_____

_____

_____

EFFECT:

14. What effect, if any, did the Salem witch hunt have on the surviving citizens? Why do you feel this way?

_____

_____

_____

_____

FACT AND OPINION:

15. The story said, "They (the Puritans) followed stringent rules of conduct based upon the Scriptures." Is this a fact or someone's opinion? How can you prove your answer?

_____

_____

_____

_____

ON YOUR OWN:

16. Write a question about the story for a teacher or another student to answer.

_____

_____

Name _____ **Date** _____

4. THE GLORIOUS TOMBS OF CHINA
Reading Level = 9.16

ABOUT THE STORY

Although many people think of the Egyptian pharaohs when the discussion turns to elaborate tombs, archaeologists have uncovered some of the most breathtaking burial sites in China. Huge tombs and spectacular treasures trace the imperial history of this ancient country.

QUOTES OF THE WEEK

Quote 1:

"Forbid it, sea gods! intercede for me with Neptune, O sweet Amphitrite, that no dull clod may fall on my coffin! Be mine the tomb that swallowed up the Pharaoh and all his hosts; let me lie down with Drake where he sleeps in the sea."[1] *(page 569)*—HERMAN MELVILLE, *WHITE JACKET*, Chapter 19

Quote 2:

"The Chinese love jade. That strange lump of stone with its faintly muddy light, like the crystallized air of the centuries, melting dimly, dully back, deeper and deeper—are not we Orientals the only ones who know its charm?"[1] *(page 796)*—TANIZAKI JUNICHIRO, *IN PRAISE OF SHADOWS*

INTERVIEW TOPIC

Interview a person of any age who has visited China. Prepare a list of literal and interpretive questions. "When did you visit China? What sites did you see? What did you learn about Chinese history? What was the most interesting thing you learned about China? How did your visit to China change your ideas about the country? If you could, would you visit China again? Why do you feel this way?"

PREVIEW WORDS

camouflage	*Prince Liu Sheng*
Mount Lishan	*Emperor Ch'in Shih Huang-Ti*
enterprising	*Princess Yung T'ai*

WORD-ORIGIN STUDY

jade: The word *jade* is a corruption of the Spanish phrase *piedra de yjada*, meaning "stone of the side." It was once believed that jade was a cure for pains emanating from the side of the body. Jade is a hard ornamental stone of translucent green or white color.

---

[1] Refer to *Quotation Footnotes for Level 9* on page 406.

camouflage: Camouflage is derived from the French word meaning "disguise." To *camouflage* is to disguise yourself to blend into the surrounding environment. Armies often camouflage their troops, ships, tanks, etc.

enterprising: The prefix *enter-* means "in or between" while *-prise* means "to take." *Enterprise* is an undertaking or project "taken in" or accepted by a person. To be enterprising is to be bold in the acceptance of a new project or undertaking.

List other words beginning with the prefix *enter-*. Write the words and their definitions in your vocabulary notebook.

BOOKS TO READ

Aylesworth, Thomas G. *Mysteries From the Past*. Garden City, NY: The Natural History Press, 1971.

Ballinger, Bill S. *The Lost City of Stone*. New York: Simon & Schuster, 1978.

Barry, Iris. *Discovering Archaeology*. Chicago: Stonehenge, in association with the American Museum of Natural History, 1981.

Bell, William. *Forbidden City: A Novel*. New York: Bantam Books, 1990.

Beshore, George. *Science in Ancient China*. New York: Franklin Watts, 1998.

Buckley, Michael. *China*. Berkeley, CA: Lonely Planet Publications, 1994.

Chinoy, Mike. *China Live: Two Decades in the Heart of the Dragon*. Atlanta: Turner Publishing, 1997.

Cohen, Joan Lebold. *China Today and Her Ancient Treasures*. New York: Harry N. Abrams, Inc., 1974.

Cooney, Eleanor. *Shangri-la: The Return to the World of the Lost Horizon*. New York: William Morrow, 1996.

Groushko, Michael. *Lost Treasures of the World*. London, England: Multimedia Books Limited, 1993.

Harrer, Heinrich. *Seven Years in Tibet*. New York: G.P. Putnam's Sons, 1996.

Hole, Frank. *An Introduction to Prehistoric Archaeology* (3rd ed.). New York: Holt, Rinehart and Winston, 1973.

Hull, Mary. *The Travels of Marco Polo*. San Diego: Lucent Books, 1995.

Lord, Bette. *The Middle Heart*. New York: Alfred A. Knopf, 1996.

Major, John S. *The Land and People of China*. Philadelphia: Lippincott, 1989.

Murowchick, Robert E. *China: Ancient Culture, Modern Land*. Norman: University of Oklahoma Press, 1994.

Palden, Gyatso. *Fire Under the Snow*. New York: Grove Press, 1997.

Paterson, Katherine. *Rebels of the Heavenly Kingdom*. New York: Avon Books, 1984.

Schafer, Edward H. *Ancient China*. New York: Time–Life Books, 1967.

Starr, John Bryan. *Understanding China: A Guide to China's Economy, History, and Political Structure*. New York: Hill and Wang, 1997.

Swetz, Frank. *The Sea Island Mathematical Manual: Surveying and Mathematics in Ancient China*. University Park: Pennsylvania State University Press, 1992.

Swinburne, Irene. *Behind the Sealed Door: The Discovery of the Tomb and Treasures of Tutankhamen*. New York: Sniffen Court Books, 1977.

Temple, Robert K.G. *The Genius of China: 3,000 Years of Science, Discovery, and Invention*. London, England: Prion Books, 1998.

Theroux, Paul. *Kowloon Tong*. Boston: Houghton Mifflin Co., 1997.

Vander Els, Betty. *Bomber's Moon*. New York: Farrer, Straus, Giroux, 1992.

_____. *Leaving Point*. New York: Farrer, Straus, Giroux, 1987.

Yep, Laurence. *Mountain Light*. New York: Harper & Row, 1997.

_____. *The Serpent's Children*. New York: Harper & Row, 1996.

VIDEOS

Bacon, William (producer). *Tibet: On the Edge of Change*. Chicago: Questar Video, 1997.

BOOK CLUB

Read Betty Vander Els's *The Bomber's Moon* and the sequel *Leaving Point*; or by William Bell's *Forbidden City: A Novel*.

INTRODUCTORY ACTIVITIES

DAY ONE

Objective: The students will visit a museum containing archaeological artifacts, or listen to a presentation by a collector of artifacts.

Visit a local museum containing archaeological artifacts. Many museums have traveling exhibits from foreign countries, or permanent exhibits of Native American artifacts. The students should take a note pad to draw pictures of and take notes on the artifacts they find interesting.

If this is not possible, invite a professional or amateur collector of archaeological artifacts to class to tell about his or her collection. Hold a question-and-answer session. "Why did you start your collection? What type of pieces do you enjoy collecting? Where did you find your pieces? Do you believe archaeology is an important branch of science? Why do you feel this way?" If the collector brings in some of his or her artifacts, allow time for the students to take notes on and draw pictures of each piece.

DAY TWO

STORY LESSON

Follow the *Presenting the Story Lesson* instructions in the Introduction. Each story lesson follows the same procedure; however, say the following in step 4: "The title of the story we're reading today is *The Glorious Tombs of China*. What do you think the story is about? What do you already know about China?"

EXTENSION ACTIVITIES

1. Review the notes and drawings the students made of the artifacts they saw on Day One. "Which pieces did you find particularly interesting? Why did you feel this way? Did you learn something about the civilization that you did not know before?"

2. The students write a report and make models of relics. Send the students to the library to learn about specific archaeological artifacts. They can narrow their search by choosing a culture to investigate, such as Native America, Egypt, Crete, etc. The students are to focus on one particular piece, make a model of the relic, and write a report telling what the relic is, where it was found, the civilization from which the relic came, its date, its use, and other points of interest.

   For example, a student might choose a piece of Native American pottery. He or she would make a clay replica, decorate the replica with the same design, then give a history of the pottery in a written report. *Or,* the student might choose a mummified cat from an Egyptian tomb. He or she would make a model of the cat, then write a history of the cat, and tell why the cat was mummified. *Or,* a student might recreate a rock painting. Using a thin stone paver, he or she would paint a replica of a rock painting onto the paver. The image might be of Australian aborigines, Native American symbols, Ice Age cave drawings, etc. Again, the student writes a history of the drawings along with the significance of the design.

3. Set up a museum of the models. Display each model with the report. Label each model with a card stating the title of the relic, the country in which it was found, the date of the object, and the name of the student. On a bulletin board, display a large map with pins indicating the location where each relic was found. Color-code the pins by matching the colored pin head to a colored dot on the display card.

THE GLORIOUS TOMBS OF CHINA

We are all familiar with the tombs of pharaohs who believed they could carry their treasures with them to the afterlife. Egypt was not the only culture with such beliefs. Many of the most impressive tombs belong to the ancient monarchs of China.

Realizing that grave robbers would risk their lives to find the emperors' buried treasures, the Chinese built elaborately disguised graves. The architects of these tombs constructed underground palaces, then covered them with large burial mounds that resembled hills. Trees planted on the mounds attempted to further camouflage the tomb.

In 1968, archaeologists unearthed the grand tomb of Prince Liu Sheng. This wealthy monarch died in 113 B.C., yet his miraculous tomb remained undisturbed. Archaeologists discovered two large underground rooms, one of which measured 170 feet by 121 feet. Among the treasures were two spectacular jade suits. Ancient Chinese believed that covering a corpse with jade prevented decay. The prince's 74-inch long suit contained 2,498 jade wafers connected by $2\frac{1}{2}$ pounds of fine gold thread.

Another extraordinary tomb belonged to the builder of the Great Wall of China, Emperor Ch'in Shih Huang-Ti (221-210 B.C.). Under the mound known as Mount Lishan, archaeologists found 1,000 life-size terracotta warriors standing guard over the emperor's treasures.

Tomb builders also used more lethal forms of protection. Many Chinese tombs contained booby traps to ensnare would-be grave robbers. Archaeologists found the remains of one unfortunate thief near the entrance of a tunnel to the tomb of Princess Yung T'ai.

Today's archaeologists maintain a cautious respect for the hazards of grave exploration. While excavating the tomb of Emperor Ming Wan Li, scientists enlisted the aid of well-known professional grave robbers. Temporarily released from prison with the title "special archaeological assistants," these enterprising thieves quickly led archaeologists to the heart of the tomb.

QUESTIONS FOR THE GLORIOUS TOMBS OF CHINA

Literal Questions:

THE FACTS:

1. Where can you find many of the most impressive tombs?

_____

_____

_____

2. Whose tomb did archaeologists unearth in 1968?

_____

_____

_____

3. In what year did Emperor Ch'in Shih Huang-Ti die?

_____

_____

_____

4. What did archaeologists find in the tomb of Emperor Ch'in Shih Huang-Ti?

_____

_____

_____

SEQUENCE OF EVENTS:

5. Which tomb was built first: the tomb of Prince Liu Sheng or the tomb of Emperor Ch'in Shih Huang-Ti?

_____

_____

_____

6. What did the Chinese build after they realized that grave robbers would risk their lives to find the emperors' buried treasures?

_____

_____

_____

Name _____   **Date** _____

Interpretive Questions:

DRAWING CONCLUSIONS:

7. What one word best describes the tomb of Prince Liu Sheng?

_____

_____

_____

_____

MAKING INFERENCES:

8. How do the Chinese feel about the tombs of their ancient emperors? What specific information led you to your answer?

_____

_____

_____

_____

MAKING PREDICTIONS:

9. Will grave robbers continue to plunder priceless tombs? If you said yes, what could authorities do to stop the robbers? If you said no, why do you feel this way?

_____

_____

_____

_____

IDENTIFICATION OF CAUSE:

10. Why would imprisoned professional grave robbers agree to help excavate a tomb?

_____

_____

_____

_____

IDENTIFICATION OF THE MAIN IDEA:

11. Write a title for the story. Use as few words as possible.

_____

_____

Name _____ **Date** _____

COMPARISON:

12. How was the tomb of Emperor Ch'in Shih Huang-Ti like that of Prince Liu Sheng? How was it different?

_____

_____

_____

_____

SUMMARIZE:

13. In your own words, describe the tomb of Prince Liu Sheng.

_____

_____

_____

_____

EFFECT:

14. What effect have grave robbers had on the historical records of China? Why do you feel this way?

_____

_____

_____

_____

FACT AND OPINION:

15. The story said, "Many of the most impressive tombs belong to the ancient monarchs of China." Is this a fact or an opinion? Why do you feel this way?

_____

_____

_____

_____

ON YOUR OWN:

16. Write a question about the story for a teacher or another student to answer.

_____

_____

Name _____   Date _____

5. AUTOMATON
Reading Level = 9.18

ABOUT THE STORY

Ancestors of the robot, automata are life-like moving toys. The story gives a brief look into the history of the fascinating world of the automaton from 60 A.D. to Thomas Edison's automaton of the late 1800s.

QUOTES OF THE WEEK

Quote 1:

"This new development (automation) has unbounded possibilities for good and for evil."[1] *(page 831)*—NORBERT WIENER, *CYBERNETICS*

Quote 2:

"The future offers very little hope for those who expect that our new mechanical slaves will offer us a world in which we may rest from thinking. Help us they may, but at the cost of supreme demands upon our honesty and our intelligence. The world of the future will be an ever more demanding struggle against the limitations of our intelligence, not a comfortable hammock in which we can lie down to be waited upon by our robot slaves."[1] *(page 832)*—NORBERT WIENER, *GOD AND GOLEM, INC.*

Quote 3:

"The danger of the past was that men became slaves. The danger of the future is that men may become robots."[3] *(page 474)*—ERICH FROMM

INTERVIEW TOPIC

Interview a person over the age of 50 about clockwork toys. Prepare a list of interpretive and literal questions: "As a child, did you own a clockwork toy? If not, do you remember clockwork toys that were available during your childhood? What were the toys? What could they do? Were they popular? Do you have a picture of the toy, or perhaps still own the toy?" (Ask the subject if you could have a copy of a photograph of the toy. If the person does not have one, look in your public library for a photograph of the toy. Look in books about collecting antique toys, or ask the reference librarian for help. If at all possible, include an illustration of the toy with your interview.)

PREVIEW WORDS

automaton	*Igashichi Iizuka*	*cockerel*
Jacques de Vaucanson	*Jaquet-Droz*	

---

[1] Refer to *Quotation Footnotes for Level 9* on page 406.

[3] Refer to *Quotation Footnotes for Level 9* on page 406.

WORD-ORIGIN STUDY

clockwork: The original meaning of the word *clock* was "bell." Prior to battery-operated clocks, clocks worked by the movement of toothed wheels operated by springs or weights. Clocks required regular winding and setting of the springs by the turning of a key. The tightened springs slowly unwound over set intervals allowing the clock to tick off the time. *Clockwork* uses similar springs and gears to produce movement, and is used in some mechanical toys.

android: The prefix *andro-* refers to "man or male." An *android* is something that resembles a man. In science fiction or computer science, an android is an automated machine that resembles a person.

robot: The term *robot* first appeared in a play written in 1921 by Karel Capek called *R.U.R.* (*Rossum's Universal Robots*). In the play, Rossum created robots to take over the manual labor of man.

automaton: *Automaton* (plural: *automata* or *automatons*) finds its roots in the Greek word *automatos*, meaning "acting of one's own will, or self-moving." An *automaton* is any device that is self-moving, and imitates the movement of people or animals. The term *automaton* can also refer to a person or animal whose actions become so automatic that they appear to act without thought.

List other words beginning with the prefix *auto-*, meaning "oneself." Write the words and their definitions in your vocabulary notebook.

BOOKS TO READ

Allen, Roger MacBride. *Isaac Asimov's Inferno*. New York: Ace Books, 1994.

Asfahl, C. Ray. *Robots and Manufacturing Automation*. New York: Wiley, 1985.

Asimov, Isaac. *Robots and Empire*. Garden City, NY: Doubleday, 1985.

_____. *The Robots of Dawn*. Garden City, NY: Doubleday, 1983.

Asimov, Isaac and Karen A. Frenkel. *Robots: Machines in Man's Image*. New York: Harmony Books, 1985.

Asimov, Isaac and Robert Silverberg. *The Positronic Man*. Garden City, NY: Doubleday, 1993.

Asimov, Isaac, Patricia S. Warrick, and Martin H. Greenberg (eds.). *Machines That Think: The Best Science Fiction Stories About Robots and Computers*. New York: Holt, Rinehart, and Winston, 1984.

Asimov, Janet. *The Norby Chronicles*. New York: Berkley Pub., 1986.

Greene, Carol. *Robots*. Chicago: Children's Press, 1983.

Lambert, Mark. *Fifty Facts About Robots*. New York: Warwick Press, 1983.

Leroe, Ellen. *Robot Romance*. New York: Harper and Row, 1985.

Litterick, Ian. *The Age of Computers: Robots and Intelligent Machines*. New York: The Bookwright Press, 1984.

Marrs, Texe W. *Careers with Robots*. New York: Facts on File, 1988.

Milton, Joyce. *Here Come the Robots*. New York: Hasting House Publishers, 1981.

Skurzynski, Gloria. *Robots: Your High-Tech World*. New York: Bradbury Press, 1990.

Sloan, Frank. *Titanic*. New York: Franklin Watts, 1987.

Thro, Ellen. *Robotics Careers*. New York: Franklin Watts, 1987.

Time–Life Books, editors of. *Understanding Computers: Robotics*. Alexandria, VA: Time–Life Books, 1986.

BOOK CLUB

Read Ellen Leroe's *Robot Romance*, or *The Robots of Dawn* by Isaac Asimov.

INTRODUCTORY ACTIVITIES

DAY ONE

Objective: The students discuss and compare/contrast the definitions of robot, automaton, and android.

Write the words ROBOT, AUTOMATON, and ANDROID on a chart along with their definitions (see Word-Origin Study). Engage the students in a discussion on how robots, automata, and androids are alike. How are they different? Make three columns on the chart paper—one for each heading of ROBOTS, *automata*, and ANDROIDS. Under each heading, ask the students to list examples of robots, automata, and androids found in fact or science fiction. Compare and contrast the objects listed. For example: "How are the robots alike, yet different from automata or androids?"

DAY TWO

STORY LESSON

Follow the *Presenting the Story Lesson* instructions in the Introduction. Each story lesson follows the same procedure; however, say the following in step 4: "The title of the story we're reading today is *Automaton*. What do you think the story is about? What do you already know about automata?"

EXTENSION ACTIVITIES

1. The students write a report about a factual robot, automaton, or android. They cannot use science fiction characters. Each report should be three to five pages in length with no less than five references. The students write the report in standard form, and include an illustration of their subject.

2. The students create a model of their own creation of a robot, automaton, or android. The model can be made of any material without limiting their creativity. They can use tin cans, appliance boxes, plastic bottles, papier-mâché, etc. Their creations might move or be stationary. With each model the students must include the robot's (automaton's, android's) name, functions, and use. Hold a model "Show and Tell."

3. Ask the students to bring to class toys that move. The students tell the class whether their toys are robots, automata, or androids, and explain what characteristics make the toys robots, automata, or androids.

AUTOMATON

Automata, life-like moving toys, fascinated people as early as 60 A.D. when Hero of Alexandria described moving objects powered by water. By the Middle Ages, with the arrival of clockwork and springs, human- and animal-like machines became popular entertainment. Many people call these objects ancestors of the robot, but they were simply nonthinking mechanical toys known as "automata" or self-moving machines.

There are many examples of complex and fascinating automata. For over 400 years, on the Strasbourg Cathedral in France, a cockerel crowed with the striking of the hour. The mechanical bird raised its head, flapped its wings, and crowed three times.

Igashichi Iizuka, a Japanese inventor, created an automaton to go to market and fetch saké. Iizuka's clockwork servant knew when to turn and when to walk straight until it reached its destination. In order to send the doll home, the merchant had to fill the flask correctly. Only then would the life-like servant return to its master.

In India, the sultan of Mysore enjoyed the "political statement" portrayed in his automaton. The six-foot-long toy, called *Tipu's Tiger*, attacked and mauled a mechanical British soldier. Lying under the claws of the tiger, the soldier flailed and shrieked.

In 1738, Jacques de Vaucanson made a clockwork duck of over 4,000 parts. Used to raise money for experiments to create artificial life, the copper duck "quacked, bathed, drank water, ate grain, digested it, and voided." After passing through the hands of several owners, the duck eventually disappeared.

Perhaps the most enchanting automaton is Jaquet-Droz's *Scribe* or *Writer*. The boy sits at a desk with his ink well, quill, and paper. The toy dips the pen into the well, then writes a message up to forty characters in length. By adjusting the gears inside the chest, the user can change the message.

Most automata were elaborate toys made for kings and the wealthy. Still others served as clever advertising tools. Even Thomas Edison employed a talking automaton to introduce his phonograph in 1891.

QUESTIONS FOR AUTOMATON

Literal Questions:

THE FACTS:

1. What are automata?

_____

_____

_____

2. What did the cockerel of the Strasbourg Cathedral do with the striking of the hour?

_____

_____

_____

3. What did Igashichi Iizuka invent?

_____

_____

_____

4. How many parts did Jacques de Vaucanson use to make his clockwork duck?

_____

_____

_____

SEQUENCE OF EVENTS:

5. Which automaton was created first: the cockerel of Strasbourg Cathedral or Jacques de Vaucanson's clockwork duck?

_____

_____

_____

6. What does Jaquet-Droz's *Scribe* do after the automaton dips the pen into the well?

_____

_____

_____

Name _____   Date _____

Interpretive Questions:

DRAWING CONCLUSIONS:

7. What one word best describes Jacques de Vaucanson's clockwork duck?

_____

_____

_____

_____

MAKING INFERENCES:

8. How did the sultan of Mysore feel about the British? What specific information in the story led you to your answer?

_____

_____

_____

_____

MAKING PREDICTIONS:

9. Would an intricate automaton such as the clockwork duck fascinate today's audiences? Why do you feel this way?

_____

_____

_____

_____

IDENTIFICATION OF CAUSE:

10. Why did Igashichi Iizuka create his automaton?

_____

_____

_____

_____

IDENTIFICATION OF THE MAIN IDEA:

11. Write a title for the story. Use as few words as possible.

_____

_____

Name _____   Date _____

COMPARISON:

12. Compare the cockerel of Strasbourg Cathedral to Jacques de Vaucanson's duck.

_____

_____

_____

_____

SUMMARIZE:

13. In your own words, describe one of the automatons discussed in the story.

_____

_____

_____

_____

EFFECT:

14. What effect, if any, would a talking automaton have on the sales of Thomas Edison's phonograph? Why do you feel this way?

_____

_____

_____

_____

FACT OR OPINION:

15. The story said, "Perhaps the most enchanting automaton is Jaquet-Droz's _Scribe_ or _Writer._" Is this a fact or an opinion? Why do you feel this way?

_____

_____

_____

_____

ON YOUR OWN:

16. Write a question about the story for a teacher or another student to answer.

_____

_____

Name _____ **Date** _____

6. AMERICA MOURNS
Reading Level = 9.18

ABOUT THE STORY

This is a *Moments in Time* story announcing the death of President James Abram Garfield. President Garfield worked to abolish the common practice of appointing campaign supporters to important political office. After failing to secure a position as foreign consul, Charles J. Guiteau shot President Garfield on July 2, 1881.

QUOTES OF THE WEEK

Quote 1:

"All free governments are managed by the combined wisdom and folly of the people."[3] *(page 275)*—JAMES A. GARFIELD

Quote 2:

"Ideas are the great warriors of the world, and a war that has no ideas behind it is simply brutality."[3] *(page 282)*—JAMES A. GARFIELD

Quote 3:

"Next in importance to freedom and justice is popular education, without which neither freedom nor justice can be permanently maintained."[3] *(page 332)*—JAMES A. GARFIELD

Quote 4:

"We may divide the struggles of the human race into two chapters: first, the fight to get leisure; and second, what to do with our leisure when we have won it. Like all blessings, leisure is a bad thing unless it is well used."[3] *(page 348)*—JAMES A. GARFIELD

Quote 5:

"Fellow citizens! God reigns, and the Government at Washington still lives!"[1] *(page 609)*—JAMES A. GARFIELD in a speech on the assassination of Abraham Lincoln, New York (April 15, 1865)

Quote 6:

"For mere vengeance I would do nothing. This nation is too great to look for mere revenge. But for the security of the future I would do everything."[1] *(page 609)*—JAMES A. GARFIELD in a speech on the assassination of Abraham Lincoln, New York (April 15, 1865)

Quote 7:

"I am not willing that this discussion should close without mention of the value of a true teacher. Give me a log hut, with only a simple bench, Mark Hopkins on one end and I on the other, and you may have all the buildings, apparatus and libraries without him."[1] *(page 609)*—JAMES A. GARFIELD in an address to Williams College Alumni, New York (December 28, 1871)

---

[3] Refer to *Quotation Footnotes for Level 9* on page 406.

[1] Refer to *Quotation Footnotes for Level 9* on page 406.

INTERVIEW TOPIC

Interview a person of any age concerning the most important historical event he or she witnessed in his or her lifetime. Prepare a list of literal and interpretive questions. "What is the most important historical event of your lifetime? Why do you feel this way? Why did this event have such an impact on you? What was the political and/or social atmosphere of the time that might have contributed to the event? Do you have any souvenirs of the event or time period?" (Take a photograph of the souvenirs with the interview subject. Be sure to obtain written permission if you intend to use this photograph in any form of public display.)

PREVIEW WORDS

James Abram Garfield	*unutterable*	*influential*
foreign consul	*Charles J. Guiteau*	

WORD-ORIGIN STUDY

campaign: The word *campaign* is related to the word *camp* (campus) meaning "field." A *campaign* is a military mission or expedition. It was later attached to an organized political competition for the election of officials.

assassination: The word *assassin* literally means "hashish-eater." (Hashish is an intoxicating narcotic.) An *assassin* was a member of a secret band of hashish-eating Moslems who murdered Christian leaders during the Crusades. It has been modified to refer to any person hired to murder political delegates. An *assassination* is murder by an assassin.

president: Using the prefix *pre-*, meaning "before," the word *preside* means "to sit before." A president *presides* over, or sits before, a company, university, organization, club, etc. According to Webster's Dictionary, a *President* is (a) the chief executive of a republic having no prime minister, or (b) in parliamentary governments, the formal head with little or no executive power, usually the presiding member of the legislative assembly or council.

List other words beginning with the prefix *pre-*. Write the words and their definitions in your vocabulary notebook.

BOOKS TO READ

Dallek, Robert. *Flawed Giant: Lyndon Johnson and His Times, 1961-1973*. New York: Oxford University Press, 1998.

Furer, Howard B. *James A. Garfield 1831-1881; Chester A. Arthur 1830-1889: Chronology—Documents—Biographical Aids*. Dobbs Ferry, NY: Oceana Publications, Inc., 1970.

Goodwin, Doris Kearns. *No Ordinary Time: Franklin and Eleanor Roosevelt: The Home Front in World War II*. New York: Simon & Schuster, 1995.

Hake, Theodore L. *Hake's Guide to Presidential Campaign Collectibles: An Illustrated Price Guide to Artifacts From 1789-1988*. Radnor, PA: Wallace–Homestead Book Co., 1992.

Hersh, Seymour M. *The Dark Side of Camelot*. Boston: Little, Brown and Co., 1997.

Hope, Bob. *Bob Hope's Dear Prez, I Wanna Tell Ya!: A Presidential Jokebook*. Los Angeles: General Pub. Group, 1996.

Hoyt, Edwin Palmer. *James A. Garfield*. Chicago: Reilly & Lee Co., 1964.

Jennison, Keith Warren. *The Humorous Mr. Lincoln: A Profile in Wit, Courage, and Compassion*. Woodstock, VT: Countryman Press, 1992.

Lillegard, Dee. *James A. Garfield: Twentieth President of the United States*. Chicago: Children's Press, 1987.

Matalin, Mary. *All's Fair: Love, War, and Running for President*. New York: Random House, 1994.

McClendon, Sarah. *Mr. President, Mr. President!: My Fifty Years of Covering the White House*. Los Angeles: General Pub. Group, 1996.

Morris, Dick. *Behind the Oval Office: Winning the Presidency in the Nineties*. New York: Random House, 1997.

Renehan, Edward. *The Lion's Pride: Theodore Roosevelt and His Family in Peace and War*. New York: Oxford University Press, 1998.

Severn, Bill. *Teacher, Soldier, President*. New York: Washburn Ives, 1964.

Stephanopoulos, George. *All Too Human: A Political Education*. Boston: Little, Brown and Co., 1999.

Woodward, Bob. *The Agenda: Inside the Clinton White House*. New York: Simon & Schuster, 1994.

BOOK CLUB

Read a biography or autobiograpy of a United States President. Break the students into groups. Each group reads about the *same* President; however, each group reads a *different* book. After reading the books, compare the information found in each biography. "Are there differences between stated facts from one biography to the next? If yes, why do these differences exist?"

INTRODUCTORY ACTIVITIES

DAY ONE

Objective: The students will read copies of newspapers dating back to July 1881 to learn about the events of the time.

Obtain copies of the front pages of newspapers surrounding the week of July 2, 1881, and the front page of the September 19, 1881 newspaper. Charles J. Guiteau shot President Garfield on July 2, 1881, yet the President did not die of his wounds until September 19, 1881. Your local library or newspaper offices can assist you in your search. Many libraries have copies of newspapers dating to this time period on microfilm. Laminating the copies will help preserve your copies.

Pass out copies of newspaper front pages dated just prior to July 2, 1881. Read the papers as a group, and discuss the local and national concerns of the time period. Do not read the front page for July 2, 1881, or after. This lesson is to prepare students to read the story about the assassination of President Garfield by learning about the national atmosphere of the time. Save the front pages dated July 2, 1881, and after, for the Extension Activities.

DAY TWO

STORY LESSON

Follow the *Presenting the Story Lesson* instructions in the Introduction. Each story lesson follows the same procedure; however, say the following in step 4: "The title of the story we're reading today is *America Mourns*. It is a *Moments in Time* story dated September 19, 1881. What do you think the story is about? What do you already know about the time period?"

EXTENSION ACTIVITIES

1. Hand out copies of newspaper front pages dated July 2, 1881. As a class, read and discuss the world, national, and local events as well as information concerning President Garfield. Continue the activity by reading the newspapers from the week following the shooting. "How did the country react to the shooting? What were the initial reports? When did they learn the motives for the shooting? What were some of the repercussions in the form of policy changes, foreign policy concerns, national economics, etc.?" Finally, read the front page of the newspaper dated September 19, 1881. "How did America mourn the death of the president? What information did you learn from this newspaper that you did not know before?"

2. In a teacher's file, collect front pages from newspapers on important dates in American history such as the moon landing, the assassination of President Kennedy, the space shuttle Challenger explosion, etc. Hand out one newspaper front page to each student. What can they learn about the time period—from fashion to national and international political trends—by reading their newspapers? Save the newspapers in your file for future use.

3. Using the date of the newspaper front page they read in Extension Activity 2, each student writes his or her own newspaper. Students need a front page, editorial page, sports page, entertainment page, local/state/international news, and extras such as crossword puzzles and comics. The newspapers must reflect the time period in the language used, topics of editorials and comics, as well as a crossword puzzle using terms of the period. Include direct quotes from important people of the time period. These quotes can be found in reference books of quotes in the local or school library.

4. Students spend a day sharing the newspapers written in Extension Activity 3.

AMERICA MOURNS

President Garfield died today among his family in Elberon, New Jersey. His daughter Mollie, age fourteen, spoke for the nation as she wrote, "Oh! it is so hard to lose him . . . ."

James Abram Garfield, born on November 19, 1831, in northern Ohio, will perhaps be the last president raised in a log cabin. As the youngest of four children, he proved himself of infinite curiosity and intelligence. Garfield became an avid reader at an early age who enjoyed learning. He later graduated from Williams College in Williamstown, Massachusetts, with honors.

His political career began in 1859 when he campaigned for a seat in the state senate. Garfield's speeches focused on anti-slavery themes and the importance of free labor.

During the Civil War, Garfield ascended to the rank of major general. As witness to the horrors of war he once wrote, "No blaze of glory" could redeem us from the "unutterable horror" of the war.

In 1862, Garfield reentered public office in the U.S. House of Representatives, a post to which he was reelected eight times. Garfield worked to abolish the practice of appointing campaign supporters to influential government offices. Garfield found that those hunting for office appointments "infest every public place . . . and thrust their papers in your face as a highwayman would his pistol." Amplifying the problem was the lack of quality among office seekers. "The war has brought to the surface of National politics many men who are neither fitted in character, nor ability, to be leaders of public thought or representative of the true men of the country." In the end, it would be these statements, not the cry for the rights of slaves, which would bring the fatal blow.

On July 2, Charles J. Guiteau shot President Garfield after being refused a position as foreign consul. The bullet remained lodged in the president's body. Even Alexander Graham Bell could not locate the bullet with an electrical device he invented for the task. After serving only 200 days as president, James A. Garfield died. America and Lady Liberty mourn the passing of our beloved president.

QUESTIONS FOR AMERICA MOURNS

Literal Questions:

THE FACTS:

1. Where and when did President Garfield die?

_____

_____

_____

2. When did his political career begin?

_____

_____

_____

3. Who shot President Garfield?

_____

_____

_____

4. What was the motive for killing President Garfield?

_____

_____

_____

SEQUENCE OF EVENTS:

5. What happened first: the Civil War or Garfield's graduation from Williams College?

_____

_____

_____

6. During the late 1880s, what did campaign supporters expect after their candidate entered political office?

_____

_____

_____

Name _____   Date _____

Interpretive Questions:

DRAWING CONCLUSIONS:

7. What were some of the possible negative consequences of appointing campaign supporters to political office?

_____

_____

_____

_____

MAKING INFERENCES:

8. How did the author feel about the death of President Garfield? What specific information led you to your answer?

_____

_____

_____

_____

MAKING PREDICTIONS:

9. Will campaign supporters continue to expect favors from a candidate after he or she enters office? Why do you feel this way?

_____

_____

_____

_____

IDENTIFICATION OF CAUSE:

10. Give two reasons for President Garfield's disapproval of the practice of appointing campaign supporters.

_____

_____

_____

_____

IDENTIFICATION OF THE MAIN IDEA:

11. Write a title for the story. Use as few words as possible.

_____

_____

Name _____   Date _____

COMPARISON:

12. Go to the library or use the Internet to research current efforts to reform political campaign practices. How are the practices of today similar to those of Garfield's time? How are they different?

_____

_____

_____

_____

SUMMARIZE:

13. In your own words, explain why Charles J. Guiteau shot President Garfield.

_____

_____

_____

_____

EFFECT:

14. What effect, if any, did President Garfield's efforts to reform campaign practices have on the process? You can find information on the subject at your library.

_____

_____

_____

_____

FACT AND OPINION:

15. The story said, "Even Alexander Graham Bell could not locate the bullet with an electrical device he invented for the task." Is this statement a fact or an opinion? How can you prove your answer?

_____

_____

_____

_____

ON YOUR OWN:

16. Write a question about the story for a teacher or another student to answer.

_____

_____

Name _____   **Date** _____

7. DREAMING TO REMEMBER
Grade Level = 9.28

ABOUT THE STORY

Researchers throughout the world study sleep, dreams, and the correlation between dreams and memory. The article investigates the impact of sleep on an individual's ability to learn and retain information.

QUOTES OF THE WEEK

Quote 1:

"Dreaming permits each and every one of us to be quietly and safely insane every night of our lives."[3] *(page 201)*—DR. WILLIAM C. DEMENT

Quote 2:

"Sleep is the best meditation."[3] *(page 201)*—DALAI LAMA

Quote 3:

"We are the music-makers,
And we are the dreamers of dreams, . . ."[1] *(page 659)*—ARTHUR WILLIAM EDGAR O'SHAUGHNESSY, *ODE, STANZA. 1*

INTERVIEW TOPIC

Interview a person 16 years old or older. Inquire into the subject's ability to learn and retain information when he or she is deprived of sleep. Prepare a list of literal and interpretive questions. "On average, how many hours of sleep do you get each night? In general, do you feel rested throughout the day? Do you notice a difference in your work performance when you don't sleep well the night before? How is your work affected by lack of sleep? Is it more difficult for you to retain new information when you get less sleep? Why do you think you experience these changes?"

PREVIEW WORDS

pontine	*John Horgan*	*Ottawa*
Weizman Institute	*embedded*	*Gini Kopecky*

WORD-ORIGIN STUDY

dream: The word *dream* can be traced to the Anglo-Saxon word meaning "joy or music." Although *dream* refers to images passing through a sleeper's mind, the term *dream* generally holds a positive connotation of hope and reverie.

---

[3] Refer to *Quotation Footnotes for Level 9* on page 406.
[1] Refer to *Quotation Footnotes for Level 9* on page 406.

nightmare:	The second half of this compound word, *mare*, is based on a Middle English word meaning "demon." It was once believed that a *nightmare* was the visitation of an evil spirit that haunted and tormented its sleeping victim. Today *nightmare* refers to any terrifying dream that often causes the sleeper to feel a sense of helplessness.
embedded:	Also spelled *imbed*, the term is based on the base word *bed*, meaning "a plat of ground." The prefix *em-*, meaning "in," creates the word *embedded*, or in a plat of ground. *Embed* means to set plants into the ground. It also has come to mean anything that is surrounded by and fixed in a mass. An idea *embedded* in the mind is fixed or implanted into the memory.

List other words beginning with the prefix *em-*. Write the words with their definitions in your vocabulary notebook.

BOOKS TO READ

Alkon, Daniel L. *Memory's Voice: Deciphering the Brain-Mind Code.* New York: HarperCollins, 1992.

Berry, Marilyn. *Help Is on the Way: Memory Skills.* Chicago: Children's Press, 1985.

Bolles, Edmund Blair. *Remembering and Forgetting: An Inquiry Into the Nature of Memory.* New York: Walker and Co., 1988.

Borbely, Alexander A. *Secrets of Sleep.* New York: Basic Books, 1986.

Brooks, Martha. *Bone Dance.* New York: Orchard Books, 1997.

Bstan-'dzin-rgya-mtsho, Dalai Lama XIV. *Sleeping, Dreaming, and Dying: An Exploration of Consciousness With the Dalai Lama.* Boston: Wisdom, 1997.

Coville, Bruce. *A Glory of Unicorns.* New York: Scholastic Press, 1998.

Dement, William C. *The Sleepwatchers.* Stanford, CA: Stanford Alumni Association, 1992.

Dunkell, Samuel. *Sleep Positions: The Night Language of the Body.* New York: Morrow, 1977.

Fritz, Roger. *Sleep Disorders: America's Hidden Nightmare.* Naperville, IL: Publishers Distribution Service, 1993.

Gallant, Roy A. *Memory: How It Works and How to Improve It.* New York: Four Winds Press, 1980.

Galloway, Priscilla. *Snake Dreamer.* New York: Delacorte Press, 1998.

Graber, Richard. *How to Get a Good Night's Sleep: More than 100 Ways You Can Improve Your Sleep.* Minneapolis: Chronimed Pub., 1995.

Hartmann, Ernest. *The Nightmare: The Psychology and Biology of Terrifying Dreams.* New York: Basic Books, 1984.

Herrmann, Douglas J. *Super Memory: A Quick-Action Program for Memory Improvement.* New York: Wings Books, 1992.

Hilton, Hermine. *The Executive Memory Guide: The Surefire Way to Remember Names, Numbers, and Important Information.* New York: Simon & Schuster, 1986.

Leviton, Richard. *Brain Builders!: A Lifelong Guide to Sharper Thinking, Better Memory, and an Ageproof Mind.* West Nyack, NY: Parker Publishing Co., 1995.

McPhee, Charles. *Stop Sleeping Through Your Dreams: A Guide to Awakening Consciousness During Dream Sleep.* New York: Henry Holt, 1995.

Meltzer, Milton. *The Landscape of Memory.* New York: Viking Kestrel, 1987.

Sykes, Shelley. *For Mike.* New York: Delacorte Press, 1998.

Wynne-Jones, Tim. *Stephen Fair: A Novel.* New York: DK Publishing, 1998.

CDs, Records, and Cassettes

Moidel, Steve. *Memory Power* (Cassette). Boulder, CO: Careertrack, 1992.

Montgomery, Robert L. *Executive Memory Program* (Book/Cassette). Mount Laurel, NY: Learn Incorporated, 1985.

Articles

Begley, Sharon. "Lights of Madness: Physiology of Schizophrenic Hallucinations." *Newsweek*, vol. 126, no. 21 (November 20, 1995), 76(2).

Horgan, John. "Daydreaming: Experiments Reveal Links Between Memory and Sleep." *Scientific American*, vol. 271, no. 4 (October 1994), 32(2).

"How to Build a Dream (How the Brain Creates Dreams)." *Psychology Today*, vol. 28, no. 6 (November-December 1995), 47(6).

Kopecky, Gini. "Make Your Dreams Work for You." *American Health* (November 1995), 78(3).

Rudavsky, Shari. "If Practice Makes Perfect, Deep Sleep Helps Even More." *The Wall Street Journal* (July 29, 1994), B2(W), B3(E), col. 6.

INTRODUCTORY ACTIVITIES

Day One

Objective: The students will make a graph comparing hours of sleep to grade average.

Hold a class discussion about sleep. "How do you feel when you get a good night's sleep? How does a good night's sleep affect your grades? In general, do you get eight hours of sleep each night?" Ask for explanations of their answers.

Hand out copies of the following Sleep Questionnaire to each student. They are not to write their names on the paper. Collect the papers. As a group, design a graph using a format the students deem most effective to illustrate the correlation between hours of sleep and grade average. Discuss the results.

SLEEP QUESTIONNAIRE

Grade Average: _____

Average Hours of Sleep Each Night: _____

DAY TWO

STORY LESSON

Follow the *Presenting the Story Lesson* instructions in the Introduction. Each story lesson follows the same procedure; however, say the following in step 4: "The title of the story we're reading today is *Dreaming to Remember*. What do you think the story is about?"

EXTENSION ACTIVITIES

1. Each student keeps a diary of his or her sleep. (Suggest keeping the diary next to the bed.) Students write down the hour they went to bed and the hour they got up. They are to note any hours they were awake during the night, and the number of times they woke up. They record any dreams they had immediately after waking. Students keep the diary for one month. Compare the diaries to look for any correlations between absenteeism and grade averages. Did those who dreamed more make higher grades?

2. Give the students a list of 100 basic foreign language terms, such as boy, table, walk, etc. Choose a language they do not speak. They don't need to pronounce the words; only match the words to their English counterparts in writing. At the end of the week, give a test listing the foreign words. The students will write the English word next to each foreign language term. Grade the papers. Test example:

   1. hermano: brother
   2. mesa: table
   3. chico: little boy
   4. hablar: to speak

Compare the grades to the sleep diary entries. Did those who dreamed the most during the week score the highest grades? Review the last paragraph of *Dreaming to Remember*. Did your results confirm or contradict the University of Ottawa study? Discuss the results.

3. Invite a counselor or psychologist trained in progressive relaxation to teach the class this relaxation technique. (Progressive relaxation is an exercise aimed at achieving deep relaxation through the conscious relaxation of major muscle groups.) Instruct the students to practice progressive relaxation prior to going to sleep each night. After two weeks, check the sleep diary entries. Are there changes in sleep patterns? Are there changes in grade averages? Discuss the results.

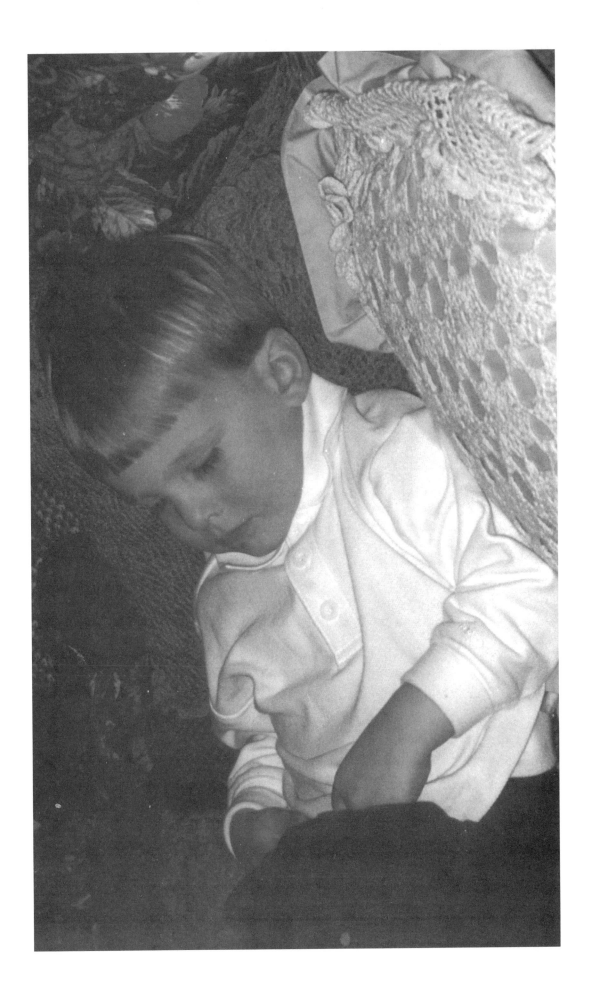

DREAMING TO REMEMBER

Why do we dream? Are dreams important? Through the centuries scientists and psychiatrists debated these questions. Some believe dreams are windows to our psyche. Others regard dreams as nothing more than images caused by random, meaningless impulses of a sleeping brain. Nevertheless, current research attributes the dreaming process to our good physical and mental health, and even our ability to learn.

In 1995, Harvard researchers designed a model of the brain as it creates dreams. Initiated from the lowest part of the brain, the pontine brainstem, dreams are simply meaningless images. The brain, in an attempt to rationalize these images, assigns emotions to the dream determining if it is a peaceful episode or a nightmare.

If the brain assigns logic to dream images, can we utilize these messages from the unconscious mind? Gini Kopecky presented information that indicates people can use dreams to help them lead better lives. Dream images arise from data and experiences embedded in the brain's "memory file." Exploring these files allows us to learn more about ourselves and our perceptions of our environments.

According to John Horgan, the mind incorporates important memories as we sleep. During deep slumber, we enter a stage called REM (rapid-eye-movement) sleep. It is at this stage that we experience dreams. During REM sleep, rats appeared to "fast-forward" their memories, swiftly repeating their recollection of mazes. Could task performance in humans improve with the occurrence of REM sleep?

Israeli researchers explored this question at the Weizman Institute. Retention of repetitious learning improved during dreams. The study concluded, "learning takes place during specific stages of brain activity such as REM sleep."

At the University of Ottawa, researchers looked at the effect of REM sleep on students enrolled in an intensive language course. Students who demonstrated an increase in learning also experienced an increase in REM sleep. Poor sleepers tended to earn the lowest test scores.

QUESTIONS FOR DREAMING TO REMEMBER

Literal Questions:

THE FACTS:

1. What did Harvard researchers design in 1995?

_____

_____

_____

2. What information about dreams did Gini Kopecky present?

_____

_____

_____

3. What do we enter during deep slumber?

_____

_____

_____

4. What did the Israeli researchers conclude about learning and sleep?

_____

_____

_____

SEQUENCE OF EVENTS:

5. Which information did the article present first: the views of John Horgan or the research at the University of Ottawa?

_____

_____

_____

6. What did John Horgan learn after he studied rats during REM sleep?

_____

_____

_____

Name _____   Date _____

Interpretive Questions:

DRAWING CONCLUSIONS:

7. Based on the information presented in the article, who would earn the highest grade on a test naming the states and capitals of the United States: a student who stayed up all night studying, or a student who slept and dreamed? On what specific information do you base your conclusion?

_____

_____

_____

_____

MAKING INFERENCES:

8. Based on the conclusion of the Israeli study, in which subject areas would a student most likely improve performance by getting a good night's sleep?

_____

_____

_____

_____

MAKING PREDICTIONS:

9. Could you improve your grades if you improved your sleeping habits? Why do you feel this way?

_____

_____

_____

_____

IDENTIFICATION OF CAUSE:

10. Why are researchers interested in the study on improved learning?

_____

_____

_____

_____

IDENTIFICATION OF THE MAIN IDEA:

11. Write a title for the story. Use as few words as possible.

_____

_____

Name _____   **Date** _____

COMPARISON:

12. Compare the studies conducted by the Israeli researchers and the researchers at the University of Ottawa. How were the studies alike? How were they different?

_____

_____

_____

_____

SUMMARIZE:

13. In your own words, describe the research of John Horgan and the conclusion he reached.

_____

_____

_____

_____

EFFECT:

14. Imagine a research study at a university where officials enforced a nine-hour sleep period for students in a specific dormitory. How might this affect the students' grades? Why do you feel this way?

_____

_____

_____

_____

FACT OR OPINION:

15. The story said, "Gini Kopecky presented information that indicates people can use dreams to help them lead better lives." Is this a fact or Kopecky's opinion? Why do you feel this way?

_____

_____

_____

_____

ON YOUR OWN:

16. Write a question about the story for a teacher or another student to answer.

_____

_____

Name _____   Date _____

8. SUMMER CAMP ISN'T WHAT IT USED TO BE
Reading Level = 9.28

ABOUT THE STORY

Throughout the country, unique and exciting summer camps are available for students of all ages, backgrounds, and interests. From music to sports, academics to recreation, there are summer camps for everyone. This article lists and describes many of the camps offered for teenagers.

QUOTES OF THE WEEK

Quote 1:

"Summer afternoon—summer afternoon; to me those have always been the two most beautiful words in the English language."[1] *(page 654)*
—HENRY JAMES, *QUOTED BY EDITH WHARTON, A BACKWARD GLANCE*, Chapter 10

Quote 2:

"Summertime an' the livin' is easy,
Fish are jumpin', an' the cotton is high."[11] *(page 122)*—Words by DU BOSE HEYWARD, music by GEORGE GERSHWIN, *SUMMERTIME*

INTERVIEW TOPIC

Interview any person of any age who has attended a summer camp. Prepare a list of literal and interpretive questions. "What was the name of the camp you attended? When did you go to the camp? How old were you? Did the camp have a theme, such as sports, music, religion, or academics? Where was the camp held? Did you enjoy the camp? Why did you feel this way? What are some of your memories of summer camp?" (If possible, ask the person for a photograph of him- or herself at the summer camp. Mount the photograph next to the interview.)

PREVIEW WORDS

concurrently	*enthusiasts*
audio	*lacrosse*

WORD-ORIGIN STUDY

camp: The word *camp* is based on the Latin word *campus*, or field. A *camp* is an area or field where tents or other temporary housings are set up. The word *camp* also refers to a vacation destination for children that includes recreational facilities.

---

[1] Refer to *Quotation Footnotes for Level 9* on page 406.
[11] Refer to *Quotation Footnotes for Level 9* on page 406.

lacrosse:	*Lacrosse* has its origins in the French words *la* ("the") and *crosse* ("crutch, hockey stick, or cross"). The game *lacrosse* began among Native American tribes of North America. There are ten members on each team. Players move the ball along the field of play using long-handled, netted rackets.
concurrently:	The prefix *con-* means "together." When attached to *-currence*, "to run," the word *concurrence* means "to run together." *Concurrently* means to run together, or happen at the same time.

List other words beginning with the prefix *con-*. Write the words and their definitions in your vocabulary notebooks.

BOOKS TO READ

Arnold, Eric H., Jeffrey Loeb, and True Kelley. *Lights Out!: Kids Talk About Summer Camp.* Boston: Little, Brown, and Co. 1986.

Crew, Linda. *Fire on the Wind.* New York: Bantam Doubleday Dell Books for Young Readers, 1995.

Kalman, Bobbie. *Summer Camp.* New York: Crabtree Publishing Co., 1995.

Kaye, Marilyn. *Phoebe: A Novel.* San Diego: Harcourt, Brace, Jovanovich, 1987.

Kroll, Steven. *Breaking Camp.* New York: Macmillan, 1985.

Levinson, Nancy Smiler. *Your Friend, Natalie Popper.* New York: Lodestar Books, 1991.

Levitin, Sonia. *Annie's Promise.* New York: Atheneum, 1993.

Pascal, Francine. *Love and Betrayal & Hold the Mayo!* New York: Viking Kestrel, 1985.

Peterson's Summer Opportunities for Kids and Teenagers, 1997. Princeton, NJ: Peterson's, 1997.

Stine, Megan and H. William Stine. *Camp Zombie.* New York: Random House, 1994.

Ware, Cheryl. *Sea Monkey Summer.* New York: Orchard Books, 1996.

BOOK CLUB

Read *Annie's Promise* by Sonia Levitin.

INTRODUCTORY ACTIVITIES

DAY ONE

Objective:	The students will discuss and describe various summer camps they have attended or know about.

Prior to the day of the lesson, ask the students to bring pictures of people at summer camp to class. The photographs might be of themselves, family members, friends, or pictures from magazines. The students and parents need to understand that the photographs will stay in the classroom on display throughout the week.

Hold a class discussion about summer camp. "Have you been to a summer camp? What was it like? Was it a traditional camp with fishing, canoeing, or swimming, or a nontraditional camp? Did you enjoy attending the camp? Why do you feel this way?"

Make a bulletin board with the title *SUMMER CAMP*. Ask each student to tell about the picture he or she brought to class. "Who is at the camp in the picture? Is it a traditional or nontraditional camp? Why do you feel this way?" Mount the pictures onto the bulletin board.

DAY TWO

STORY LESSON

Follow the *Presenting the Story Lesson* instructions in the Introduction. Each story lesson follows the same procedure; however, say the following in step 4: "The title of the story we're reading today is *Summer Camp Isn't What It Used to Be*. What do you think the story is about? What do you already know about summer camp?"

EXTENSION ACTIVITIES

1. The students research camps available for campers with special needs such as illness, disabilities, or children facing the death of family members. Each student chooses a camp and writes a short report describing the camp, its goals, the children it serves, and its history. Each report ends with a paragraph explaining why this camp is important. Information about such camps might be found on the Internet or in *Peterson's Summer Opportunities for Kids and Teenagers* (see Books to Read).

2. The students design a "Dream Camp." Their camp plans must include a theme, a map of the camp, a list of activities, a menu based on the theme, and the name of the best location for the site. They prepare a logo and motto to match their camp's theme.

3. (Complete this activity with the cooperation of a local elementary school.) Help your students prepare a half-day camp for local elementary students. It is best to work with one elementary grade level. Choose a theme for the camp, such as "Say No to Drugs" or "Dinosaur Camp," and allow your students to create activities around the theme. Include games and art projects based on the topic. If possible, design and paint T-shirts for the elementary students based on the theme of the camp.

SUMMER CAMP ISN'T WHAT
IT USED TO BE

Summer camp: tents, sleeping bags, campfires, bugs, bugs, bugs . . . . Today's summer camps are no longer the same-old-thing. There is something for everyone no matter what you like, where you live, or how much money you have.

Perhaps you'd like to learn more about a major subject you're considering for college. There are camps dedicated to every academic field you can imagine. You can go to geology camps, aerospace science camps, architecture camps, or prelaw camps.

In the fields of art, you can find camps focusing on everything from music to clowning. You can look into the Institute for Television, Film, and Radio Productions, the Athens Centre Program of Greek Theater in Greece, or the Duke Young Writers' Workshop. At the Aspen Music School, campers train in every musical discipline from orchestral instruments to audio recording. The camp lasts an entire nine weeks, and runs concurrently with the Aspen Music Festival.

There are even camps for sports enthusiasts ready to escape the classroom. You can practice your archery or aerobic skills. There are even camps for badminton lovers and all-terrain vehicle fans. The Philadelphia Flyers professional coaching staff teaches lacrosse, roller hockey, and more at the JKST Roller Hockey Camp.

Rub elbows with the animal population. Zoos throughout the country offer opportunities to work with the animals. Road's End Farm Horsemanship Camp, Camp Allen, and BROADREACH Adventures in Scuba and Sailing offer hands-on animal studies. Sea World/Busch Gardens Adventure Camps invite students in grades 6-12 to learn about "animals, science, and the outdoors." Students actually interact with the animals as they learn about animal care and veterinary science.

No matter who you are or what your interests are, there's a camp somewhere tailor-made for you. Many camps offer financial aid or services for "economically disadvantaged children." There's no doubt about it: Summer camp just isn't what it used to be.

QUESTIONS FOR SUMMER CAMP ISN'T WHAT IT USED TO BE

Literal Questions:

THE FACTS:

1. List three academic fields you can study at camp.

_____

_____

_____

2. List two camps where you can learn more about the fields of art.

_____

_____

_____

3. Who makes up the coaching staff at the JKST Roller Hockey Camp?

_____

_____

_____

4. What do students learn about at the Sea World/Busch Gardens Adventure Camps?

_____

_____

_____

SEQUENCE OF EVENTS:

5. Write the list of camp themes in the order presented in the story: the arts, sports, academics.

_____

_____

_____

6. Which camp does the article describe first: the JKST Roller Hockey Camp or the Aspen Music School?

_____

_____

_____

Name _____   Date _____

Interpretive Questions:

DRAWING CONCLUSIONS:

7. Why do summer camps offer such a wide variety of themes?

_____

_____

_____

_____

MAKING INFERENCES:

8. Are today's summer camps more entertaining than those visited by your parents? Why do you feel this way?

_____

_____

_____

_____

MAKING PREDICTIONS:

9. What summer camp themes might be available when the next generation enters the summer camp age group?

_____

_____

_____

_____

IDENTIFICATION OF CAUSE:

10. List three reasons why a teen might go to a summer camp.

_____

_____

_____

_____

IDENTIFICATION OF THE MAIN IDEA:

11. Write a title for the story. Use as few words as possible.

_____

_____

Name _____   **Date** _____

COMPARISON:

12. How is a traditional summer camp like the Sea World/Busch Gardens Adventure Camps? How are they different?

_____

_____

_____

_____

SUMMARIZE:

13. In your own words, tell about the offerings of one of the summer camps described in the story.

_____

_____

_____

_____

EFFECT:

14. What changes in family life since the 1970s might have affected the popularity of summer camps?

_____

_____

_____

_____

FACT AND OPINION:

15. The story said, "Many camps offer financial aid or services for 'economically disadvantaged children.'" Is this statement a fact or an opinion? How can you prove your answer?

_____

_____

_____

_____

ON YOUR OWN:

16. Write a question about the story for a teacher or another student to answer.

_____

_____

Name _____   Date _____

9. "MA" BARKER GUNNED DOWN BY F.B.I.
Reading Level = 9.34

ABOUT THE STORY

This is a *Moments in Time* story. On January 16, 1935, the F.B.I. tracked down and killed the notorious Karpis gang in a four- to six-hour gun battle. Led by their mother, Arizona Clark "Ma" Barker, the Barker boys and their gang committed robbery, murder, and kidnapping.

QUOTES OF THE WEEK

Quote 1:

"Evil deeds are like perfume—difficult to hide."[3] *(page 50)*—WEST AFRICAN SAYING

Quote 2:

"History . . . is indeed little more than the register of the crimes, follies, and misfortunes of mankind."[1] *(page 383)*—EDWARD GIBBON, *DECLINE AND FALL OF THE ROMAN EMPIRE*, Chapter 3

Quote 3:

"I know that I felt as if a terrific weight had been lifted from my shoulders now that the shadow of "Scarface Al" no longer hovered over Chicago—and over us. We had been lucky men to come through all in one piece."[7] *(page 248)* —ELIOT NESS, *ON THE CAPTURE OF AL "SCARFACE" CAPONE*

INTERVIEW TOPIC

Interview a person over the age of 60. Does the subject remember stories about the notorious gangs of the 1920s and 1930s, such as Bonnie and Clyde, "Ma" Barker, Al Capone, and others? Prepare a list of interpretive and literal questions. "What do you remember about these gangsters? Do you remember stories about gangsters of the period? Why did people find these gangsters fascinating? How did people feel about the gangsters during their era? Are these criminals now part of American folklore? Why do you feel this way?"

PREVIEW WORDS

culmination	*miscreant*
cache	*underworld*

WORD-ORIGIN STUDY

kidnap:	The word *kidnap* is a compound word combining the word *kid* (child) with *nap* (an alteration of the word nab).

---

[3] Refer to *Quotation Footnotes for Level 9* on page 406.

[1] Refer to *Quotation Footnotes for Level 9* on page 406.

[7] Refer to *Quotation Footnotes for Level 9* on page 406.

Originally, kidnapping referred to the stealing of a child. Today it means any forcible abduction of a person of any age.

miscreant: The prefix *mis-* (from *mes-*) meaning "less" is attached to the word *creant*, meaning "to believe." The original word meant "believing less, or unbelieving." Today a *miscreant* is an unbeliever or heretic. *Miscreant* also refers to a corrupt person or criminal, or acting in a villainous manner.

List other meanings for the prefix *mis-* along with examples of words using these meanings. Write the words and their definitions in your vocabulary notebook.

BOOKS TO READ

Bondi, Victor. *American Decades: 1930-1936*. New York: Gale Research, Inc., 1995.

Daniel, Clifton (ed.). *Chronicles of the 20th Century*. Mount Kisco, NY: Chronicle Publications, 1987.

Feder, Joshua B. *Gangsters: Portraits in Crime*. New York: Friedman Group, 1992.

Grant, Robert and Joseph Katz. *The Great Trials of the Twenties: The Watershed Decade in America's Courtrooms*. Rockville Centre, NY: Sarpedon, 1998.

MacNee, Marie J. *Outlaws, Mobsters & Crooks: From the Old West to the Internet*. Detroit, MI: UXL, 1998.

Murray, Jesse George. *Legacy of Al Capone: Portraits and Annals of Chicago's Public Enemies*. New York: G.P. Putnam, 1975.

Myers, Walter D. *The Mouse Rap*. New York: Harper & Row, 1990.

Ness, Eliot. *The Untouchables*. New York: Pocket Books, 1957.

Pace, Denny F. and Jimmie C. Styles. *Organized Crime: Concepts and Control*. Englewood Cliffs, NJ: Prentice-Hall, 1975.

Pasley, Fred D. *Al Capone: The Biography of a Self-Made Man*. Freeport, NY: Books for Libraries Press, 1971.

Schoenberg, Robert J. *Mr. Capone*. New York: Morrow, 1992.

Walker, Josh and Austin Sarat (eds.). *Organized Crime*. Philadelphia: Chelsea House Publishers, 1999.

Wolf, George. *Frank Costello: Prime Minister of the Underworld*. New York: William Morrow & Company, Inc., 1974.

Woodford, Jack and Neil Elliott (interviewer). *My Years With Capone: Jack Woodford and Al Capone, 1924-1932*. Seattle: Woodford Memorial Editions, 1985.

CDs, RECORDS, AND CASSETTES

Mary Higgins Clark Presents Malice Domestic 2 (Cassette). Los Angeles: Dove Audio, 1996. (Includes the story *The Return of Ma Barker* by Gary Alexander)

VIDEOS

Bougas, Nick and Tom Lavagnino. *The Real Stories of Al Capone, John Dillinger, Bonnie and Clyde and Others*. Chicago: Questar Video, 1994.

BOOK CLUB

Read the book *The Mouse Rap* by Walter D. Myers or *The Untouchables* by Eliot Ness.

INTRODUCTORY ACTIVITIES

DAY ONE

Objective: The students will watch a video outlining the history and biographies of gangsters of the early twentieth century.

Begin the lesson with a discussion about the American gangsters of the 1920s and 1930s. Do they know the history of such gangsters as Al Capone, Bonnie and Clyde, or John Dillinger? Who were these criminals? Why have they entered American folklore?

Watch a documentary about the gangsters of the 1920s and 1930s such as *The Real Stories of Al Capone, John Dillinger, and Bonnie and Clyde and Others*. After the movie, discuss the reasons why gang violence and unlawfulness rose during this time period. Do accounts of these mobsters' escapades glorify their violent acts? Why does the movie industry continue to show interest in violent gansters in movies such as *Bonnie and Clyde, The Untouchables*, or *The Godfather*?

On the chalkboard, list factual information about each criminal. List public opinion and folklore surrounding these individuals. "Is there a discrepancy? Why do you feel this way? If there are discrepancies, how does this affect our understanding of these criminals, their victims, and American history?"

DAY TWO

STORY LESSON

Follow the *Presenting the Story Lesson* instructions in the Introduction. Each story lesson follows the same procedure; however, say the following in step 4: "The story we're reading today is a *Moments in Time* article entitled '*Ma' Barker Gunned Down By F.B.I.* What do you think the story is about?"

EXTENSION ACTIVITIES

1. The students research the causes of the increase in gang violence during the 1920s and 1930s. They list at least five reasons for this outbreak, and describe the gang activities of the time. Next, students research five reasons for the current outbreak of gang violence, and describe the gangs' activities. "Can parallels be drawn between the two? Why do you feel this way?"

2. Invite a gang task force officer from your local police department to talk to the class. Ask the officer to prepare a discussion about the history of gang violence in America with a comparison between the gangs of the early twentieth century with current gangs. "What information can the officer present on the management of today's gang violence? What are the current trends? Is gang activity increasing or decreasing? What are the causes of these trends? Can we learn any lessons from the 1920s and 1930s that can be applied today? Why do you feel this way?"

3. Have the students investigate gang violence in the United States in the early twentieth century compared with other countries' criminal trends during the same time period. "Was the escalation of violence seen solely in America? On what facts do you draw your conclusions? If other countries suffered from different types and intensity of crimes, what is the cause of these differences?" The students write a report in standard form using at least five references explaining the results of their investigation.

"MA" BARKER GUNNED DOWN BY F.B.I.

F.B.I. officials announced that Ma Barker, age 55, and her son Fred, age 32, died today after a four- to six-hour gun battle. At the culmination of an extensive manhunt, F.B.I. agents discovered the Barkers, prominent members of the vicious Karpis gang, in a rented cottage in Lake Weir, Florida. According to reports, none of the dozen or more agents at the violent confrontation sustained injury.

Arizona Clark Barker, known more commonly by the name "Ma" Barker, was born and raised in Springfield, Missouri. It is there she once met the infamous Jesse James. In 1892, she entered into an unhappy marriage to farm laborer George Barker. The marriage produced four sons: Herman, Lloyd, Arthur ("Doc"), and Fred. Many believe Ma's guilt laid not in her crimes, but in her blind devotion to her sons.

Becoming increasingly miscreant, the boys entered a world of violent crime. After killing a watchman during a botched robbery, an Oklahoma jury sentenced Doc to life in prison. In 1927, when stopped by a pair of police officers in Wichita, Kansas, Herman opened fire, fatally shooting one officer in the head. Herman committed suicide in fear of capture, sending his mother into a deep and bitter depression.

It is this depression many blame for Ma's increased, yet unproven, involvement in the underworld. Obtaining Doc's pardon in 1933, Ma, with her surviving sons, joined the brutal Karpis gang.

The gang turned to kidnapping, abducting William Hamm, a successful Minneapolis brewer, and later Minneapolis banker Edward Bremer. The gang secured a two-hundred-thousand-dollar ransom from the Bremer kidnapping. During this time Ma's crimes included murder, not only of civilians, but members of her own gang.

Earlier this month, federal agents arrested Doc. According to reliable sources, Ma retrieved the ransom money just prior to the fatal shoot-out; however, officers never located the cache.

Questions for "Ma" Barker Gunned Down by F.B.I.

Literal Questions:

THE FACTS:

1. When does the story take place?

_____

_____

_____

2. Name "Ma" Barker's four sons.

_____

_____

_____

3. Why was Doc Barker sentenced to life in prison?

_____

_____

_____

4. Who was William Hamm?

_____

_____

_____

SEQUENCE OF EVENTS:

5. Write the following events in chronological order: Ma Barker met Jesse James; The gang secured a two-hundred-thousand-dollar ransom from the Bremer kidnapping; Ma Barker and her son Fred died after a four- to six-hour gun battle.

_____

_____

_____

6. Which happened first: an Oklahoma jury sentenced Doc to life in prison or Herman Barker committed suicide?

_____

_____

_____

Name _____   Date _____

Interpretive Questions:

DRAWING CONCLUSIONS:

7. What one word best describes Ma Barker? Why do you feel this way?

_____

_____

_____

_____

MAKING INFERENCES:

8. How did Herman Barker feel about being captured? What might have influenced his feelings?

_____

_____

_____

_____

MAKING PREDICTIONS:

9. Will Ma Barker become part of America's folklore? Why do you feel this way?

_____

_____

_____

_____

IDENTIFICATION OF CAUSE:

10. Why did Ma Barker become involved in her sons' criminal activities?

_____

_____

_____

_____

IDENTIFICATION OF THE MAIN IDEA:

11. Write a title for the story. Use as few words as possible.

_____

_____

_____

Name _____   **Date** _____

COMPARISON:

12. Compare the gang activity of the Barkers with the gang violence of today.

_____

_____

_____

_____

SUMMARIZE:

13. In your own words, tell about the events leading to the deaths of Ma and Fred Barker.

_____

_____

_____

_____

EFFECT:

14. What effect did Herman's suicide have on his mother? What specific information led you to your answer?

_____

_____

_____

_____

FACT AND OPINION:

15. The story said, "Many believe Ma's guilt laid not in her crimes, but in her blind devotion to her sons." Is this a fact or someone's opinion? Why do you feel this way?

_____

_____

_____

_____

ON YOUR OWN:

16. Write a question about the story for a teacher or another student to answer.

_____

_____

Name _____ **Date** _____

10. JOSEPH CARDINAL BERNARDIN
Reading Level = 9.44

ABOUT THE STORY

Joseph Bernardin was a priest following the words of Pope John XXIII, make "the human sojourn on earth less sad." When diagnosed with pancreatic cancer, Cardinal Bernardin embarked on his "cancer ministry." Two months before his death, Cardinal Bernardin was awarded the Medal of Freedom.

QUOTES OF THE WEEK

Quote 1:

"Faith and knowledge lean largely upon each other in the practice of medicine."[1] *(page 464)*—PETER MERE LATHAM, *COLLECTED WORKS*

Quote 2:

"He who has courage and faith will never perish in misery!"[1] *(page 909)* —ANNE FRANK, *ANNE FRANK: THE DIARY OF A YOUNG GIRL* (March 7, 1944)

Quote 3:

"What I would like to leave behind is a simple prayer that each of you may find what I have found-God's special gift to us all: the gift of peace."[8] *(page 152)*—JOSEPH CARDINAL BERNARDIN

INTERVIEW TOPIC

Interview any person asking him or her to give a definition for the term *role model*. Prepare a list of literal and interpretive questions. "What is your definition of the term *role model*? Are role models important? Why do you feel this way? Who are your role models? Why do you find this person, or people, inspiring?"

PREVIEW WORDS

Joseph Cardinal Bernardin *sojourn* *chaplin*
pancreatic *affliction*

WORD-ORIGIN STUDY

sojourn: The word *sojourn* comes from words meaning "under a day." To *sojourn* means to stay in a place only a short time; a temporary resident. A sojourner is a person who only stays for a visit. Pope John XXIII was quoted, make "the human sojourn on earth less sad." Based on the definition of *sojourn*, what does this quote mean?

---

[1] Refer to *Quotation Footnotes for Level 9* on page 406.
[8] Refer to *Quotation Footnotes for Level 9* on page 406.

affliction: The prefix *af-* is a form of the prefix *ad-* meaning "to, unto, or toward." The word *affliction* originally meant "to strike down." An *affliction* is a state of distress, pain, or anguish.

List other words beginning with the prefix *af-*. Write the words and their definitions in your vocabulary notebook.

BOOKS TO READ

Bernardin, Joseph Louis. *The Gift of Peace*. Chicago: Loyola Press, 1997.

Kennedy, Eugene. *My Brother Joseph: The Spirit of a Cardinal and the Story of a Friendship*. New York: St. Martin's Press, 1997.

Lucas, Eileen. *Peace on the Playground: Nonviolent Ways of Problem-Solving*. New York: Franklin Watts, 1991.

Naylor, Phyllis Reynolds. *The Agony of Alice*. New York: Atheneum Book Club, 1985.

Westridge Young Writers Workshop. *Kids Explore America's Hispanic Heritage*. Santa Fe, NM: John Muir Publications, 1992.

VIDEOS

Kerwin, John (producer). *The Positive Parent*. Carlsbad, CA: Bridgestone Group, 1977.

Perrone, Charlene (writer and producer). *The Entrepreneurs*: Ebony/Jet *Guide to Black Excellence: Program 1*. Chicago: Public Media Video, 1991.

_____. *The Leaders*: Ebony/Jet *Guide to Black Excellence: Program 2*. Chicago: Public Media Video, 1991.

_____. *The Entertainers*: Ebony/Jet *Guide to Black Excellance: Program 3*. Chicago: Public Media Video, 1991.

BOOK CLUB

Students read an autobiography or biography of their favorite role model. The teacher can assign biographies to avoid an abundance of books about sports figures and entertainers. This is an opportunity to expose students to lesser known role models such as Joseph Cardinal Bernardin or Clara "Mother" Hale.

INTRODUCTORY ACTIVITIES

DAY ONE

Objective: The students will define the term *role model* and list attributes of a role model.

Discuss the term *role model*. "What does it mean? Why are people concerned about young people having good role models? Are role models important?"

Write the information on chart paper. Help the students work together to write a clearly stated, precise definition of the term *role model*. Under the definition, list attributes one must have in order to be a role model. Display the chart throughout the lesson week.

DAY TWO

STORY LESSON

Follow the *Presenting the Story Lesson* instructions in the Introduction. Each story lesson follows the same procedure; however, say the following in step 4: "The title of the story we're reading today is *Joseph Cardinal Bernardin*. What do you think the story is about?"

EXTENSION ACTIVITIES

1. The students research three role models. They will write a brief description of the individual's life history, and explain why the person is a role model based on the definition written on Day One of the Introductory Activities. Students also list which of the attributes listed on Day One are possessed by their role model. Each of the three reports should be written separately. Encourage the students to look for people in history and in their local community. Do not use only entertainment or sports figures. Examples of community role models might be found in local volunteer organizations such as the Big Brothers and Sisters, a foster parent program, etc.

2. Make a bulletin board entitled "I Found My Role Models." Display the reports around the chart written on Day One of the Introductory Activities.

3. Using the reports on role models, the students vote for the Role Model of the Week. Display the report and a photograph of the role model in a prominent place in the school. Send a card, letter, or computer-generated certificate to the role model telling him or her of the selection as Role Model of the Week, and why. Addresses for celebrities and other famous personalities—such as architects, authors, public representatives, etc.—can be located through your public library. If the role model is deceased, your public library might help you locate that person's estate (surviving family).

JOSEPH CARDINAL BERNARDIN

Born to Italian immigrants in 1928, Joseph Bernardin began life amid the hopelessness of the Depression. Joseph's father worked in the darkness of the marble mines, but brought sunshine through his spirit to his young family.

By the time Joseph was six, his father passed away from the ravages of cancer. "What stands out most vividly," Cardinal Bernardin recalled, "are the many times he (his father) expressed his love for our family, even in the worst days of his illness." In the end, this was a lesson Joseph learned well.

Joseph Bernardin chose the path of a priest. In this role, he became a shepherd to many Christians. They admired his kindness and dedication to the people. He lived his life by the words of Pope John XXIII. He wanted to make "the human sojourn on earth less sad."

Joseph Bernardin served as an Auxiliary Bishop of Atlanta after his ordination into priesthood for the Diocese of Charleston in 1952. He went on to become General Secretary of the U.S. Bishops' Conference in Washington, D.C., Archbishop of Cincinnati, President of the Bishops' Conference, and Archbishop of Chicago. In 1983, he became a cardinal.

Throughout his service, Cardinal Bernardin earned the love and devotion of not only Catholics, but the American public at large. When doctors diagnosed Cardinal Bernardin with pancreatic cancer, the entire nation paused.

With dignity and devote faith, Cardinal Bernardin coped with the anguish of his own cancer. He inspired a nation as he reached out to others suffering with the same affliction. Soon he embarked on his "cancer ministry."

Cardinal Bernardin's dedication to those "suffering with heavy burdens" as he himself faced death inspired the nation. Two months before his death, America honored its "unofficial chaplain" to cancer patients with the Medal of Freedom.

QUESTIONS FOR JOSEPH CARDINAL BERNARDIN

Literal Questions:

THE FACTS:

1. Where and when was Joseph Bernardin born?

_____

_____

_____

2. How did Joseph's father die?

_____

_____

_____

3. What words did Joseph Bernardin live by?

_____

_____

_____

4. What honor was bestowed on Cardinal Bernardin two months before his death?

_____

_____

_____

SEQUENCE OF EVENTS:

5. Write the following events in chronological order: Joseph Bernardin became a cardinal; Joseph's father died of cancer; America honored Cardinal Bernardin with the Medal of Freedom.

_____

_____

_____

6. Which event occurred last in the story: doctors diagnosed Cardinal Bernardin with pancreatic cancer or Cardinal Bernardin embarked on his "cancer ministry?"

_____

_____

_____

Name _____   **Date** _____

Interpretive Questions:

DRAWING CONCLUSIONS:

7. What one word best describes Cardinal Joseph Bernardin?

_____

_____

_____

_____

MAKING INFERENCES:

8. During his lifetime, did Cardinal Bernardin make "the human sojourn on earth less sad?" Why do you feel this way?

_____

_____

_____

_____

MAKING PREDICTIONS:

9. Will the effects of Cardinal Bernardin's devotion to his fellow human beings continue to touch people long after his death? Why do you feel this way?

_____

_____

_____

_____

IDENTIFICATION OF CAUSE:

10. Why did Cardinal Bernardin embark on his "cancer ministry" rather than hiding himself away until his death?

_____

_____

_____

_____

IDENTIFICATION OF THE MAIN IDEA:

11. Write a title for the story. Use as few words as possible.

_____

_____

Name _____ **Date** _____

COMPARISON:

12. Compare Cardinal Bernardin's illness, attitude, and death to his father's. What do you believe the cardinal learned from his father?

_____

_____

_____

_____

SUMMARIZE:

13. In your own words, describe the career of Cardinal Bernardin.

_____

_____

_____

_____

EFFECT:

14. How might meeting Cardinal Bernardin during his cancer ministry affect those suffering from terminal illness?

_____

_____

_____

_____

FACT AND OPINION:

15. The story said, "He inspired a nation as he reached out to others suffering with the same affliction." Is this statement a fact or an opinion? Why do you feel this way?

_____

_____

_____

_____

ON YOUR OWN:

16. Write a question about the story for a teacher or another student to answer.

_____

_____

Name _____   **Date** _____

11. WHAT DOES "QWERTY" MEAN?

Reading Level = 9.45

ABOUT THE STORY

The letter arrangement on a computer keyboard appears confusing and illogical. However, there is a reasonable explanation that dates back to the original manual typewriter. The story investigates the progression of advancements in typing machines that led us to the current computer keyboard layout.

QUOTES OF THE WEEK

Quote 1:

"The computer is more than a tool, it is a medium. Just as the typeface standardized information—changing us from a society where information was at the mercy of monks busy with hand copying into a fact-loving society where nonfiction outsells fiction—so the computer will change the way we look at the world."[3] *(page 463)*—JOHN SCULLEY

Quote 2:

"I am pleased that history recognizes the first to invent something, but I am more concerned with the first person to make it work."[9] *(page 27)* —GRACE HOPPER

INTERVIEW TOPIC

Interview a person over the age of 40. Discuss the development of computers and how they affected the subject's life. Prepare a list of literal and interpretive questions. "When did you first hear the word *computer*? When did you use your first computer? What is the history of computers in your personal life? How have computers changed your life? Have the changes been for the better or worse? Why do you feel this way? What do you see as the influence of the computer on future generations?" Ask the subject if he or she has a photograph of or user's manual from an early computer model. Make a drawing of the picture and mount it with your interview.

PREVIEW WORDS

hodgepodge	*dubbed*	*Christopher Sholes*
Carlos Glidden	*Samuel W. Soule*	

WORD-ORIGIN STUDY

hodgepodge: *Hodgepodge* finds its origins in an Old Dutch phrase for a stew of beef or mutton cut into small pieces, mixed together, then boiled. It later took on the meaning of a "mingled mass." Today *hodgepodge* still refers to a stew of

---

[3] Refer to *Quotation Footnotes for Level 9* on page 406.
[9] Refer to *Quotation Footnotes for Level 9* on page 406.

various meats and vegetables mixed together, but it is often used to describe anything mixed in a mass.

illogical: *Logic* refers to reason, or the analyzing of information through sound reasoning. The prefix *il-* means "not." To be *illogical* is to not use sound reasoning.

List other words beginning with the prefix *il-*. Write the words with their definitions in your vocabulary notebook.

BOOKS TO READ

Coleman, Bob and Deborah Neville. *The Great American Idea Book.* New York: W.W. Norton, 1993.

James, Peter. *Ancient Inventions.* New York: Ballantine Books, 1994.

King, Buzz. *Silicon Songs.* New York: Delacorte Press, 1990.

Mazer, Harry. *City Light.* New York: Scholastic, 1988.

Mount, Ellis and Barbara A. List. *Milestones in Science and Technology: The Ready Reference Guide to Discoveries, Inventions, and Facts.* Phoenix: Oryx Press, 1994.

Readers Digest Staff. *Strange Stories, Amazing Facts: Stories That Are Bizarre, Unusual, Odd, Astonishing & Often Incredible.* Pleasantville, NY: Reader's Digest Association, Inc., 1976.

Rubinstein, Gillian. *Skymaze.* New York: Orchard Books, 1991.

Yenne, Bill. *100 Inventions That Shaped World History.* San Francisco: Bluewood Books, 1993.

BOOK CLUB

Read *Skymaze* by Gillian Rubinstein, *City Light* by Harry Mazer, or *Silicon Songs* by Buzz King.

INTRODUCTORY ACTIVITIES

DAY ONE

Objective: The students will conduct research to learn about the first computers.

Discuss the development of the computer. Do the students know the history of computers? As the students relate their ideas about the first computers, write their answers on a chart. Save the chart to use in the Extension Activities.

Send the students on a "Hunt for the First Computers." They can use a variety of references including the Internet. The students must bring the following information to class for the Extension Activities:

- When was the first computer invented?
- What was the computer called?
- Who invented the computer?
- What was the purpose of the computer?
- What was the computer's capabilities?
- What did the computer look like? (Include a drawing or picture.)
- How large was the computer?
- How was it different from the personal computers we use today?

The students must be prepared to tell about the computers they found, and participate in a discussion about the evolution of computer technology.

DAY TWO

STORY LESSON

Follow the *Presenting the Story Lesson* instructions in the Introduction. Each story lesson follows the same procedure; however, say the following in step 4: "The title of the story we're reading today is *What Does "QWERTY" Mean? What do you think the story is about?"

EXTENSION ACTIVITIES

1. Review the information written on the chart of the Introductory Activity for Day One. Now that the students have completed their research on computers, which ideas in Day One were correct? Which were incorrect?

   Discuss the results of the "Hunt for the First Computer." Index each report according to the date of the computer the students found. Begin to lay out a Computer Family Tree. The oldest computer is at the top of the tree, with successive computers trailing down the branches like a genealogical family tree. (See the example of the family tree in Extension Activity 3.)

2. As a group, finish the Computer Family Tree tracing the "roots" of the computer to the present. Next, predict what the descendants of today's computers will look like and how they will work. Continue to branch the tree down for three more generations.

3. Each student chooses an example of modern technology, such as the automobile, microwave, automated teller machine, etc. Make sure the students do not choose the same subject. Each student makes a family tree for his or her subject, and predicts the future development of the subject for the next three generations.

For example:

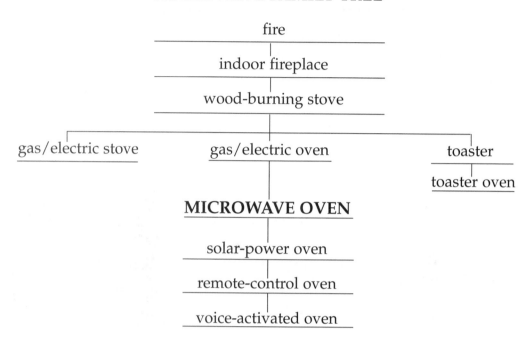

MICROWAVE FAMILY TREE

fire

indoor fireplace

wood-burning stove

gas/electric stove   gas/electric oven   toaster

                                                                toaster oven

MICROWAVE OVEN

solar-power oven

remote-control oven

voice-activated oven

4. The story *What Does "QWERTY" Mean?* investigates why keyboards developed their unique layout. The students explore the placement of the steering wheel in American automobiles. Present the question "Why do American automobiles have the steering wheel on the left side of the car while other countries place the steering wheel on the right?" Send them on a research hunt to discover the answer. Students might have similar questions they would like to examine. List the questions on a chart, and send students to the library or computers to unearth the answers.

WHAT DOES "QWERTY" MEAN?

Anyone can tell you the letter arrangement on a computer keyboard appears confusing and illogical. It's hard to believe there is actually a rational explanation for this hodgepodge of letters.

England granted the first patent for a typewriter in 1714 to a London engineer named Henry Mill; however, no one knows what Mill's typewriter looked like. In 1829, William Austin Burt of Detroit received a patent for a typewriter called the "Burt's Family Letter Press." A wooden box about 12 inches in length and height encased the press. On the front of the box was a dial resembling a clock that showed the amount of paper in the machine. The user turned a large crank at the top of the box, lined it up with a letter, then pressed down. With the help of an ink pad, the letter printed onto the paper.

In 1868, Christopher Sholes, Carlos Glidden, and Samuel W. Soule made the next important advancement in typewriter design. Like today's manual typewriter, individual letters sat on the end of long-armed bars. Using an alphabetically arranged keyboard, the typist pressed a key that activated the corresponding bar. The bar raised up, striking the paper, and printing the letter.

Although this was a significant advancement in typewriter design, it had one major flaw. When operated by a fast typist, the letter bars often crossed, locked together, and jammed. To reduce the occurrence of "jamming," Sholes studied the English language looking for the most commonly used letters, then he rearranged the keys to distribute these letters throughout the keyboard. By separating the most common letters, Sholes reduced the chances of striking two adjacent letter bars and causing a "jam."

Dubbed the QWERTY keyboard for the first letters on the top line, Sholes called his invention "A blessing to mankind—especially to womankind." As typewriters continued to develop from large office models to portable manuals to electric typewriters and on to computers, the QWERTY system remained.

QUESTIONS FOR WHAT DOES "QWERTY" MEAN?

Literal Questions:

THE FACTS:

1. Who was granted the first patent for a typewriter?

_____

_____

_____

2. When did Sholes, Glidden, and Soule make the next important advancement in typewriter design?

_____

_____

_____

3. How did Sholes reduce the occurrence of jamming?

_____

_____

_____

4. Why was Sholes's keyboard called the QWERTY keyboard?

_____

_____

_____

SEQUENCE OF EVENTS:

5. Which country issued the first patent for a typewriter, England or the United States?

_____

_____

_____

6. What did the Sholes, Glidden, and Soule typewriter do after the typist pressed a key?

_____

_____

_____

Name _____   Date _____

Interpretive Questions:

DRAWING CONCLUSIONS:

7. Although computer keys do not jam like manual typewriters, why do they still use the QWERTY keyboard rather than an alphabetical keyboard?

_____

_____

_____

_____

MAKING INFERENCES:

8. Why did Sholes say the QWERTY keyboard design was especially a blessing to womankind?

_____

_____

_____

_____

MAKING PREDICTIONS:

9. As computer technology advances, will we still use the QWERTY keyboard design? Why do you feel this way?

_____

_____

_____

_____

IDENTIFICATION OF CAUSE:

10. Why did Sholes want to reduce the occurrence of jamming on his typewriter design?

_____

_____

_____

_____

IDENTIFICATION OF THE MAIN IDEA:

11. Write a title for the story. Use as few words as possible.

_____

_____

Name _____ **Date** _____

COMPARISON:

12. Compare a manual typewriter to a computer.

_____

_____

_____

_____

SUMMARIZE:

13. In your own words, tell about the development of the typewriter.

_____

_____

_____

_____

EFFECT:

14. What effect, if any, might the QWERTY design have had on the sales of Sholes's typewriters?

_____

_____

_____

_____

FACT AND OPINION:

15. Sholes called his invention "A blessing to mankind—especially to womankind." Is this statement a fact or Sholes's opinion? Why do you feel this way?

_____

_____

_____

_____

ON YOUR OWN:

16. Write a question about the story for a teacher or another student to answer.

_____

_____

Name _____   **Date** _____

12. ADOPT-A-SENIOR
Reading Level = 9.46

ABOUT THE STORY

Adopt-a-Senior is a unique program that reaches out to at-risk seniors at Smoky Hill High School in Aurora, Colorado. Seniors at risk of dropping out choose a faculty member as their adopted mentor. The mentors give these students special attention, and work with parents in an attempt to avoid failure, or drop-outs. Seventy-five percent of the students in the program graduated.

QUOTES OF THE WEEK

Quote 1:

"The object of education is to prepare the young to educate themselves throughout their lives."[2] *(page 172)*—ROBERT MAYNARD HUTCHINS

Quote 2:

"Education is helping a child realize his potentialities."[2] *(page 173)*
—ERICH FROMM

Quote 3:

"The great end of education is to discipline rather than to furnish the mind; to train it to the use of its own powers, rather than fill it with the accumulation of others."[2] *(page 173)*—TRYON EDWARDS (1809-1894)

Quote 4:

"A child miseducated is a child lost."[2] *(page 173)*—JOHN F. KENNEDY

INTERVIEW TOPIC

Interview a person over the age of 20 concerning the importance of a high school diploma. Prepare a list of literal and interpretive questions. "Why is it important to earn a high school diploma? What did you learn about the importance of a high school diploma after you left high school that you did not know as a teen? If you did not graduate from high school, do you regret not earning a diploma? Why do you feel this way? If you did graduate from high school, what benefits did you receive by earning a diploma?" If possible, ask the subject for a copy of a graduation photograph to include with your interview.

PREVIEW WORDS

mentor   distinctive   implement

---

[2] Refer to *Quotation Footnotes for Level 9* on page 406.

WORD-ORIGIN STUDY

mentor:	In the mythological epic the *Odyssey*, Mentor was the name of a friend and counselor to Ulysses and his son Telemachus. Because Mentor was a trusted counselor, Athena occasionally took his form to advise Telemachus. Today a *mentor* is a person who takes on the role of counselor and friend.
distinctive:	The prefix *dis-* indicates separation, negation, or reversal. To be *distinctive* is to possess qualities that separate or distinguish the subject from others.

List other words beginning with the prefix *dis-*. List the words and their definitions in your vocabulary notebook.

BOOKS TO READ

Bautista, Veltisezar B. *Improve Your Grades: A Practical Guide to Academic Excellence.* Farmington Hills, MI: Bookhaus Publishers, 1990.

Burgess, Melvin. *Smack.* New York: Henry Holt and Company, 1996.

Coman, Marcia J. *What You Need to Know About Developing Study Skills, Taking Notes & Tests, Using Dictionaries and Libraries.* Lincolnwood, IL: NTC Pub. Group, 1995.

Dellabough, Robin. *101 Ways to Get Straight A's.* Mahwah, NJ: Troll Associates, 1994.

Fry, Ronald W. *Improve Your Reading.* Hawthorne, NJ: Career Press, 1991.

_____. *Take Notes.* Hawthorne, NJ: Career Press, 1991.

_____. *Write Papers.* Hawthorne, NJ: Career Press, 1991.

Greene, Lawrence J. *1001 Ways to Improve Your Child's Schoolwork: An Easy-to-Use Reference Book of Common School Problems and Practical Solutions.* New York: Dell, 1991.

Nathan, Amy. *Surviving Homework: Tips From Teens.* Brookfield, CT: Millbrook Press, 1996.

Wirths, Claudine G. *I Hate School.* New York: Harper/Crowell, 1986.

VIDEOS

Class Act. Fairfield, CT: Prevention Publishing, 1992.

Pomeroy, Johanna. *Test Taking Techniques.* Freeport, NY: Educational Activities Video, 1994.

There's an A in Your Day: How to Earn Straight A's in School. Mesa, AZ: Premier American Educational Publishers, 1992.

BOOK CLUB

Read *Smack* by Melvin Burgess (awarded the Carnegie Medal and Guardian Prize for fiction).

INTRODUCTORY ACTIVITIES

DAY ONE

Objective: The students will review the drop-out and failure rates of their school and school district.

Through the use of the Internet and information on public record as well as reports obtained from the principal and school district, the students review the drop-out and failure rates of their school and school district. "What information can you learn from these reports? How does our school compare with other schools in the district? How does the school compare nationally? How does the failure rate compare to previous years?" Using the information, predict the possible drop-out rate for the upcoming year.

DAY TWO

STORY LESSON

Follow the *Presenting the Story Lesson* instructions in the Introduction. Each story lesson follows the same procedure; however, say the following in step 4: "The title of the story we're reading today is *Adopt-a-Senior*. The story tells about a unique education program for high school seniors."

EXTENSION ACTIVITIES

1. Through a class discussion, develop a plan to reduce drop-out and failure rates for your school using a brainstorming session. Use information about successful intervention programs such as the Adopt-a-Senior program for reference.

2. Invite the principal to the class to hold a discussion on the drop-out and failure rates of the school. What information can he or she share about the problem? The students share with the principal their ideas and strategies devised in Activity One.

3. Look into statistics concerning the affect of high school drop-outs on the economy nationally, statewide, and locally, as well as the affect on the personal lives of citizens not holding high school degrees. Based on these statistics, each student writes a report in standard form using at least five references.

ADOPT-A-SENIOR

Throughout the country, high school students fail to graduate at alarming rates. Statistics tell us that these students reduce their chances of creating a fulfilling adult life.

One school, Smoky Hill High School of Aurora, Colorado, began a unique program aptly named Adopt-a-Senior. This special program relies on faculty and staff volunteers. These volunteers act as mentors for at-risk students.

Teachers, counselors, and deans follow the progress of students as they work their way through high school. Seniors identified as at-risk for failure or drop-out become eligible for "adoption." In the 1995-1996 school year, mentors adopted more than 60 out of 533 students.

Adopted seniors look over the names of the volunteers and select their own mentor. The ability to choose adds a personalized dimension to the adoption process.

Mentors and students meet often during the school year. The students share their interests, and their mentors help them set educational and personal goals. Parents receive monthly progress reports.

How effective is the Adopt-a-Senior program? Mary G. Jarvis, principal of Smoky Hill High School, reports, "Our graduation rate has steadily risen in the five years since program inception; the current rate is more than 93 percent, an increase of 4 percent." Seventy-five percent of the Adopt-a-Senior participants graduated between the years 1990 and 1995.

To read more about the Adopt-a-Senior program, look for articles by Mary G. Jarvis in *The High School Magazine* (June/July 1996, pp. 12–17) and *The Education Digest* ("Personalizing High School," September 1996, pp. 19-22). Through personalized attention, every high school student can enter his or her adult life knowing someone cared enough to listen.

QUESTIONS FOR ADOPT-A-SENIOR

Literal Questions:

THE FACTS:

1. Which school implemented the Adopt-a-Senior program?

_____

_____

_____

2. Who acted as mentors for at-risk students?

_____

_____

_____

3. How often did parents receive progress reports?

_____

_____

_____

4. What percentage of the Adopt-a-Senior participants graduated between the years 1990 and 1995?

_____

_____

_____

SEQUENCE OF EVENTS:

5. What was the first step of the Adopt-a-Senior program: the students chose their own mentor or the students set educational and personal goals?

_____

_____

_____

6. What happened before the students met with their mentors?

_____

_____

_____

Name _____ **Date** _____

Interpretive Questions:

DRAWING CONCLUSIONS:

7. Was the Adopt-a-Senior program successful? What specific information led you to your conclusion?

_____

_____

_____

_____

MAKING INFERENCES:

8. Did most of the participating students follow the advice of their mentors? Why do you feel this way?

_____

_____

_____

_____

MAKING PREDICTIONS:

9. Would your school benefit from a program such as Adopt-a-Senior? Why do you feel this way?

_____

_____

_____

_____

IDENTIFICATION OF CAUSE:

10. Why were teachers, counselors, and deans willing to volunteer as mentors?

_____

_____

_____

_____

IDENTIFICATION OF THE MAIN IDEA:

11. Write a title for the story. Use as few words as possible.

_____

_____

Name _____   **Date** _____

COMPARISON:

12. Compare the possible future of an Adopt-a-Senior participant with the possible future of a student who chose not to participate?

_____

_____

_____

_____

SUMMARIZE:

13. In your own words, tell about the Adopt-a-Senior program.

_____

_____

_____

_____

EFFECT:

14. What effect did the mentors have on the lives of the adopted students? Why do you feel this way?

_____

_____

_____

_____

FACT AND OPINION:

15. The story said, "Seventy-five percent of the Adopt-a-Senior participants graduated between the years 1990 and 1995." Is this statement a fact or someone's opinion? How can you prove your answer?

_____

_____

_____

_____

ON YOUR OWN:

16. Write a question about the story for a teacher or another student to answer.

_____

_____

Name _____   Date _____

13. 1,200 DEAD IN CAMEROON
Reading Level = 9.55

ABOUT THE STORY

This is a *Moments in Time* story. On August 25, 1996, 1,200 people died in Cameroon (West Africa) when a toxic cloud swept over several villages. Many residents were asphyxiated in their sleep. According to geologists, a dormant volcano hidden at the bottom of Lake Nios suddenly erupted, spewing poisonous gas over its victims.

QUOTES OF THE WEEK

Quote 1:

"To destroy is still the strongest instinct in nature."[3] *(page 376)*
—MAX BEERBOHM

Quote 2:

"But perhaps the universe is suspended on the tooth of some monster."[3]
(page 377)—ANTON CHEKHOV

Quote 3:

"It is far from easy to determine whether nature has proved to man a kind parent or a merciless stepmother."[3] *(page 377)*—PLINY THE ELDER

INTERVIEW TOPIC

Interview any person who survived a natural disaster. Prepare a list of interpretive and literal questions. "What was the natural disaster you experienced? When did it occur? How old were you at the time? What was your immediate reaction? What was the long-term affect of the disaster on your life? What did you learn about surviving a natural disaster? What advice would you give others?"

PREVIEW WORDS

Cameroon	*Paul Biya*	*Lake Nios*
Lake Mounoun	*asphyxiating*	*hindered*

WORD-ORIGIN STUDY

volcano:	The word *volcano* comes from the name of the god Vulcan, god of fire.
asphyxiating:	*Asphyxia* or *asphyxy* originated from two Greek words meaning "the stopping of the pulse, and to beat violently." *Asphyxiation* is death by suffocation caused by a lack of oxygen, or "too much carbon dioxide in the blood."

---

[3] Refer to *Quotation Footnotes for Level 9* on page 406.

> **hindered:** The word *hinder* comes from *hind,* "back, or behind." To *hinder* is to hold back or impede. It can also mean the hind, rear, or back as in "the hinder part of the ship." If you stand in back of a person, you are be<u>hind</u> him or her.

List the multiple meanings of the prefix *be-* along with examples of words using *be-* in its various meanings. Write the words and their definitions in your vocabulary notebook.

BOOKS TO READ

Brindze, Ruth. *Hurricanes: Monster Storms From the Sea.* New York: Atheneum, 1973.

Daily News (Longview, WA) and the *Journal–American* (Bellevue, WA). *Volcano, The Eruption of Mount St. Helens.* Longview, WA: Longview Publishing Co., 1980.

Foster, Robert J. *Geology,* 3rd ed. Columbus, OH: Charles E. Merrill Publishing Company, 1976.

Lauber, Patricia. *Volcano: The Eruption and Healing of Mount St. Helens.* New York: Bradbury Press, 1986.

Legrand, Jacques (publisher). *Chronicles of the 20th Century.* Mount Kisco, NY: Chronicle Publications, Inc., 1987.

Lehman, Yvonne. *Tornado Alley.* Minneapolis: Bethany House Publishers, 1996.

Simpson, Robert H. and Herbert Riehl. *The Hurricane and Its Impact.* Baton Rouge: Louisiana State University Press, 1981.

Smith, Roland. *Sasquatch.* New York: Hyperion Books for Children, 1998.

Thomas, Joyce Carol. *Marked by Fire.* New York: Avon Books, 1982.

Tufty, Barbara. *1001 Questions Answered About Storms, and Other Natural Air Disasters.* New York: Dodd, Mead, 1970.

VIDEOS

The American Experience: The Great San Francisco Earthquake. Boston: WGBH; New York: WNET; Los Angeles: KCET; Public Broadcasting Service, 1989.

The Hawaiian Volcanoes: A Force for Creation. Hilo, HI: Harada Productions, 1989.

Nature: The Volcano Watchers. Beverly Hills, CA: PBS Home Video, 1990.

Volcano! Washington, D.C.: National Geographic Video, 1992.

BOOK CLUB

Read *Sasquatch* by Roland Smith.

INTRODUCTORY ACTIVITIES

DAY ONE

Objective: The students will discuss the geographical features of the area they live in. They make a map of the area indicating land formations.

Invite a local geologist to the class to discuss and illustrate the unique geological features of the land on which your community is built. Ask the speaker to outline the geological history of the area. Are there unique land formations in the area?

With the help of the geologist, the students make maps of the geological features of the area. Include features perhaps hidden under vegetation, such as fault lines. Look for areas not suitable for construction. Are developers building on this land? Why did they choose this location?

As a group, write a brief summery of the geological history of your community. "How were the mountains formed? Was the land once part of a seabed? Are there extinct volcanoes in the region? Why did they become extinct?"

End the class with a question-and-answer session.

DAY TWO

STORY LESSON

Follow the *Presenting the Story Lesson* instructions in the Introduction. Each story lesson follows the same procedure; however, say the following in step 4: "The title of the story we're reading today is *1,200 Dead in Cameroon*. What do you think the story is about?"

EXTENSION ACTIVITIES

1. Watch the video *Volcano!* or *Nature: The Volcano Watchers*. Discuss how the eruptions featured in the video are like the Cameroon eruption described in the story. How are they different?

2. The students research a natural disaster in the history of their community. "What was the disaster: a flood, tornado, hurricane, or earthquake? What was the impact of the disaster on the community and individuals? What changes were made, if any, in local policy or construction to reduce the damage and deaths associated with the reoccurrence of such a disaster?" Contact your local newspaper. There might be photographs available to the students featuring the damage caused by the disaster.

3. As a class, prepare a list of possible natural disasters that could occur in your area. Students will use this list for activities in the next story lesson, *Predicting the Next Earthquake*.

1,200 DEAD IN CAMEROON

About 1,200 people died in Cameroon (West Africa) when a rapidly moving toxic cloud swept over several villages. According to President Paul Biya, the cloud erupted from Lake Nios in Northeastern Cameroon. Local officials reported a large explosion which sent toxic gas spewing from the lake. The source of the gas appears to be a dormant volcano at the bottom of the lake. The toxic gas enveloped three villages on shore, asphyxiating many residents as they slept.

Scientists believe the gas was a mixture of carbon dioxide and hydrogen which combined to create an acidic vapor that burned the lungs of its victims. Observers compare this incident to a similar eruption in 1984 at Lake Mounoun. In that tragedy nearly a dozen people lost their lives.

Geologists explained that such a release of toxic gas from volcanos is fairly common. Robert J. Foster compared the release of gases from a volcano to bubbles suddenly pouring from an opened soda bottle.[1] Liquid in soda dissolves carbon dioxide when the contents are under pressure. Opening the bottle releases the pressure, and the gas fizzes out from the liquid.

At Lake Nios, the earthen "lid" over the volcano kept the toxic gas dissolved within the magma. Years of built-up tension blasted the lid off the volcano. This sudden release of pressure allowed the rapid escape of gases. The high-pressure release sent poisonous fumes racing through the atmosphere leaving no time to escape.

Medical personnel from around the world rush to Cameroon in fear of an epidemic. Hindered by remaining pockets of toxic gas, rescuers are unable to reach the decaying bodies of the victims.

---

[1] Foster, Robert J. *Geology,* 3rd ed., Columbus, OH: Charles E. Merrill Publishing Company, 1976, page 25.

QUESTIONS FOR 1,200 DEAD IN CAMEROON

Literal Questions:

THE FACTS:

1. Where is Cameroon located?

_____

_____

_____

2. What appeared to be the source of the gas that killed 1,200 people in Cameroon?

_____

_____

_____

3. How many villages did the toxic gas envelop?

_____

_____

_____

4. What hindered rescuers from reaching the dead?

_____

_____

_____

SEQUENCE OF EVENTS:

5. Which happened last: the eruption at Lake Mounoun or the eruption at Lake Nios?

_____

_____

_____

6. What happened after the blast suddenly released the pressure built up inside the volcano?

_____

_____

_____

Name _____   Date _____

Interpretive Questions:

DRAWING CONCLUSIONS:

7. The word *dormant* means "to sleep." Why was the volcano under Lake Nios described as dormant, rather than extinct?

_____

_____

_____

_____

MAKING INFERENCES:

8. How did the world feel about the deaths of the Cameroon citizens? On what specific information in the story do you base your answer?

_____

_____

_____

_____

MAKING PREDICTIONS:

9. Will an eruption similar to the one in Lake Nios happen in the future? Why do you feel this way?

_____

_____

_____

_____

IDENTIFICATION OF CAUSE:

10. What caused the eruption of the volcano in Lake Nios?

_____

_____

_____

_____

IDENTIFICATION OF THE MAIN IDEA:

11. Write a title for the story. Use as few words as possible.

_____

_____

Name _____ **Date** _____

COMPARISON:

12. Compare the eruption in Lake Nios with the eruption in Lake Mounoun. How were the eruptions alike? How were they different?

_____

_____

_____

_____

SUMMARIZE:

13. In your own words, explain how the eruption of the volcano was like bubbles suddenly pouring from an opened soda bottle.

_____

_____

_____

_____

EFFECT:

14. What effect, if any, might the eruption of the volcano have on the planning of village development in Cameroon? Why do you feel this way?

_____

_____

_____

_____

FACT AND OPINION:

15. The story said, "Geologists explained that such a release of toxic gas from volcanos is fairly common." Is this a fact or the geologists' opinion? How can you prove your answer?

_____

_____

_____

_____

ON YOUR OWN:

16. Write a question about the story for a teacher or another student to answer.

_____

_____

Name _____   Date _____

14. PREDICTING THE NEXT EARTHQUAKE
Reading Level = 9.59

ABOUT THE STORY

Throughout history, scientists looked for ways to predict earthquakes. An accurate and timely warning could save thousands of lives. The story traces the history of earthquake prediction dating back to 132 A.D.

QUOTES OF THE WEEK

Quote 1:

"It is a test of true theories not only to account for but to predict phenomena."[1] *(page 472)*—WILLIAM WHEWELL, *PHILOSOPHY OF THE INDUCTIVE SCIENCES*, Aphorism 39

Quote 2:

"Lots of new buildings just recently finished are completely destroyed. They are blowing up standing buildings that are in the path of flames with dynamite. Now water. It's awful. There is no communication anywhere and entire phone system busted. I want to get out of here or be blown up."[10] *(page 122)*—CHIEF TELEGRAPH OFFICER, SAN FRANCISCO, APRIL 18, 1906, 2:20 P.M. (THE FINAL MESSAGE FROM SAN FRANCISCO AFTER THE EARTHQUAKE)

INTERVIEW TOPIC

Interview a person at or above the age of 21. How has this person prepared for the possibility of a natural disaster, such as an earthquake, tornado, or flood? Prepare a list of literal and interpretive questions. "Have you made provisions for the possibility of a natural disaster? What type of precautions have you taken? If a natural disaster should occur, have you a plan of action? In your opinion, what should people do to protect themselves from the effects of a natural disaster?

PREVIEW WORDS

seismology   *Panayiotis Varotsos*
Chang Heng   *instantaneously*

WORD-ORIGIN STUDY

seismology: The prefix *seismo-* is derived from the Greek word meaning "to shake, or earthquake." *Seismology* is the science or study of earthquakes.

prediction: The prefix *pre-* means "before." To make a *prediction* is to foretell an event, or tell people about the possibility of the event before it happens.

---

[1] Refer to *Quotation Footnotes for Level 9* on page 406.
[10] Refer to *Quotation Footnotes for Level 9* on page 406.

List other words beginning with the prefix *pre-*. Write the words and their definitions in your vocabulary notebook.

BOOKS TO READ

Corley, Edwin. *The Genesis Rock*. Garden City, NY: Doubleday, 1980.

Cottonwood, Joe. *Quake!: A Novel*. New York: Scholastic Inc., 1995.

Goodman, Jeffrey. *We Are the Earthquake Generation: Where and When the Catastrophes Will Strike*. New York: Seaview Books; trade distribution by Simon & Schuster, 1978.

Iacopi, Robert. *Earthquake Country*. Menlo Park, CA: Lane Books, 1971.

Kehret, Peg. *Earthquake Terror*. New York: Cobblehill Books/Dutton, 1996.

Levy, Matthys and Mario Salvadori. *Earthquake Games: Earthquakes and Volcanoes Explained by 32 Games and Experiments*. New York: MK McElderry Books, 1997.

National Geographic Society. *Nature on the Rampage*. Washington, D.C.: National Geographic Society, 1986.

_____. *Powers of Nature*. Washington, D.C.: National Geographic Society, 1978.

Paananen, Eloise. *Earthquake*. New York: The John Day Company, 1966.

Reader's Digest Staff. *Strange Stories, Amazing Facts: Stories That Are Bizarre, Unusual, Odd, Astonishing & Often Incredible*. Pleasantville, NY: The Reader's Digest Association, Inc., 1976.

Stern, Richard Martin. *Flood*. Garden City, NY: Doubleday & Co., 1979.

Thomas, Gordon and Max Morgan-Witts. *The San Francisco Earthquake*. New York: Stein and Day, 1971.

Thomas, Joyce Carol. *Marked by Fire*. New York: Avon Books, 1982.

Verschuur, Gerrit L. *Cosmic Catastrophes*. Reading, MA: Addison-Wesley Publishing Co., 1978.

Waltham, Tony. *Catastrophe: The Violent Earth*. New York: Crown Publishers, 1978.

VIDEOS

The American Experience: The Great San Francisco Earthquake. Boston: WGBH; New York: WNET; Los Angeles: KCET; Public Broadcasting Service, 1989.

Grazulis, Tom (writer, producer, and director). *Twisters!: Nature's Fury/Channel 1000*. Thousand Oaks, CA: Goldhil Video, 1996.

MacLeod, Anne. *Natural Disasters*. New York: Dorling Kindersley Vision, 1997.

ARTICLES

Carlson, Shawn. "Detecting Natural Electromagnetic Waves (Using a Radio Detector to Predict Earthquake Activity)." *Scientific American*, vol. 274, no. 5 (May 1996), 98(3).

Kerr, Richard. "Quake Prediction Tool Gains Ground (Electromagnetic Changes in the Crust Used to Predict Earthquakes)." *Science*, vol. 270, no. 5238 (November 10, 1995), 911(2).

BOOK CLUB

Read *Quake!: A Novel* by Joe Cottonwood.

INTRODUCTORY ACTIVITIES

DAY ONE

Objective: The students will learn about ways in which natural disasters are predicted in their area, and how the public is warned.

Prior to the lesson, learn what natural disasters are likely to occur in your area. (See Extension Activities for the Level 9 story *1,200 Dead in Cameroon*). Is your community prone to earthquakes, tornadoes, hurricanes, floods, etc.? Invite a person employed in public safety to speak to your class about prediction, warning systems, and disaster-management plans in your community. This speaker might be a member of the weather service or an employee of the town or city. End the lesson with a question-and-answer session.

DAY TWO

STORY LESSON

Follow the *Presenting the Story Lesson* instructions in the Introduction. Each story lesson follows the same procedure; however, say the following in step 4: "The title of the story we're reading today is *Predicting the Next Earthquake*. What do you think the story is about? What do you already know about earthquakes? What do you already know about earthquake prediction?"

EXTENSION ACTIVITIES

1. Invite a representative from the Red Cross or other disaster relief organization to talk about preparing for emergencies, such as natural disasters. The procedures will vary depending on your area. The students are to list supplies to keep on hand at home in case of an emergency: bottled water, flashlights, can opener, canned foods, etc. Next, make a list of procedures students should follow when an emergency occurs: turn off the gas, leave the building, locate a shelter, etc. Finally, make a list of how and where to seek information during an emergency: listen for weather sirens, turn on a weather radio run on batteries, listen for special announcements on television or radio, etc. Again, all the information will vary from city to city, town to town. Include information for stu-

dents living in houses as well as those living in apartments. Also, discuss the importance of keeping personal records, such as wills, insurance policies, etc., in safe deposit boxes.

2. Each student makes a poster to mount at home. The poster should consist of three lists: emergency supplies, emergency procedures, and where to listen for information during an emergency. Include space to list locations of personal records such as wills, insurance policies, etc. Make each list clear, but concise. Laminate the poster to protect it from moisture. Avoid elaborate decorations that might detract from the vital information.

3. Make extra posters. Send students to local elementary schools, senior citizen centers, etc., to spread the word about personal preparation for emergencies. Supply the schools and centers with the extra posters to display as public-awareness information.

PREDICTING THE NEXT EARTHQUAKE

Throughout history, scientists have tried to predict earthquakes. Successful earthquake prediction could save incalculable lives. Every country prone to earthquake activity invests millions of dollars in the science of earthquake prediction.

Greek physicist Panayiotis Varotsos and his co-workers believe they found a dependable form of Earthquake prediction. Varotsos measured changes in the Earth's crust's electrical activity using giant voltmeters. Many seismologists believe such changes in electrical activity precede earthquakes. Using this method, Varotsos predicted three earthquakes in Greece.

Chinese seismologists successfully predicted three out of seven earthquakes in a three-month period using information from ongoing seismic activity. China evacuated 150,000 people using this prediction method, possibly saving thousands of lives.

However, many scientists believe that earthquake prediction is an impossible goal. Fractures in geological faults occur instantaneously. Even small tremors can set off massive quakes. Sudden quakes give little or no warning, leaving no time for evacuation. Many scientists believe earthquake funding should concentrate on the development of earthquake-proof buildings and roads.

Perhaps the most amazing instrument developed to detect earthquakes came from China in 132 A.D. A Chinese astronomer, Chang Heng, invented an early "earthquake alarm." This beautiful instrument resembled an urn placed upside down. The urn stood eight-feet tall. Eight dragons dangled from the top of the vessel, hanging by their tails. Each dragon pointed to a direction of the compass. In their mouths, the dragons held a small ball. Below the snout of each dragon sat a small, open-mouthed frog patiently waiting for the next quake.

Heng suspended a pendulum inside the urn like a clapper hanging in a bell. When an earthquake hit, the pendulum swung in the direction of the quake. The swinging pendulum triggered the jaw of the dragon facing the earthquake to open, dropping the ball into the open mouth of the frog waiting below.

QUESTIONS FOR PREDICTING THE NEXT EARTHQUAKE

Literal Questions:

THE FACTS:

1. Who believe they have found a dependable form of earthquake prediction?

_____

_____

_____

2. Who successfully predicted three out of seven earthquakes in a three-month period?

_____

_____

_____

3. Where do many scientists believe agencies should concentrate earthquake funding?

_____

_____

_____

4. Who invented an early "earthquake alarm"?

_____

_____

_____

SEQUENCE OF EVENTS:

5. What did Heng's "earthquake alarm" do after it detected an earthquake?

_____

_____

_____

6. What do many seismologists believe precede earthquakes?

_____

_____

_____

Name _____   Date _____

Interpretive Questions:

DRAWING CONCLUSIONS:

7. Why do you believe many of the advancements in earthquake prediction occurred in China?

_____

_____

_____

_____

MAKING INFERENCES:

8. Based on what you read in the story, have scientists focused on predicting earthquakes or making earthquake-proof buildings?

_____

_____

_____

_____

MAKING PREDICTIONS:

9. Will scientists and architects work together to develop earthquake-proof buildings and roads? Why do you feel this way?

_____

_____

_____

_____

IDENTIFICATION OF CAUSE:

10. Why has every country prone to earthquake activity invested millions of dollars in the science of earthquake prediction?

_____

_____

_____

_____

IDENTIFICATION OF THE MAIN IDEA:

11. Write a title for the story. Use as few words as possible.

_____

_____

Name _____   Date _____

COMPARISON:

12. How is developing techniques to predict earthquakes like building earthquake-proof buildings and roads? How is it different?

_____

_____

_____

_____

SUMMARIZE:

13. In your own words, describe Chang Heng's "earthquake alarm."

_____

_____

_____

_____

EFFECT:

14. What effect, if any, would the ability to predict earthquakes have on southern California?

_____

_____

_____

_____

FACT AND OPINION:

15. The story said, ". . . many scientists believe that earthquake prediction is an impossible goal." Is this statement a fact or the scientists' opinion? How can you prove your answer?

_____

_____

_____

_____

ON YOUR OWN:

16. Write a question about the story for a teacher or another student to answer.

_____

_____

Name _____ Date _____

15. CHARLES KURALT: JOURNALIST OF THE PEOPLE

Reading Level = 9.64

ABOUT THE STORY

Charles Kuralt started working at CBS as a travelling reporter. In 1967, Kuralt began his series *On the Road*, which consisted of interviews taken along the back roads of America. Winning several awards, including Emmys and George Foster Peabody awards, Charles Kuralt became the "journalist of the people." Kuralt died of lupus at the age of 62 in 1997.

QUOTES OF THE WEEK

Quote 1:

"Thanks to the interstate highway system, it is now possible to travel across the country coast to coast without seeing anything."[3] *(page 338)*
—CHARLES KURALT

Quote 2:

"Along with responsible newspapers we must have responsible readers."[2] *(page 323)*—ARTHUR HAYS SULZBERGER

Quote 3:

"The only authors whom I acknowledge as American are the journalists. They, indeed, are not great writers, but they speak the language of their countrymen, and make themselves heard by them."[2] *(page 325)*
—ALEXIS DE TOCQUEVILLE (1805-1859)

INTERVIEW TOPIC

Interview people who remember the *On the Road* series by Charles Kuralt. Prepare a question list that includes literal and interpretive questions. "Did you enjoy the *On the Road* series? Why do you feel this way? What is the most memorable story from the series? Why do you remember it so vividly? What was your opinion of Charles Kuralt as a journalist? Why do you feel this way?"

PREVIEW WORDS

venal   *accolades*   *succumbed*   *lupus*

WORD-ORIGIN STUDY

reporter: *Report* originally meant "to carry again." To *report* is to carry back, or relate information. A *reporter* carries back, or relates, information either in newspapers, or in legal or legislative proceedings.

---

[3] Refer to *Quotation Footnotes for Level 9* on page 406.
[2] Refer to *Quotation Footnotes for Level 9* on page 406.

journalist: The word *journey* originally meant "a day's journey, a day's work, or daily." A *journal* refers to writing completed in a day, or a daily newspaper. Originally, *journalist* referred to a reporter writing for the daily newspaper.

List other words based on the word *journey*. Write the words and their definitions in your vocabulary notebook.

BOOKS TO READ

Bliss, Edward. *Now the News: The Story of Broadcast Journalism*. New York: Columbia University Press, 1991.

Broder, David S. *Behind the Front Page: A Candid Look at How the News Is Made*. New York: Simon & Schuster, 1987.

Cloud, Stanley and Lynne Olson. *The Murrow Boys: Pioneers on the Front Lines of Broadcast Journalism*. Boston: Houghton Mifflin, 1996.

Cohl, H. Aaron. *Are We Scaring Ourselves to Death?: How Pessimism, Paranoia, and a Misguided Media Are Leading Us Toward Disaster*. New York: St. Martin's Griffin, 1997.

Fallows, James M. *Breaking the News: How the Media Undermine American Democracy*. New York: Pantheon Books, 1996.

Fry, Ronald W. (ed.). *Newspapers Career Directory, 3rd ed*. Hawthorne, NJ: Career Press, 1990.

Jones, Daniel and John D. Jorgenson. *Contemporary Authors New Revision Series*. Farmington, MI: Gale Research, 1999.

Kronenwetter, Michael. *Journalism Ethics*. New York: Franklin Watts, 1988.

Kuralt, Charles. *Charles Kuralt's America*. New York: G.P. Putnam's Sons, 1995.

_____. *Charles Kuralt's America* (Large-type edition). Thorndike, ME: Thorndike Press, 1996.

_____. *A Life on the Road*. New York: G.P. Putnam's Sons, 1990.

_____. *On the Road with Charles Kuralt*. New York: G.P. Putnam's Sons, 1985.

(Other books by Charles Kuralt: *Dateline: America; North Carolina Is My Home;* and *To the Top of the World*

Malmgren, Dallin. *The Ninth Issue*. New York: Delacorte Press, 1989.

McNeill, Robert *UPI Stylebook: The Authoritative Handbook for Writers, Editors & News Directors*. Lincolnwood, IL: National Textbook Co., 1993.

O'Rourke, P.J. *Age and Guile Beat Youth, Innocence, and a Bad Haircut: Twenty-Five Years of P.J. O'Rourke*. New York: Atlantic Monthly Press, 1995.

Patten, Jim. *Opportunities in Journalism Careers*. Lincolnwood, IL: VGM Career Horizons, 1991.

Pfeffer, Susan Beth. *A Matter of Principle: A Novel*. New York: Delacorte Press, 1982.

Pinkwater, Jill. *Buffalo Brenda*. New York: Macmillan, 1989.

Robertson, Nan. *The Girls in the Balcony: Women, Men, and the New York Times*. New York: Random House, 1992.

Rodowsky, Colby F. *Sydney, Invincible*. New York: Farrar, Straus and Giroux, 1995.

Sabato, Larry. *Feeding Frenzy: How Attack Journalism Has Transformed American Politics*. New York: Free Press, 1991.

Schami, Rafik. *A Hand Full of Stars*. New York: Dutton Children's Book, 1990.

Selditch, Dianne. *My First Year as a Journalist: Real-World Stories From America's Newspaper and Magazine Journalists*. New York: Walker and Co., 1995.

Witt, Leonard. *The Complete Book of Feature Writing: From Great American Feature Writers, Editors, and Teachers*. Cincinnati: Writer's Digest Books, 1991.

BOOK CLUB

Read *A Hand Full of Stars* by Rafik Schami, *The Ninth Issue* by Dallin Malmgren, or *Buffalo Brenda* by Jill Pinkwater.

INTRODUCTORY ACTIVITIES

DAY ONE

Objective: The students will compare/contrast local interest stories written in neighborhood newspapers with the writings of Charles Kuralt.

Discuss stories of local interest printed in the school newspaper or the local newspaper. "Do the stories tell about the people living in your community? What can you learn about the personality of your community and the country at large when you read these stories? Why would people enjoy reading such anecdotes? What is the purpose of the stories?"

Read to the class a local news story about an individual living in your community. "How did the journalist express him- or herself in the story? Did he or she simply state the facts, or did the journalist use special writing techniques to paint a picture in words? Did you enjoy the story? Why did you feel this way?"

Read a chapter from *On the Road with Charles Kuralt*. Choose a story that would compliment the local news article the students just heard. Conduct a compare/contrast discussion analyzing how the local story and the story by Charles Kuralt are alike and different. "Which story did you enjoy more? Why do you feel this way? What special writing techniques did Charles Kuralt use to tell his story? Were his techniques similar to the ones used by the local journalist? How did the expressions and writing techniques used by each writer affect the telling of the story?"

DAY TWO

STORY LESSON

Follow the *Presenting the Story Lesson* instructions in the Introduction. Each story lesson follows the same procedure; however, say the following in step 4: "The title of the story we're reading today is *Charles Kuralt: Journalist of the People*. What do you think the story is about? What do you already know about Charles Kuralt?"

EXTENSION ACTIVITIES

1. Each day read to the class a story from *On the Road with Charles Kuralt*. Discuss the characters Kuralt meets, and how these personalities reflect the American community.

2. Send each student out in the community to interview a person he or she feels reflects the spirit of the community, or who is part of the history of the town/city. The stories should illustrate, through words, the subject's interesting personality and contributions.

   If possible, ask each student to return with a photograph of his or her interview subject. Be sure to obtain written permission to use the photograph and story in a class book.

3. As a class, the students edit and arrange the stories and photographs from Extension Activity 3 into a book. Use a looseleaf notebook, a photo album, a computer, or binder. The students should give a title to their book, and create and design a proper cover page.

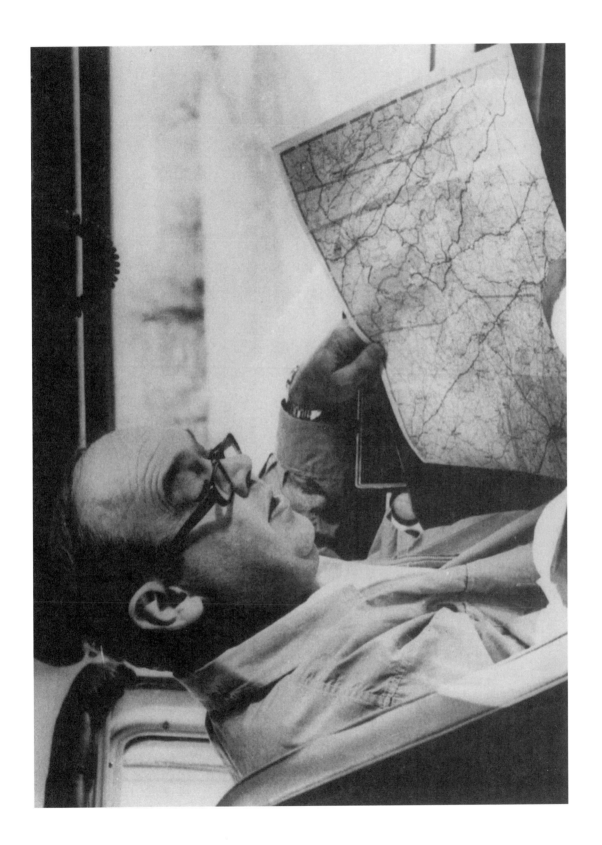

CHARLES KURALT: JOURNALIST OF THE PEOPLE

In the beginning, he was just another journalist. Working for CBS, Charles Kuralt reported from Vietnam to the North Pole. "I was a real reporter once," he later recalled, "but I was not suited for it by physique or temperament." Charles Kuralt's temperament was that of a poet, whose skill as a writer set him in a class of his own. So, in 1967, Charles Kuralt set out "On the Road," looking for the heart of America.

Little did he know that families across the country watched the evening news waiting for his reports from small towns and kindly people along his road to America: The America of compassionate, brave, caring folk who, in our quiet dreams, made up the soul of our country. In times of turmoil, Kuralt found our countrymen, told their stories, and set our minds at ease.

"To read the front pages," wrote Kuralt, "you might conclude that Americans are mostly out for themselves, venal, grasping and mean-spirited. . . . But you can't travel the back roads very long without discovering a multitude of gentle people doing good for others with no expectation of gain or recognition."

The *On the Road with Charles Kuralt* series won accolades from mainstream journalism, as well as the public, winning two Emmys and two George Foster Peabody awards. The International Radio and Television Society named him "Broadcaster of the Year" in 1983. According to his colleague Jim Lehrer, "To go 'On the Road with Charles Kuralt' is to go with humor, understanding and affection to see and hear and feel America. It is good for the soul."

In 1997, Charles Kuralt's wanderings ended when he succumbed to lupus at the age of 62. America will remember him as the laureate of our heartland. We imagine he is still on the road, looking for the next story. "We are out there now," Kuralt wrote, "leaving the motel parking lot with the sun coming up."

QUESTIONS FOR CHARLES KURALT: JOURNALIST OF THE PEOPLE

Literal Questions:

THE FACTS:

1. Which network did Charles Kuralt work for?

_____

_____

_____

2. When did Charles Kuralt begin his *On the Road* series?

_____

_____

_____

3. From where did Charles Kuralt report in his series *On the Road*?

_____

_____

_____

4. List the awards earned by *On the Road with Charles Kuralt.*

_____

_____

_____

SEQUENCE OF EVENTS:

5. What did Charles Kuralt do first: report from Vietnam or work on his *On the Road* series?

_____

_____

_____

6. List these events in chronological order: The International Radio and Television Society named Kuralt "Broadcaster of the Year;" Charles Kuralt succumbed to lupus; Charles Kuralt set out "On the Road"; Charles Kuralt reported from the North Pole.

_____

_____

_____

Name _____   **Date** _____

Interpretive Questions:

DRAWING CONCLUSIONS:

7. What one word describes the style of journalism practiced by Charles Kuralt?

_____

_____

_____

_____

MAKING INFERENCES:

8. How did Charles Kuralt feel about the small towns and people he reported about? What specific information led you to your answer?

_____

_____

_____

_____

MAKING PREDICTIONS:

9. Would it be possible today to develop a successful news series about small-town America? Why do you feel this way?

_____

_____

_____

_____

IDENTIFICATION OF CAUSE:

10. Why did Charles Kuralt report on events and people along the back roads of America?

_____

_____

_____

_____

IDENTIFICATION OF THE MAIN IDEA:

11. Write a title for the story. Use as few words as possible.

_____

_____

Name _____ **Date** _____

COMPARISON:

12. How was *On the Road with Charles Kuralt* like today's evening news reports? How was it different?

_____

_____

_____

_____

SUMMARIZE:

13. In your own words, tell about Charles Kuralt's *On the Road* series.

_____

_____

_____

_____

EFFECT:

14. What effect did *On the Road with Charles Kuralt* have on the author of the story? Why do you feel this way?

_____

_____

_____

_____

FACT AND OPINION:

15. Jim Lehrer said, "To go 'On the Road with Charles Kuralt' is to go with humor, understanding and affection to see and hear and feel America." Is this statement a fact or Mr. Lehrer's opinion? Why do you feel this way?

_____

_____

_____

_____

ON YOUR OWN:

16. Write a question about the story for a teacher or another student to answer.

_____

_____

Name _____ **Date** _____

REFERENCES FOR LEVEL 9

OMEN IN THE SKY

Asimov, Isaac. *Asimov's Guide to Halley's Comet*. New York: Walker and Company, 1985, pp. 1-7.

Flaste, Richard, Holcomb Noble, Walter Sullivan, and John Noble Wilford. *The New York Times Guide to the Return of Halley's Comet*. New York: Random House, 1985, pp. 53, 61-84.

Sagan, Carl and Ann Druyan. *Comet*. New York: Ballantine Books, 1997, pp. 14-33.

"COSMIC ROCKET:" SOVIETS WINNING THE SPACE RACE

Daniel, Clifton (ed.). *Chronicles of the Twentieth Century*. Mount Kisco, NY: Chronicle Publications, 1987, pp. 806, 807, 823, 832.

WITCHES AND LIES: THE SALEM WITCH HUNT

Johnson, Thomas H. "Puritanism." *Encyclopedia Americana* (1963), 23, 28-30.

Krensky, Stephen. *Witch Hunt: It Happened in Salem Village*. New York: Random House, 1989.

Rice, Earle, Jr. *The Salem Witch Trials*. San Diego: Lucent Books, 1997.

Van Der Linde, Laurel. *The Devil in Salem Village: The Story of the Salem Witchcraft Trials*. Brookfield, CT: Millbrook Press, 1992.

THE GLORIOUS TOMBS OF CHINA

Groushko, Michael. *Lost Treasures of the World*. London, England: Multimedia Books Limited, 1993, pp. 92-94.

AUTOMATON

Asimov, Isaac and Karen A. Frenkel. *Robots: Machines in Man's Image*. New York: Harmony Books, 1985, p. 5.

Lambert, Mark. *50 Facts About Robots*. New York: Warwick Press, 1983, pp. 3-4.

Litterick, Ian. *The Age of Computers: Robots and Intelligent Machines*. New York: The Bookwright Press, 1984, pp. 9-10.

Milton, Joyce. *Here Comes the Robots*. New York: Hasting House Publisher, 1981, pp. 15-24.

AMERICA MOURNS

"Garfield, James A." *Pictorial Encyclopedia: People Who Made America*. Skokie, IL: United States History Society, Inc., 1973, pp. 430-431.

Lillegard, Dee. *Encyclopedia of Presidents: James A. Garfield*. Chicago: Children's Press, 1987.

Dreaming to Remember

"Behavior: Dream to Learn." *Nature-Science Annual* (1978). Alexandria, VA: Time/Life Books, 1977, p. 169.

Rudavsky, Shari. "If Practice Makes Perfect, Deep Sleep Helps Even More." *The Wall Street Journal*, July 29, 1994, B2(W), B3(E), col. 6.

Summer Camp Isn't What It Used to Be

Peterson's Summer Opportunities for Kids and Teenagers (1997). Princeton, NJ: Peterson's, 1997.

"Ma" Barker Gunned Down by F.B.I.

Bondi, Victor. *American Decades: 1930-1936*. New York: Gale Research, Inc., 1995, pp. 288-289.

Daniel, Clifton (ed.). *Chronicles of the Twentieth Century*. Mount Kisco, NY: Chronicle Publications, 1987, p. 440.

Joseph Cardinal Bernardin

Bernardin, Joseph Louis. *The Gift of Peace*. Chicago: Loyola Press, 1997.

Kennedy, Eugene. *My Brother Joseph: The Spirit of a Cardinal and the Story of a Friendship*. New York: St. Martin's Press, 1997.

What Does "Qwerty" Mean?

Merrill, Peter D. "Typewriter." *Encyclopedia Americana* (1963), 27, 318-319.

Reader's Digest Staff. *Strange Stories, Amazing Facts: Stories That Are Bizarre, Unusual, Odd, Astonishing & Often Incredible*. Pleasantville, NY: Reader's Digest Association, Inc., 1976, p. 209.

Adopt-a-Senior

Jarvis, Mary G. "Personalizing High School: Mentoring Programs for High School Students." *Education Digest*, vol. 62, no. 1 (September 1996), 19(4).

1,200 Dead in Cameroon

Daniel, Clifton (ed.). *Chronicles of the Twentieth Century*. Mount Kisco, NY: Chronicle Publications, 1987, p. 1285.

Predicting the Next Earthquake

Geller, Robert J., David D. Jackson, Yan Y. Kagan, and Francesco Mulargia. "Earthquakes Cannot Be Predicted." *Science*, vol. 275, no. 5306 (March 14, 1997), 1616(2).

Kerr, Richard A. "Warnings Precede Chinese Temblors: Earthquakes Predicted." *Science*, vol. 276, no. 5312 (April 25, 1997), 526

Reader's Digest Staff. *Strange Stories, Amazing Facts: Stories That Are Bizarre, Unusual, Odd, Astonishing & Often Incredible.* Pleasantville, NY: The Reader's Digest Association, Inc., 1976, p. 176.

CHARLES KURALT: JOURNALIST OF THE PEOPLE

"Died: Charles Kuralt." *Maclean's*, vol. 110, no. 28 (July 14, 1997), 11.

Kuralt, Charles. *On the Road With Charles Kuralt.* New York: G.P. Putnam's Sons, 1985.

QUOTATION FOOTNOTES FOR LEVEL 9

[1] Bartlett, John. *Bartlett's Familiar Quotations.* Boston: Little, Brown and Company, 1980.

[2] Peter, Laurance J. *Peter's Quotations: Ideas of Our Times.* New York: William Morrow and Company, Inc., 1977.

[3] Applewhite, Ashton, William R. Evans III, and Andrew Frothingham. *And I Quote: The Definitive Collection of Quotes, Sayings, and Jokes for the Contemporary Speechmaker.* New York: St. Martin's Press, 1992.

[4] Rowes, Barbara. *The Book of Quotes.* New York: E.P. Dutton, 1979.

[5] Sagan, Carl and Ann Druyan. *Comet.* New York: Ballantine Books, 1997.

[6] Rice, Earle, Jr. *The Salem Witch Trials.* San Diego: Lucent Books, 1997.

[7] Ness, Eliot. *The Untouchables: The Real Story.* New York: Pocket Books, 1957.

[8] Bernardin, Joseph Louis. *The Gift of Peace.* Chicago: Loyola Press, 1997.

[9] Ceruzzi, Paul E. *A History of Modern Computing.* Cambridge, MA: The MIT Press, 1998.

[10] Thomas, Gordon and Max Morgan Witts. *The San Francisco Earthquake.* New York: Stein and Day, 1971.

[11] Haag, John L. (producer). *Phenomenal: Music, Words, Chords.* Los Angeles: West Coast Publications, Inc., and New York: Gershwin Publishing Corporation, 1971.

WORD-ORIGIN STUDY REFERENCE FOR LEVEL 9

Unless otherwise noted:

Webster, Noah. *Webster's New Twentieth Century Dictionary of the English Language.* New York: The World Publishing Company, 1964.